Withdrawn/ABCL

America's Obsessives

America's Obsessives

The Compulsive Energy That Built a Nation

JOSHUA KENDALL

GRAND CENTRAL
PUBLISHING

NEW YORK   BOSTON

Grand Central Publishing
Hachette Book Group
237 Park Avenue
New York, NY 10017

www.HachetteBookGroup.com

Printed in the United States of America

RRD-C

First Edition: June 2013
10 9 8 7 6 5 4 3 2 1

Grand Central Publishing is a division of Hachette Book Group, Inc.
The Grand Central Publishing name and logo is a trademark of Hachette Book Group, Inc.

The publisher is not responsible for websites (or their content) that are not owned by the publisher.

Library of Congress Cataloging-in-Publication Data
Kendall, Joshua C.
  America's obsessives : the compulsive energy that built a nation / Joshua Kendall. — First edition.
    pages cm
  Summary: "Behind every great man (or woman), there's a compulsion" — Provided by the publisher.
  Includes bibliographical references and index.
  ISBN 978-1-4555-0238-7 (hardcover) — ISBN 978-1-4555-0236-3 (ebook) — ISBN 978-1-61113-832-0 (audiobook) 1. United States—Biography.
2. Successful people—United States—Biography. 3. Scholars—United States—Biography. 4. Inventors—United States—Biography. 5. Motivation (Psychology)—United States—Case studies. 6. Compulsive behavior—Social aspects—United States—Case studies. I. Title.
  CT215.K46 2013
  609.2'273—dc23
                          2012051196

For Andrew Brink (1932–2011)

The truly strong and sound mind is the mind that can embrace equally great things and small. I would have a man great in great things, and elegant in little things.

—Samuel Johnson

Contents

The Obsessive Innovator

The Archetypal Super-Achiever

> When you grow up you tend to get told the world is the way it is
> and your life is just to live your life inside the world. Try not to
> bash into the walls too much. Try to have a nice family life, have
> fun, save a little money. That's a very limited life....You can
> change it, you can influence it, you can build your own things
> that other people can use.
>
> —Steve Jobs

I'm on my way to the factory. Meet me there." *Click.*

It was shortly after 8 a.m. on a Sunday in the fall of 1984. Steve Jobs was about to hop into his black Mercedes sedan to make the forty-minute trek from his home in Woodside to Fremont where Apple was churning out its latest product—the Macintosh computer.

On the receiving end of the phone line was Debi Coleman, the company's head of manufacturing, who had been sitting on her porch in Cupertino, buried in the Sunday paper. After two and a half years at Apple, she was accustomed to her boss's demanding and eccentric behavior—the rage attacks, the intrusions during off-work hours, and the sudden disappearances for days at a time. "I was less surprised by the timing of Steve's call than by what I saw when I got there," recalled Coleman, now a partner at SmartForest, a Portland, Oregon–based venture capital firm.

Eager to build the perfect factory, Jobs had been badgering Coleman for months. After deciding in late 1983 that the initial site—Dallas, Texas—would not do, Jobs became consumed with every detail. He wanted to bring to America the elegantly designed machines that he had seen in Germany such as Braun appliances and BMW cars. But his focus went way beyond acquiring state-of-the-art equipment. He insisted that the walls all be painted white. "No white was too white for Steve," stated Coleman. Jobs would also don white gloves to do frequent dust checks. Whenever he spotted a few specks on either a machine or on the floor, which he was determined to keep clean enough to eat off, Coleman had to arrange for an instant scrubbing. Despite her frequent exasperation, Coleman did not think about quitting. "I was mesmerized by his genius and charm. And like several other women in the company, I was a little bit in love with him," she added.

When Coleman arrived that Sunday, she noticed a side of Jobs that she had never seen before. "He was particularly reserved and eager to please," Coleman noted. The reason? The normally high-octane entrepreneur, then still several months shy of his thirtieth birthday, had brought along a special guest—his adoptive father, Paul Jobs. From nine to eleven, Coleman escorted father and son around the nearly empty factory; in contrast to a weekday, when two shifts of workers would file in, only a few members of the security staff were present that morning. "The facility was not yet completely finished," added Coleman, "but Steve couldn't wait to show his father what he had created." A master craftsman himself, Paul Jobs, who had supported his family by working as a repo man, liked to build cabinets and fences. The elder Jobs also had a knack for fixing used cars. "While his father was impressed by how everything worked," stated Coleman, "he asked a lot of questions. He, too, paid attention to details."

While Steve Jobs did many great things at both Apple and Pixar, where he revolutionized the animation industry, he also never failed to keep track of the small things. And this intensity rattled many of his employees besides Coleman. Pamela Kerwin was the marketing director at Pixar when Jobs arrived in 1986, as his first stint at Apple was coming to an end. She was terrified whenever she printed anything for him to read, even memos. "He was a control freak and perfectionist in all things," recalled Kerwin, now a principal at the Los Angeles tech firm Luminous Publishing. "He would carefully go over every document a million times and would pick up on punctuation errors such as misplaced commas."

Commas. Cleanliness. Jobs could obsess and go ballistic about minutiae that would not even register on the radar screens of most CEOs. A tad mad, Jobs suffered from what psychiatrists call obsessive-compulsive personality disorder (OCPD). Though little studied, this condition affects as much as 8 percent of the U.S. population, according to a survey of more than forty thousand Americans published in 2012 in the *Journal of Psychiatric Research*. The current edition of psychiatry's bible, the *Diagnostic and Statistical Manual*, defines OCPD as a "preoccupation with orderliness...and mental and interpersonal control" and lists a total of eight common symptoms, four of which need to be present to reach the diagnosis. The key ones are:

- preoccupation with details, rules, order, lists, organization, or schedules
- perfectionism
- excess devotion to work
- inflexibility about matters of morality, ethics, or values
- reluctance to delegate tasks unless others submit to exactly his way of doing things
- rigidity and stubbornness

But for Jobs, these emotional difficulties didn't just impede his ability to get along with others; paradoxically, they also emerged as assets—the very skill set that enabled him to create the behemoth that is now Apple. After all, in our fiercely competitive culture, being results oriented rather than relationship oriented has its advantages.

And Jobs is just one in a long ticker-tape parade of American icons—beginning with Founding Fathers such as Thomas Jefferson and continuing through Pittsburgh entrepreneur Henry J. Heinz and Boston Red Sox star Ted Williams—whose obsessions and compulsions have fueled their stratospheric success. This list includes librarian Melvil Dewey, author of the pioneering search engine the Dewey Decimal Classification System, sexologist Alfred Kinsey, aviator Charles Lindbergh, and cosmetics tycoon Estée Lauder, all of whom also led the way in their chosen fields. Like Jobs, the author of the Declaration of Independence kept sweating the small stuff. The man who gave us the penny—his 1784 paper "Notes on the Establishment of a Money Unit, and of a Coinage for the United States" organized our national currency—couldn't help but keep track in his copious account books of every cent that he ever spent. And Jefferson's attention to detail was also responsible for the better-known chunks of his legacy—his brilliant writing, his pioneering architecture, and the University of Virginia, the exemplary public institution of higher learning that he founded. Like Jefferson, Heinz, who turned ketchup into our national sauce at the dawn of the twentieth century, had an obsession with counting, which he used to create one of the most successful slogans in advertising history, "57 Varieties." Slavishly devoted to his craft, Ted Williams was also an order and cleanliness nut. When visiting the Red Sox spring training facility in the late 1970s, the retired Hall of Famer would pester the clubhouse attendant about why he used Tide on the team's laundry. This ballplayer didn't hit to live, he lived to hit; and until the day he died, he loved nothing more than talking about the perfect swing.

To describe this exclusive group of archetypal super-achievers, of whom Jobs is the most prominent recent example, I prefer to use a term of my own coinage: "obsessive innovator." Current nomenclature can be misleading because we tend to associate obsessives solely with careful, plodding performance. While the consultant Jim Collins, author of the megaselling *Good to Great: Why Some Companies Make the Leap... and Others Don't* (2001), puts obsessives at the top of his leadership pyramid, he contends that these "Level 5 Leaders" are mild-mannered, self-effacing types and not creative trailblazers. Making the same assumption about those suffering from OCPD, authors who have recently explored the link between madness and greatness assign other psychiatric maladies to our biggest movers and shakers. For example, in *The Hypomanic Edge: The Link Between (a Little) Craziness and (a Lot of) Success in America* (2005), a study of a half dozen American leaders including Alexander Hamilton and Andrew Carnegie, Johns Hopkins psychologist John D. Gartner argues that hypomania, a mild form of bipolar disorder, "helped make America the richest nation on Earth." Likewise, in *Narcissistic Leaders* (2007), management guru Michael Maccoby lumps Jobs together with his fellow techie Oracle's Larry Ellison, calling them "productive narcissists." According to Maccoby, who notes that "productive obsessives" make excellent middle managers or CFOs rather than CEOs, the highest rung to which an obsessive can aspire is to play a fastidious Sancho Panza to a visionary Don Quixote. To make his case, Maccoby cites the steady Ray Lane, Larry Ellison's longtime number two at Oracle. But Apple's stupendous growth in the first decade of the twenty-first century occurred precisely because Steve Jobs was both an obsessive like Ray Lane and a narcissist like Larry Ellison; he was a two-for-one. While obsessive innovators also possess the grandiosity and self-absorption characteristic of narcissists, they are driven primarily by their particular obsessions and compulsions; and it is precisely this connection between unremitting internal pressures and extraordinary external achievements that has received surprisingly little attention.

To illustrate the distinction between obsessive innovators and narcissists, consider how Larry Ellison stacks up against his contemporary and close friend Jobs. While the two tech titans had similar early histories and shared several common behavioral traits, their internal preoccupations appear to have been quite different. In her unauthorized biography, *Everyone Else Must Fail* (2003), the late technology journalist Karen Southwick describes Oracle's domineering CEO as "a modern-day Genghis Khan who has elevated ruthlessness in business to a carefully cultivated art form.... Ellison runs through and discards [subordinates] with unusual ferocity." Like Jobs, Ellison was abandoned by both his parents shortly after birth. When Ellison was nine months old, his unwed mother shipped him off to Lillian and Louis Ellison, his grandmother's sister and her husband. In contrast to Jobs, who bonded with both his adoptive parents — particularly his father — Ellison got along with his mother but feared his father, who constantly belittled him.

"Larry hated that man and had nothing but venom toward him," Nancy Wheeler Jenkins, the second of Ellison's four ex-wives, told me in a recent interview. When Ellison was a sophomore in college, Lillian Ellison died of cancer, leaving him without much of a support system. He would end up bouncing around a couple of colleges and never earned a bachelor's degree. The self-taught programmer, who began working in northern California tech firms in the late 1960s, was nothing if not ambitious. "If I needed information to build something," Ellison told an interviewer in 1995, "I was relentless. I could not stop thinking about a problem that had to be solved in order to build something. I was obsessive." But in contrast to Jobs, Ellison was obsessive only about success — not about cleanliness, order, or details. According to Jenkins, who married Ellison in 1977 — the union lasted only eighteen months — just as he was starting Oracle, his first manual for the company was littered with spelling mistakes. "He thought it a total waste of time to fix those errors," she stated. Jenkins, who found Ellison brilliant and witty, believes that his drive for vast wealth stemmed from his difficult childhood: "Larry wanted to show everyone that he was legitimate — he wanted to be a somebody." While fellow adoptee Jobs struggled with a similar, if not larger, batch of insecurities — his routine failure to attend to his own personal hygiene in early adulthood suggests that unlike Ellison, he also endured a period of neglect in childhood — the Apple founder viewed the accumulation of material possessions as secondary to the pursuit of his obsessions.

In contrast to narcissists like Ellison, obsessive innovators like Jobs aren't consumed solely by raw ambition. He did not design "insanely great products" just to build a great company; he built a great company so that he could keep designing "insanely great products." So compelled was Jobs to pursue this obsession, which dated back to his childhood in Mountain View, California, that he could not *think* of stopping. Becoming a master craftsman was his way to earn the approval of his beloved father; it was thus forever associated with his deepest needs for both validation and connection. This was something that mattered more to the adult Jobs than life itself. When the sedated cancer patient was lying in his hospital bed, he once ripped off his oxygen mask, railing that he hated its design. Much to the surprise of his doctors, Jobs then ordered them to begin work on five different options for a new mask. Similarly, Estée Lauder was also a prisoner to her own compulsions. As a little girl, she assisted her mother in her daily beauty rituals; and for the rest of her life, she could not stop putting makeup on women's faces.

Like narcissists, obsessive innovators are made more than born. While it is not possible to rule out a genetic component, as a general rule OCPD constitutes a direct response to adverse circumstances in early childhood. The seven super-achievers profiled in this book all faced more than their fair share of early stressors; medical illness, neglect, emotional abuse, parental mental illness, loss of a parent, and severe family discord are common in their histories. "The obsessive personality type emerges in response to unmet emotional needs. Children who have little control over the key events and people in their lives begin to focus on something that they can control, such as details," says psychiatrist Kerry Sulkowicz, founder of the Boswell Group, which provides advice to CEOs and corporate boards. Sulkowicz, also a clinical professor of psychiatry at New York University, emphasizes that over time this strategy of adapting to the environment becomes ingrained. Paradoxically, the cure to the child's stressful predicament is this lifelong disease.

Behind every obsessive innovator is a unique constellation of family circumstances that derails normal parent-child bonding. And the same obsessions and compulsions, which originally constitute an ingenious resolution to this existential crisis, eventually beget the legacy. By adolescence, these future dynamos are typically friendless loners who are much more attached to things than to other people. As a child, Ted Williams was neglected by both his parents, who couldn't stand each other and rarely spent much time at home. The baseball bat was not just his ticket to stardom; it was also his emotional anchor. In high school, Williams lacked the social skills to do the basics, such as go out on a date. The same was true for Lindbergh and Kinsey. The Lone Eagle's tempestuous parents were also constantly bickering with each other; as a teenager, he ogled not girls but the gadgets at the local hardware store. His closest ties were to the machines and animals on the family's Minnesota farm. Likewise, Kinsey's favorite boyhood pastime was bonding with bugs and ferns during his long, solitary hikes in suburban New Jersey.

In contrast to these three obsessive innovators, who never learned to connect in childhood, Henry Heinz and Melvil Dewey became hyperobedient—the byproduct of having grown up in families run by domineering women who bent their numerous children (as well as their passive husbands) to their wills. Both Anna Heinz and Eliza Dewey were strict disciplinarians who ruled by repeating harsh parental maxims. Eliza Dewey's favorite was "Praise to the face is an open disgrace." In grade school, Heinz and Dewey were already working overtime to please their "Tiger Mothers." While little Henry was feverishly helping Anna grow fruits and vegetables to sell to neighbors, little Melvil was busy classifying and arranging the contents of Eliza's pantry. And thus were born the vocations of two future American icons.

The case studies of Heinz and Dewey illustrate a point often obscured in the recent national debate about child-rearing unleashed by Amy Chua's controversial memoir, *Battle Hymn of the Tiger Mother* (2011)—like the Chinese, Americans also have a long history of "extreme parenting" designed to instill success. Anna Heinz and Eliza Dewey were both mid-nineteenth-century versions of Grace Welch, the hard-charging mother of former General Electric CEO Jack Welch. In his bestselling autobiography, *Jack: Straight from the Gut* (2001), Welch talks about an incident in high school when he flung his hockey stick across the rink after his team suffered a bitter defeat. Startling his teammates and everyone else in sight, his fiery Irish mother rushed into the locker room and grabbed him by the collar, yelling, "You punk! If you don't know how to lose, you'll never know how to win." Like Heinz, who also idealized his mother, Welch calls his "the most influential person in my life...who taught me the value of competition."

While Tiger Mothers can produce exceptional leaders, the same humiliations that teach lifelong lessons also have the potential to create long-term emotional problems. "Neutron Jack," the man who constantly trimmed his staff at GE, has often been described as a narcissist incapable of empathy. "His egocentrism is everywhere," observes Joseph Nocera in his review of *Jack* for the *New York Times*

Book Review. A likely reason why Heinz and Dewey developed into two-for-ones rather than pure narcissists is that unlike Jack Welch, they both also experienced maternal neglect. Eliza Dewey was forty-two when she had Melvil and, as he later recalled, "had no time to fuss with babies." Whatever early bonding the future decimal man experienced came at the hands of his elder sister, Mate, to whom his mother entrusted his care.

While obsessive innovators all have obsessive-compulsive personality disorder (OCPD), they do not necessarily suffer from obsessive-compulsive disorder (OCD). These two psychiatric conditions, while often considered synonymous, are actually cousins. Broadly speaking, obsessions are things that one can't stop thinking about, and compulsions are things that one can't stop doing. While the content of these thoughts and actions can be similar in the two disorders, the person's internal experience is very different. Whereas in OCD, the obsessions—say, fears of dirt—are unwelcome, in OCPD the opposite is true. In psychiatryspeak, this is the distinction between egodystonic and egosyntonic. Compare the elderly Howard Hughes, who would spend all day sitting naked in the middle of hotel rooms—the germ-free zone—with the thirty-something Steve Jobs, who would do his quick dust checks on the factory floor. In contrast to Hughes, who was paralyzed by his OCD, Jobs basked in his OCPD; he was proud of his company's cleanliness. Likewise, Melvil Dewey celebrated his childhood fixation with the number 10, turning it into his signature achievement, the decimal classification system that bears his name. And in contrast to those with OCD, who often seek psychiatric treatment, those with OCPD rarely acknowledge that anything is wrong. That's because the personality disorder typically improves rather than impairs normal functioning. "OCPD is a method of avoiding suffering. Those with the disorder come for help only if someone else—say, a spouse—demands it," explained Lorrin Moran, a professor emeritus of psychiatry at Stanford University who ran the Medical Center's OCD Clinic for many years. But this rarely happens. More often than not, like the inflexible Charles Lindbergh, who insisted that his wife, the writer Anne Morrow Lindbergh, keep track of all household expenditures in detailed ledgers, those with OCPD tend to drive other family members into treatment. And Anne Lindbergh had to fight with her husband in order to see a psychotherapist, because he hated everything to do with psychiatry.

OCPD is also sometimes confused with Asperger's syndrome. "Aspies" do have some of the same core symptoms, such as rigidity, anger outbursts, and lack of empathy; they, too, can get caught up in repetitive or ritualistic behavior such as collecting bits of information (though they gravitate even more toward the totally useless variety). But the hallmark of this autistic spectrum disorder is the inability to read the social or emotional cues of others—something that doesn't apply to obsessives. While obsessives can also be cold and distant, they are capable of occasional warmth and charm. For example, Estée Lauder had a remarkable knack for relating to customers, but not necessarily to anyone else; with both employees and family members, she was often demanding and unpredictable. And the characteristically tight-lipped Lindbergh eventually learned a thing or two about how to seduce women—techniques that he would need to feed his sexual addiction. If he had been a true Aspie, he would not have been able to maintain his long-term affairs with his three German mistresses, with whom he fathered a total of seven children. Aspies, who often have trouble connecting with their dates, certainly can't do that kind of thing (nor, for that matter, can most of us, as it takes an obsessive innovator to build four families).

While several of these seven super-achievers found a degree of happiness in marriage—including Lindbergh, who developed a deep and meaningful bond with Anne, even though he spent as little as two months a year with her—they all lived as fragmented individuals. Uncomfortable in their own skin, they often fiddled with their identity or created new identities. Estée Lauder (née Josephine Esther Mentzer) hid her Jewish background by inventing not only a new name, but also a bogus aristocratic family, whose origins she kept changing. Much to the amusement of his library colleagues, Melvil (né Melville) Dewey changed his last name to "Dui" after a business failure in his late twenties. On his love trips to Germany, Charles Lindbergh borrowed Superman's pseudonym, Careu Kent; and the swinging bachelor Ted Williams would sometimes check himself into hotel rooms as G. C. Luther ("How do you doubt," the perspicacious dissembler explained, "a name like G. C. Luther?"). While Thomas Jefferson didn't hide his identity, he also had a secret lover—his slave Sally Hemings.

These larger-than-life figures were several fully realized Shakespearean characters all rolled into one. Besides the sybarite and the upstanding family man (or woman), they housed a host of other contradictory selves such as the saint, the sinner, the rule maker, and the rule breaker. Like the young Steve Jobs, who rarely showered, Alfred Kinsey was a cleanliness nut who flirted with filth; the sex doctor enjoyed hanging around public bathrooms in order to count (and to hook up with) gay men searching for anonymous sex partners. Ted Williams helped save the lives of thousands of cancer patients through his tireless advocacy on behalf of the Jimmy Fund, a charity affiliated with the Dana-Farber Cancer Institute in Boston; however, he also was, as he admitted, "horseshit" with his own three children. The Red Sox star was even two different people on the baseball diamond; the hyperfocused hitter coexisted with the lackadaisical outfielder, who sometimes turned his back to home plate in order to take phantom swings. For Williams, as for the others, the core obsessions and compulsions could rarely be held in check for very long.

Part One

———

Founding Farmers and Factoid Finders

Thomas Jefferson
A Philosopher a Patriote and a Friend
Dessiné par son Ami Tadée Kosciuszko.
Et Gravé par Mr Sokolnicki

1.

Politics: Thomas Jefferson

Omniscient Organizer

A mind always employed is always happy. This is the true secret,
the grand recipe for felicity.
— Thomas Jefferson, letter to his daughter Martha,
May 21, 1787

On the morning of Monday, July 1, 1776, Thomas Jefferson had, it can safely be said, a lot on his mind.

On that fateful day, the Second Continental Congress in Philadelphia was to consider the resolution, first introduced on June 7 by his fellow Virginian Richard H. Lee, to dissolve "all political connection between [the Colonies] and the state of Great Britain." And as soon as that resolution passed, as Jefferson expected it would, his draft of the Declaration of Independence, which he had completed the previous Friday, was due to come to the floor for a vote. Hypersensitive to criticism, the assiduous thirty-three-year-old wordsmith dreaded the thought of any tinkering with his text. (In fact, for the rest of his life, Jefferson would be bitter about the "mutilations" that his congressional colleagues were about to make, which reduced its length by about 25 percent.) He was also unnerved because the war effort of the new nation-to-be was not going well; the American troops in Canada, who lacked essential provisions due to a shortage of money, had just been hit by a smallpox epidemic. "Our affairs in Canada," Jefferson wrote later that day to William Fleming, a delegate to Virginia's new independent state legislature, "go still retrograde."

The six-foot-two-and-a-half-inch delegate with the angular face, sandy complexion, and reddish hair was also dogged by a host of domestic concerns. He was still recovering from the sudden death—her illness lasted less than an hour—of his fifty-six-year-old mother, Jane Randolph Jefferson, three months earlier. For most of April and the first part of May, Jefferson was detained by incapacitating migraines at Monticello, his five-thousand-acre estate, then a two-week journey by horseback from Philadelphia. And with his frail wife, Martha, pregnant for the third time in six years, he felt, as he informed Virginia's de facto governor, Edmund Pendleton, on June 30, that it was "indispensably necessary ... [to] solicit the substitution of some other person" to take his seat in the Continental Congress by the end of the year. As it turned out, an anxious Jefferson couldn't even wait that long; on September 2, he would submit his resignation and return to his "country," as he still called his native Virginia.

Amid all the uncertainty and anxiety that he faced early on that sweltering July morning, Jefferson did a surprising thing. He started what turned out to be a massive list. For Jefferson, as for other obsessives, list making was a passionate pursuit that could help him get his bearings. Flipping his copy of *The Philadelphia Newest Almanack, for the Year of Our Lord 1776* upside down, he wrote on the first interleaved blank page at the back, "Observations on the weather." Below this heading, he set up three columns, "July, hour, thermom." At 9 a.m., he recorded 81½. With the debate on Lee's resolution taking up most of the day, Jefferson did not do another temperature reading until 7 p.m., when he recorded 82. But for the rest of that momentous week and for years on end, he would record the temperature at least three times a day. On the fourth, when the mercury hit 68 at 6 a.m. before reaching a fitting high of 76 at 1 p.m., he even managed to squeeze in a total of four readings. On the day that the Declaration was signed, Jefferson also made the fifteen-minute trek from his room at Seventh and Market to John Sparhawk's book and gadget store on Second Street, where he shelled out 3 pounds, 15 shillings (the equivalent of several hundred dollars today) for a new thermometer. On Monday the eighth, as he recorded in the account book, which he kept on the interleaved pages in the front half of his almanac, he returned to Sparhawk's to purchase a barometer for 4 pounds, 10 shillings.

Jefferson had been fascinated by meteorology ever since his undergraduate days at William and Mary. In Williamsburg, he had befriended Lieutenant Governor Francis Fauquier, a London-born Fellow of the Royal Society, who was well connected in scientific circles. In 1760, Fauquier, who possessed the latest versions of the major scientific inventions of the day— the thermometer, telescope, and microscope—had begun a weather diary (which was limited to just one reading a day). Inspired by this adolescent hero, Jefferson would establish himself as an international authority in the field. In a chapter in his scientific treatise, *Notes on the State of Virginia*, first published in 1785, Jefferson summarized some preliminary findings. In the age-old debate about climate change that dated back to the ancients, Jefferson (like another prominent Southern politico who served as vice president exactly two centuries after he did) came down squarely on the side of "global warming." (But in contrast to Al Gore, who has warned of the dangers associated with greenhouse gases, Jefferson was hypothesizing about how events such as deforestation could be "very fatal to fruits.")

"A change in our climate...is taking place very sensibly," he concluded, based on his assessment of decades of data collected by himself and others. "Both heats and colds are become much more moderate.... Snows are less frequent and less deep." Jefferson, who bought about twenty thermometers during the course of his life, would continue to gather a wealth of weather data, which he crunched every which way, until 1816. Even during his presidency, he took the temperature at both dawn and 4 p.m. The National Weather Service, established in 1870 as the Weather Bureau, has hailed Jefferson as "the father of weather observers."

But a thirst for knowledge wasn't the only reason why Jefferson began this ambitious new scholarly undertaking at what turned out to be a pivotal moment in world history. Compiling and organizing information, as he well knew, could also help calm him down. "Nature intended me," he later wrote, "for the tranquil pursuits of science by rendering them my supreme delight." Distracting himself from his innermost thoughts was his way of warding off feelings of despair. While Jefferson was a gifted singer, he often used his musical talent, like his ingenuity, to hide from himself. One could "hardly see him anywhar outdoors," his slave Isaac once noted, "but that he was a-singin'." He would even sing while reading. His habitual manner of coping with stress was to do not less, but more. In contrast to most people, who become undone when they take on too much, Jefferson became energized. His constant fear was not having enough to occupy his mind. For Jefferson, whose personal credo was a mishmash of Epicureanism and Stoicism, happiness was synonymous with virtuous work. "Nothing can contribute more to it [happiness]," he later mused, "than the contracting a habit of industry and activity." In contrast, he considered idleness "the most dangerous poison of life." To be fair, his was not an introspective culture; as one historian has put it, eighteenth-century Virginians had "neither the taste nor the skill for self-examination." Even so, the vehemence with which Jefferson avoided experiencing internal distress qualifies him as an outlier.

The pedantic side of this patron saint of polymaths has often been overlooked. Most Americans associate Jefferson only with his staggering intellect. As President John F. Kennedy put it at a White House dinner honoring fifty Nobel laureates a half century ago, "I think this is the most extraordinary collection of talent, of human knowledge, that has ever been gathered together at the White House, with the possible exception of when Thomas Jefferson dined alone." Few are aware that America's "Apostle of Freedom," as President Franklin Roosevelt called the most erudite Founding Father, was as consumed by the petty as he was by the lofty. The nonstop doer was not always discriminating in what he did. Jefferson delighted in gathering factoids, regardless of how meaningful they might turn out to be. He was also eager to communicate what he reaped. "[Jefferson] scattered information," Senator William Maclay of Pennsylvania observed in 1790, "wherever he went." During his presidency, he kept a long list with the equally long-winded title, "A statement of the vegetable market in Washington, during a period of 8 years, wherein the earliest and last appearance of each article is noted." As this document reveals, while entrusted with running the country, Jefferson felt compelled to keep constant tabs on the availability of twenty-nine vegetables (and seven fruits) in our nation's capital. The earliest date on which he could enjoy a watermelon at the White House was July 7; the latest was September 4. And when his eldest grandson, Thomas Jefferson Randolph, who was about to spend a year studying science in Philadelphia, visited him in Washington in 1807, the president immediately asked the fifteen-year-old to empty out his trunk so that he could personally examine every article. Having completed this inventory, Jefferson took out a pencil and paper in order to make a list of other items that he was convinced the adolescent would need.

Keeping track of minutiae was a lifelong preoccupation. Jefferson kept in his pocket an ivory notebook—a kind of proto-iPad on which he could write in pencil; and when he returned to his study, he would then transfer his data to one of his seven permanent ledger books. In his Garden and Farm books, which he kept for more than fifty years, he recorded all the goings-on at Monticello. "[H]ad the last dish of our spring peas," he wrote on July 22, 1772, in a typical entry in the Garden Book. And in his account books, which he maintained for nearly sixty years, he kept track of every cent he ever spent. "Mr. Jefferson," the overseer at Monticello once observed, "was very particular in the transaction of all his business. He kept an account of everything. Nothing was too small for him to keep an account of it."

All this financial calculating did not do much for Jefferson himself. One reason why obsessives love control—or, to be accurate, the illusion of having everything under control—is that they can easily be overwhelmed by their own impulses. A man with sumptuous tastes, Jefferson never could get a handle on his own penchant for runaway spending; during his eight years in the White House, he would shell out $10,000 ($200,000 today) on fine wines. But while he would always be in debt and would saddle Thomas Jefferson Randolph, the executor of his estate, with a $100,000 ($2 million) tab, time and time again, America benefited from his interest in systematically tracking the smallest of expenditures. After all, Jefferson created the penny as we know it—an innovation that would help put the whole country's finances in order. On account of this little-known legacy, to this day, Americans have Jefferson to thank every time they open their wallet or balance their checking account.

Jefferson loved all things decimal (as did fellow obsessive the librarian Melvil Dewey, discussed in chapter 3), and as a congressman at the end of the Revolution, he convinced Robert Morris, then the superintendent of finance, to scrap his confusing plan for establishing a uniform currency. To replace the various state currencies, which featured both pounds and dollars, Morris had proposed issuing a new federal dollar divided into 1,440 units (a measure that would have incorporated the pennies of each state without leaving any fractions). As Jefferson cogently argued in his 1784 paper, "Notes on the Establishment of a Money Unit, and of a Coinage for the United States" (of which he was so proud that he appended it to his autobiography, written in 1821), "the inconveniences of this Unit" meant that an eighty-dollar horse would "require a notation of six figures, to wit, 115,200 units." Jefferson's recommendation to divide the dollar instead into ten dimes and one hundred pennies was readily accepted. Jefferson also sought (as would Dewey a century later) to extend the decimal system to weights and measures, but his extensive report on the subject, submitted to the House of Representatives when he was secretary of state, went nowhere. However, his countrymen may well have been better off had Congress heeded his sage advice to divide the foot into ten inches and the inch into ten lines.

Jefferson was the Founding Father who could not stop organizing the fledgling nation. When the bored vice president and president of the Senate became frustrated by the chaotic ways of Congress, he did not hesitate to take on the monumental task of setting it aright. As a law student in the 1760s, he had done a systematic study of deliberative bodies through the ages, gathering quotations—a practice that he called "commonplacing"—from various British treatises. After returning to Philadelphia in 1797 to assume his position as the number two in the administration of President John Adams, Jefferson frequently relied on these old notes contained in his "Parliamentary Pocket-Book," a 105-page leather-bound duodecimo (a small volume whose pages are just 5 by 7¾ inches). In early 1800, he began to think about publishing a trimmed-down version of this guide, which he called A *Manual of Parliamentary Practice*. To put the finishing touches on his neatly written manuscript required clarifying "small matters of daily practice," as he wrote that February to George Wythe, his legal mentor from his Williamsburg days; for Jefferson, this need to go into procedural minutiae made the endeavor all that much more enjoyable.

Printed in early 1801, just as Jefferson was exchanging the vice presidency for the presidency, his manual on the legislative process was immediately put into use by the Senate, the House of Representatives, and state legislatures across the country. "It is much more material," Jefferson wrote in the first section, entitled "Importance of Rules," "that there should be a rule to go by, than what that rule is."

By this meta-rule also lived the man. Jefferson was addicted to his routines. He would rise at dawn and read before breakfast. For sixty years, he gave himself a cold foot bath every morning. At one o'clock, he would go riding—an activity he continued as president. On his return, about two or two and a half hours later, he would have his daily glass of water; dinner would then be served, during which he drank wine, but never more than three glasses. He typically retired to his chambers at nine and went to bed between ten and eleven.

Monticello, which he kept fine-tuning for decades after first moving there in 1770, celebrated the regularity and order that he loved. To construct his home, Jefferson relied on another rule-laden treatise, *The Four Books on Architecture* by the sixteenth-century architect Andrea Palladio, which he once referred to as his "Bible." During his lifetime, Jefferson owned seven editions of this masterpiece that inspired the revival of the classical style in the eighteenth century—he could not resist snapping up a couple of French translations. For each part of a villa—say, the walls or ceilings—Palladio insisted on precise proportions, based on the dimensions of ancient Roman buildings, which he himself had measured "with the utmost diligence." (This Renaissance man of numbers also encouraged architects to make "an exact calculation" of their costs before building in order to avoid leaving their creations unfinished.) Jefferson was, a French visitor noted in 1782, "the first American who has consulted the Fine Arts to know how he should shelter himself from the weather." One factor contributing to his decade of "unchequered happiness" with his wife, Martha, who died at the age of thirty-three in 1782, was her skillful administration of Monticello. "Nothing," Dumas Malone, the author of the Pulitzer Prize–winning six volume *Jefferson and His Time*, completed in 1981, "he ever did was more characteristic of him as a person or as a mind." Jefferson himself calculated the mathematical measurements and did the drawings for the three-story, twenty-one-room mansion, which he didn't finish until 1809. He also selected all the furnishings and accoutrements, down to the drapery and upholstery.

Jefferson liked mathematical precision everywhere, even in poetry. In the mid-1780s, in his daily walks in the Bois de Boulogne, America's minister to France began formulating how to put English literature in order. Jefferson's essay "Thoughts on English Prosody," completed in the fall of 1786, sought to explain "the rules" that should govern poetic composition. Mining passages from his literary commonplace book, which he began keeping as an adolescent, he presented numerous examples of different types of meter and rhyme interspersed with his commentary. The inveterate classicist came down hard on lyric poems such as Thomas Gray's "Elegy Written in a Country Churchyard" (1751) for intermingling different line lengths in the same verse and thus departing from "that simplicity and regularity of which the ear is most sensible." Though he didn't quite recommend kicking such poems out of the canon, he came close, concluding that "these pieces are seldom read twice."

Despite the overwhelming evidence of Jefferson's obsessionality, most biographers have looked the other way. Dumas Malone, whose work still remains definitive, characterized his subject as "thoughtful and observant" as he whipped out his thermometer in Philadelphia on July 4, 1776. The preeminent Jefferson scholar said nothing else about this curious incident. (Perhaps it takes one *not* to know one; Malone, who spent nearly forty years combing through Jeffersoniana, once described himself as "properly fastidious.") But such has not always been the case. The first writer to get his hands on the bulk of Jefferson's papers, Henry Stephens Randall, could not help but fixate on this central characterological tic. Like a giddy teenager, Randall, the author of a three-volume, two-thousand-page life published in 1858, used italics and exclamation points to express his initial surprise:

All the manuscripts of Thomas Jefferson present a striking and persistent coincidence in one particular—and it is one of the first ones which the examiner notices, partly from its own prominence, and partly because few out of the circle of his immediate friends are prepared for the fact it discloses. It is his remarkable *precision* down to minute details—his apparent *fondness for details*. Never was there a more methodical man from great matters down to the merest seeming trifles—never so diligent a recorder of them!...The pocket account books include the minutest items of his daily expenditure, down to two or three pennies paid for a shoe string, or tossed into a beggar's hat in Paris—and we think we remember one or two entries of a single penny, to make the inexorable *cash book* balance *exactly*!

As Randall aptly notes, to point out Jefferson's immersion in the trivial is not to diminish his greatness. "The master mind, that comes but once in a century," the biographer adds, "is stamped with universality....It has vigor to collect all, without becoming over-wearied or frittered away in the pursuit."

The more distressed Jefferson was, the more avidly he threw himself into his collecting, organizing, and list making. The loss of his wife would produce a veritable frenzy of classification. While his grief initially resulted in emotional paralysis, within a few months, he sought comfort by cranking out a host of new lists. In early 1783, the master collector created an Epistolary Record to track all his correspondence. Over the next forty-three years, he cataloged 19,000 letters of his own—he used a polygraph, not the modern day lie-detector but a primitive copy machine, as he wrote—and 25,000 from colleagues in a 656-page index. Not long after Martha's death, he also recorded a second inventory of his slaves—the total came to 204—in his Farm Book. And around the same time, he completed the first catalog of his books. Following the Renaissance philosopher Francis Bacon, Jefferson classified his 2,640 volumes into the categories of Memory (history), Reason (mathematics and philosophy), and Imagination (art and literature). To console himself, the aging Jefferson repeatedly responded to his own query of "whether my country is the better for my having lived at all" by compiling lists of his achievements. Shortly before his death in 1826, he came up with a final "short list." As he instructed his heirs, he wanted "the following inscription, and not a word more" placed on his tombstone:

HERE WAS BURIED
THOMAS JEFFERSON
AUTHOR OF THE DECLARATION OF AMERICAN INDEPENDENCE
OF THE STATUTE OF VIRGINIA FOR RELIGIOUS FREEDOM
AND FATHER OF THE UNIVERSITY OF VIRGINIA.

So attached to lists was he that he wished to be remembered by one; and this summary of his career stressed his main obsessions and compulsions—advocating for freedom and organizing knowledge—rather than the prominent offices he held—governor, secretary of state, and president.

For comfort, Jefferson often turned to data sets rather than to other people. A man who had difficulty connecting, he was convinced that "the most effectual means of being secure against pain is to retire within ourselves, and to suffice for our own happiness." A loner with few close friends, he felt uncomfortable in most social settings. In fact, in a recent paper published in the *Journal of Nervous and Mental Disease*, a team of Duke University psychiatrists, based on the evidence contained in the major biographies, concluded that Jefferson met the diagnostic criteria for social phobia. A common symptom of this anxiety disorder is an intense fear of public speaking, the very problem that derailed Jefferson's law career in the early 1770s. "His voice, if raised much above the loudness of ordinary conversation," Randall notes, "began, after a few moments' effort, to 'sink in his throat'—in other words, to become husky and inarticulate."

Jefferson never said a word in the debates held during the Second Continental Congress. As president, he gave just two speeches—his first and second Inaugural Addresses. In sharp contrast with his predecessors, George Washington and John Adams, President Jefferson hardly ever appeared in public, except at his dinner parties, where he set strict rules (he invited members of one party—either Federalists or Republicans—in groups of twelve to twenty, and any political discussion was verboten). While Jefferson could be a lively conversationalist, he related more easily to others on the page than in person. His was an epistolary presidency. In his White House study, with his pet hummingbird, Dick, often perched upon his shoulder—the president kept the cage open when no one else was around—he spent ten to thirteen hours a day at his writing desk. As per his own calculations, in the first year of his administration, Jefferson received 1,881 letters and sent out 677.

Thomas Jefferson was born on April 13, 1743, in Shadwell, Virginia. He was the third child and firstborn son of Peter Jefferson and Jane Randolph; he had nine brothers and sisters, seven of whom would survive until adulthood. A modest country squire who owned about 1,500 acres of farmland along with two slaves at the time of his marriage, Peter Jefferson was an imposing physical specimen; it was said he could lift a thousand pounds of tobacco from the ground to an upright position with each hand simultaneously. The laconic advocate of self-reliance often reminded his children, "Never ask another to do for you what you can do for yourself." The Virginia native didn't attend college, but he was an avid reader of Shakespeare who made sure that his eldest son received the best education that money could buy. At nine, Tom boarded at the house of a local clergyman, William Douglas, where he began studying the classics. No slouch with numbers, Peter Jefferson kept his own detailed account books—his payments to Douglas came to sixteen pounds per annum—and was a talented surveyor who coauthored a widely used map of the southern United States. According to Randall, "the lessons of system, punctuality, energy and perseverance" were passed down from the father, who also served his community as a justice of the peace, a colonel in the militia, and a member of the Virginia House of Burgesses.

While Thomas Jefferson later spoke affectionately about his father, he almost never mentioned his mother, even though her family stood at the center of Virginia's aristocracy. "By his own reckoning," one biographer has written, "she was a zero quantity in his life." His desire to erase his mother from his history suggests, most Jefferson scholars agree, that the relationship was marked by tension. One common hypothesis is that she had a habit of barking out injunctions to him, just as he would later do with his daughters. Whatever the source of the friction, its effects may well have been considerable; after all, Jane Randolph constantly hovered over him. Except for his student years in Williamsburg, he continued to live with her at Shadwell until he moved to Monticello at the age of twenty-seven. And the boy who felt alienated from his mother would evolve into a loner who had difficulty forging intimate bonds with other human beings, particularly women.

Details about Tom's early years are scant. Shadwell burned down in 1770, destroying many of his papers. Eager to protect his privacy, Jefferson would later burn his entire correspondence with both his mother and his wife. And his un-finished memoir, written in 1821, like his various accounts books, focuses mostly on the data. "At the age of 77," he wrote in the introduction to this hundred-page autobiographical fragment, which describes political events rather than personal experiences, "I begin to make some memoranda and state some recollections of dates and facts concerning myself, for my own ready reference and for the infor-mation of my family." The septuagenarian had little interest in remembering for himself, much less in revealing to others, his life as he had actually lived it. "I am already," Jefferson noted about a third of the way through, "tired of talking about myself."

Tom would be forced to grow up much too fast. In August 1757, when he was fourteen, his beloved father died. In his will, Peter Jefferson left his eldest son a "body servant," his library of forty-two books—then a not insignificant number—and his mathematical instruments. But Tom would not inherit any property until he reached twenty-one. In the meantime, he would have to cater to those who wielded authority over the family—namely, his mother and the five executors of his father's estate, whose approval he would need for his expenses. According to one biographer, this was the primary reason why Jefferson began counting every penny and became "obsessed by accountability." Sadly, even though the adoles-cent had little control over his own quotidian life, he was saddled with enormous responsibility. Thrust into the role of the man of the house, he was supposed to oversee the education and welfare of his six sisters and brother, whose ages then ranged from seventeen to two. "When I recollect that at 14 years of age," Jeffer-son confided to his grandson a half century later, "the whole care and direction of my self was thrown on my self entirely, without a relation or friend qualified to advise or guide me…I am astonished I did not…become…worthless to soci-ety." These feelings of anger and alienation would last well into adulthood.

In early 1758, the fourteen-year-old began attending a boarding school in nearby Fredericksville, led by a cleric named William Maury. While he enjoyed immersing himself in his studies and learning the violin, he could not escape entirely from the stressful family situation that he encountered upon his return to Shadwell every weekend. As the literary critic Kenneth Lockridge has noted, of the roughly eighty entries that Jefferson made in his literary commonplace book in the years surrounding his father's death, about half contain passages ex-pressing rage against authority. This correlation, argues Lockridge, suggests that the teenager had an "obsession with conflict." As he read John Milton's *Paradise*

Lost, Jefferson apparently sympathized with Satan, the epic poem's protagonist, who, as the schoolboy recorded in his notebook, vowed "ever to do Ill" and preferred to "reign in Hell, than serve in Heaven." Long before writing the Declaration, Jefferson was already thinking about revolution.

After two years at Reverend Maury's, he petitioned John Harvie, a family friend who served as the chief executor of his father's estate, to approve his plan to begin college at William and Mary. "I suppose I can pursue my Studies in the Greek and Latin as well there as here," he explained to Harvie in his earliest surviving letter, dated January 14, 1760, "and likewise learn something of the Mathematics." The sixteen-year-old's hunch proved prescient. Soon after his arrival in Williamsburg that March, he came under the wing of William Small, a professor of mathematics and natural philosophy (physics), who, as he later wrote, "fixed the destinies of my life." From Small, who taught Jefferson through lectures as well as informal daily chats, he learned to appreciate the scientific method and systematic thinking of all kinds. But it was mathematics about which Jefferson became downright passionate. The perfectionist could hardly resist the lure of entering a world filled only with numbers. "We have no theories there," he wrote a half century later, "no uncertainties remain on the mind; all is demonstration and satisfaction." For the same reason, this voracious intellectual would later express a reverence for all branches of knowledge except ethics and metaphysics; he had little but contempt for philosophers such as Plato. "Recondite speculation," concludes Randall, "having no connection with practical questions...could not long interest his attention." Though much more widely read than the other obsessives covered in this book (and just about anyone else), Jefferson too was a problem solver, not a reflective thinker. The Virginia plantation owner would return again and again to William Emerson's *Doctrine of Fluxions*, his beloved calculus text from college, but each time, he was motivated by a specific task. "I have imagined and executed," he wrote to John Taylor, a fellow Virginia politico and farmer, in 1794, "a mould-board [the wooden part of a plow that picks up the sod cut by the iron blade] which may be mathematically demonstrated to be perfect, as far as perfection depends on mathematical principles." While Jefferson didn't patent his famous "Moldboard of Least Resistance," which greatly facilitated plowing, most scholars consider his invention a significant contribution to agriculture.

Reading fifteen hours a day, Jefferson completed William and Mary in two years. Over the next five years, as he studied law under George Wythe, a leader of the Virginia bar to whom he had been introduced by Dr. Small, he kept up the pace. Except for his hour a day of violin practice, he would rarely have time for anything else. Wythe, whom Jefferson would later praise for "regularity in all his habits" and call a "second father," endeared himself to the future defender of individual rights by his enlightened approach to legal training. Instead of requiring Jefferson to do clerical work in his law office, the bibliophile with the perfect Greek encouraged him to learn for himself. Judging by the advice that Jefferson gave to a prospective law student in 1769, he followed a grueling reading schedule; he would begin with Agriculture at dawn, move to Law, Politics, and History during the day, and conclude with Belles-Lettres at bedtime. In the missive in which he showcased his rigorous curriculum, Jefferson mentioned all the essential books in each area (the key legal text was the *Institutes of the Lawes of England* by Sir Edward Coke, the legendary Jacobean jurist), insisting that they be "read in the order in which they are named." He also recommended summarizing "every case of value," which was exactly what he did in his own legal commonplace book. For most of the 1760s, Jefferson's deepest ties were to his texts; canonical authors such as Coke, whom he once referred to as an "old...scoundrel," were as real to him as his colleagues and family members. When a slave informed him in early 1770 that Shadwell had burned down, his thoughts didn't immediately turn to the welfare of his mother or siblings who lived there with him. "But were none of my books saved?" was instead the first question that emerged from his lips. For Jefferson, books were imaginary friends that could help insulate him from feelings of isolation.

During his student years in Williamsburg, Jefferson enjoyed the company of just a few flesh-and-blood friends. His closest was John Page, a classmate at William and Mary (and later a governor of Virginia) with whom he would chitchat about both his studies and town gossip. But in contrast to Page and other peers who found wives soon after finishing college, Jefferson was too socially obtuse to get anywhere near the altar in the 1760s. At nineteen, he developed a crush on Rebecca Burwell, a bright and attractive sixteen-year-old living at the home of her uncle, a senior member of the Governor's Council. With Rebecca, as with his books or anything else that piqued his interest, he had only one gear—the obsessional. In December 1762, of the woman of his dreams, whom he still hardly knew, he confided to Page, "There is so lively an image of her imprinted in my mind that I shall think of her too often I fear for my peace of mind." The following fall, the perpetually tongue-tied Jefferson fell into a "most melancholy fit" when she rejected his awkward proposal of marriage one evening at a dance. "When I had an opportunity of venting...[my thoughts]," he wrote to Page, "a few broken sentences, uttered in great disorder, and interrupted with pauses of uncommon length, were the too visible remarks of my strange confusion!" Not yet ready to give up, Jefferson tried again during a follow-up conversation. But rather than pleading his case by insisting upon the depth of his love, Jefferson decided to go around her; as he informed Rebecca, he now planned to ask her family for the right to her hand sometime in the future. "His idolizing dreams," Jon Kukla, author of *Mr. Jefferson's Women*, has written of this episode, "had blinded him to the existence of the real girl." Confused, if not incensed by Jefferson's second proposal, Rebecca soon made plans to marry someone else. Upon hearing the news, a devastated Jefferson came down with a "violent head ach."

The bachelor's next stab at romance was so disastrous that it would reemerge decades later as Exhibit A in America's first presidential sex scandal. In 1768, as Jefferson would acknowledge in 1805, a few years after newspapers such as the *New York Evening Post* first reported the story, he made unwelcome advances toward Betsy Walker, the wife of John Walker, a classmate at both Reverend Maury's and William and Mary. (Exhibit B would be his liaison with his slave, Sally Hemings, which began several years after his wife's death; and to these accusations he would never respond.)

In July 1768, Walker, later a U.S. senator from Virginia, asked Jefferson, his "neighbor and fast friend" and the executor of his will, to look after his wife and infant daughter while he went to New York on business. Upon his return four months later, a distressed Betsy Walker, who wouldn't mention any particulars for another decade and a half, told her husband of her objection to keeping Jefferson as his executor. She also "wondered," as Walker later reported to a friend, "why I could place such confidence in him [Jefferson]." According to Walker, his wife also informed him that Jefferson made passes at her on several other occasions over the next decade. When Walker went public with his version of events in 1805, Jefferson wrote to Robert Smith, his secretary of the navy, "You will perceive that I plead guilty to one of their charges, that when young and single, I offered love to a handsome lady. I acknowledge its incorrectness." In this "he said that she said vs. he said" debate, it's impossible to tell whether Jefferson persisted in his efforts to seduce Mrs. Walker after his marriage to Martha. But whatever the full extent of his harassment, Jefferson was guilty of a serious lapse in judgment that highlights the gulf between his intellectual and emotional intelligence.

Given Jefferson's cluelessness around women, it's surprising that he ever managed to win the heart of the accomplished Martha Wayles Skelton. Born in 1748, she was the daughter of the wealthy landowner John Wayles and his first wife, also named Martha, who died a week after her birth. In 1766, the pretty, well-read, and musically inclined five-foot-tall heiress with the expressive hazel eyes married Bathurst Skelton, another colleague of Jefferson's at William and Mary. Jefferson first met Martha around the time of her first husband's premature death in 1768 when he took on her father as a client. The young widow immediately attracted a horde of suitors. Though as gauche as ever, Jefferson made the most of his competitive advantage; he would let his musical expertise do what his clumsy and disorganized words could not. And he had some experience to draw on. Duets were what had bonded him with his elder sister, Jane, whose loss he was still mourning—his favorite sibling had died suddenly in 1765 at the age of twenty-five. His strategy worked to a tee. According to Randall, two rivals once entered Martha's house and overheard "her harpsichord and voice, accompanied by Mr. Jefferson's violin and voice, in the passages of a touching song...and took their hats and retired, to return no more on the same errand!" During their courtship, Jefferson kept plying her with music. In December 1770, he bought her a portable clavichord; six months later, he gave her a more expensive mahogany pianoforte. The couple was married on January 1, 1772. Martha was an ideal match. Among the Jefferson papers at the Library of Congress are a couple of pages from an account book that she kept from January to June 1777 in her clear handwriting. In four consecutive entries in March, Martha, then seven months pregnant, recorded her production of soap—on March 8, her output came to a staggering one hundred pounds. Such devotion to cleanliness (and accurate measurement) must have endeared her to her husband as much as her affinity for Laurence Sterne, the author of *Tristram Shandy*, the one novelist whom this man of facts adored. Sterne's signature work repeatedly attacked conventional authority, and thus appealed to the adolescent rebel that would forever remain a core part of Jefferson.

———

After his admission to the bar in early 1767, Jefferson quickly built a thriving legal practice. Though he missed the nonstop reading, he didn't mind the mundane tasks of writing briefs and filing motions; after all, for Jefferson, drudgery always held a certain appeal. He kept close track of all the relevant numbers in his copious fee and case books; the former features an eighteen-page alphabetized index of all his debtors and the latter lists all 939 cases that he handled between February 1, 1767, and November 9, 1774, when political unrest shut down the courts. By then, the husband with the growing family was already channeling most of his energy into a promising legislative career that had begun with his taking a seat in the House of Burgesses in May 1769. As he entered government, he felt it necessary to step up his reading of political philosophy. By the end of 1769, he was devouring a host of tomes by such heavyweights as England's John Locke and France's Montesquieu. While Jefferson could have become an accomplished lawyer and a legislator without the decade of systematic study— Patrick Henry, whom he called "the laziest man in reading I ever knew," did not attend college and devoted just six weeks to the study of law—his self-designed professional training would be instrumental in helping him shake up the reigning political order in both America and the world.

He got his first chance to wield his fiery pen for the cause of freedom in June 1774, when Parliament responded to the Boston Tea Party by closing the Port of Boston. Standing in solidarity with the residents of Massachusetts, the delegates to the Virginia assembly planned a meeting for early August to choose representatives to the new Continental Congress, slated to begin in September. Jefferson soon completed a twenty-three-page pamphlet of grievances, which he intended to show to his fellow legislators. While his body did not reach the capital—en route to Williamsburg, he came down with dysentery—his words did; and they caused quite a stir when published anonymously later that year in the *Virginia Gazette* and other papers across America as "A Summary View of the Rights of British America." "If it had any merit," a modest Jefferson would write a generation later of his first publication, "it was that of our taking our true ground, and that which was afterwards assumed and maintained." Jefferson had issued the most powerful challenge to date of British rule, one which got the colonists to think about their plight in an entirely new way.

In an attempt to stop Parliament from passing any more unjust laws, Jefferson marshaled a series of brilliant and original theoretical arguments. This was not philosophy for philosophy's sake, but philosophy as a means to achieve specific political ends. According to Jefferson, just like the Saxons who had emigrated to Britain a millennium earlier, the residents of America were free agents unbeholden to the mother country; but they had been too busy earning a living to be aware of the rights to which they were entitled. "Our ancestors…who migrated hither," noted the conscientious student of history and law, "were farmers, not lawyers. The fictitious principle that all lands belong originally to the king, they were early persuaded to believe real." And not only, stressed Jefferson, was America not a feudal state, but "British parliament [had] no right to exercise authority over us." That bold assertion was based on the doctrine of natural right, which he had read in Locke and elsewhere. Though Jefferson's position was radical for the time, he did not yet seek to displace King George III as America's "chief magistrate." He envisioned that America might become self-governing just as Scotland had been in the seventeenth century. And he appealed to the king for protection from parliamentary abuses. "No longer persevere," he implored, "in sacrificing the rights of one part of the empire to the inordinate desires of another."

Jefferson would move on to attacking the king in the Declaration. By June 1776, he had already acquired a reputation among his colleagues as a writer with a "peculiar felicity for expression," as John Adams would later put it; thus, he received the most votes when the Continental Congress appointed a committee of five to draft a document to explain the rationale for independence. Jefferson proposed that the older, Harvard-educated Adams, who had come in second in the balloting, take a first crack at it. Though he was one of the few Founders in Jefferson's league in the book collection and consumption department, Adams still felt compelled to demur, conceding, "You can write ten times better than I can." In contrast to "A Summary View," the Declaration would contain no new ideas. In the intervening two years, a general consensus had emerged among American Whigs that the doctrines of natural law and natural right applied to their dispute with England. "Not to find out new principles," Jefferson would write of his purpose nearly a half century later, "or new arguments, never before thought of…but to place before mankind the common sense of the subject.…It was intended to be an expression of the American mind, and to give to that expression the proper tone and spirit called for by the occasion." By crafting one of the most revered state papers ever written, which Abraham Lincoln would call that "immortal emblem of man's humanity," Jefferson would succeed in doing far more than that; he would also inspire oppressed groups from around the world for centuries to come.

The Declaration would bear Jefferson's stamp not in its content, but in its style and its passion. As the historian Carl Becker observed nearly a century ago, its text is a "model of clear, concise and simple statement." These were the prose skills that Jefferson had honed during his long years of apprenticeship in Williamsburg. The voracious reader was also a compulsive note taker, who prided himself on his ability to "seek out the pith" when summarizing legal cases in his commonplace book. "The most valuable of all talents," he once wrote, "is that of never using two words where one will do." In the storied Preamble, he squeezed in all the major arguments of Locke's *Second Treatise on Government* in just two hundred words. The urgency behind his plea also had roots in his own experience. For the thirty-three-year-old, who had still lived in his mother's home just a half dozen years earlier, personal independence had been a long time in coming. For Jefferson, the British monarch represented one more authority figure who stood in his way. And characteristically, the bulk of his achievement number one—more than half of its nearly 1,400 words—took the form of a list, which Samuel Adams later described as George III's "catalogue of crimes." In detailing the king's twenty-seven abuses in its central section, often forgotten today, Jefferson was plagiarizing from himself; the preamble of his draft of the Virginia Constitution, which he had completed that spring, was a close cousin. In the Declaration, he couldn't help but personalize the conflict, calling the king "a tyrant...unfit to be the ruler of a free people." This epithet made others squirm. "I thought the expression too passionate," John Adams would later write, "and too much like scolding, for so grave and solemn a document." Jefferson wouldn't budge on his assessment, however. In his memoir, he would refer to the English monarch, whom he met in London in 1786, as a "mulish being."

That summer, America's declaration of independence, rather than Thomas Jefferson's Declaration of Independence, was what made headlines. All that anyone seemed to care about was that the colonists had finally broken all ties with the mother country. In cities and towns across the nation, the text was read aloud to cheering throngs rather than studied. Few Americans knew who had written the document or paid attention to its particular words and phrases. That Jefferson had been the primary author was not mentioned in any newspaper until 1784. And only in the 1790s, when he sought to replace Washington as president, did Jefferson start to claim ownership. With the birth of partisan politics, his Republican party saw itself as the defender of the founding principles against its opponents, the Federalists, which it dubbed "monarchists." In 1797, a Republican paper celebrated the Declaration as a "rational discussion and definition of the rights of man and the end of civil government." After his presidency, as he started to focus on his legacy, Jefferson was visibly moved whenever he recalled the bold assertions on behalf of human dignity that he had made in his youth. He also kept close track of the relevant numbers. "Of the signers of the Declaration of Independence," he reported to John Adams in 1812, "I see now living not more than half a dozen on your side of the Potomac and on this side, myself alone."

After completing his work on the Declaration, Jefferson would have little to do with national affairs until the war ended. In October 1776, accompanied by his wife, he headed to Williamsburg, where he took up his seat in Virginia's House of Delegates. With the new Commonwealth then rebuilding itself from the ground up, Jefferson relished the chance to strike out against "every fiber...of ancient or feudal aristocracy" in order to lay a foundation for "government truly republican." This "political architect," as Dumas Malone has called him, wished to bring order and rationality to his home state by creating an "aristocracy of talent and virtue." Within a month, he notched his first victory by getting his fellow delegates to abolish primogeniture. That fall, he was also appointed to head a committee of five, which was charged with the responsibility of revising all of Virginia's laws. Two men soon dropped out, and Jefferson ended up doing the bulk of the work himself. The astute legal historian took on the monumental task of revising English common law and statutes until the reign of James I. In June 1779, shortly after he became governor, Jefferson submitted to the General Assembly a ninety-page report of his committee of revisers, which featured 126 carefully wrought bills. As in his own account and fee books, Jefferson stuck an index in the front, which listed the contents of each numbered bill. In the revisions of the outdated laws, precise prose reigned. As Jefferson later noted in his memoir, he thought it useful to eliminate "endless tautologies...involutions of case within case, and parenthesis within parenthesis, and...multiplied efforts at certainty by *saids* and *aforesaids*, by *ors* and *ands*." The bills addressed everything from property rights and education to the penal code and religion.

His pride and joy was Bill Number 82, "For Establishing Religious Freedom," which he first introduced in 1779. This cause célèbre, too, had its source in childhood hurts. The adolescent railing against authority had also felt alienated from his Anglican instructors, Douglas and Maury; in his memoir, he insulted the former as "a superficial Latinist, less instructed in Greek." (Jefferson's assessment of Douglas was much harsher than the similar one rendered by the poet Ben Jonson of Shakespeare—"small Latin and less Greek"—because clas-

sical languages were supposed to be this clergyman's bailiwick.) Baptized into
the Church of England like everyone else in his family, Jefferson did not hate
religion per se; but as a deist, who saw God solely as the omnipotent creator of
the universe, he hated the dogma spread by organized religions. To come up
with the text for his famous bill, Jefferson once again mined his reading notes.
Paraphrasing Locke's A *Letter Concerning Toleration*, he stressed the connection between true religious belief and rationality, noting that "the opinions and
belief of men...follow involuntarily the evidence proposed to their minds." De-
cried by critics as "diabolical," his bill didn't pass until several years later when
it was revived by his protégé, James Madison, then a key member of the Virginia
legislature. By the end of 1786, Madison would help transform nearly half of
Jefferson's 126 bills, which he called a "mine of legislative wealth," into law. Virginia's Act for Religious Freedom, which created "a wall of separation between
church and state," as Jefferson would later put it, was soon reworked into the
First Amendment of the Bill of Rights. Thanks to Jefferson, all Americans would
enjoy both the freedom of religion and the freedom from religion. No longer
could the government, as states such as Virginia had done before the Revolution, use tax dollars to support any officially sanctioned church or churches.
The socially awkward Jefferson, who experienced most human connections as
an annoyance, had gotten another group of intruders—the clergy—to leave him
alone. Jefferson's political philosophy, often summed up as "that government is
best which governs least" (even though these words were penned not by him,
but by Henry David Thoreau), was inseparable from his personal predilection
for solitude.

Jefferson's two one-year terms as Virginia's governor proved to be the low
point of his political career. Elected by the legislature on June 1, 1779, to
replace Patrick Henry, who was prohibited by law from serving a fourth consecutive term, he accepted the post reluctantly. "[E]specially in times like these,"
Jefferson wrote to Richard Henry Lee a couple of weeks later, "public offices
are burthens to those appointed to them." Inflation in Virginia, as in the rest
of the struggling nation, was spiraling out of control; the price of a duck, just
a few shillings in 1779, would skyrocket to fifty pounds by 1781. And British
forces, having recently taken Savannah, Georgia, were starting to attack the Virginia coast. Despite—or perhaps because of—all the stress, Jefferson's minutiae
mania was as fervent as ever. When presented by his assistants with a list of all
the furniture in the Governor's Palace after a few weeks in office, he person-

ally checked off each of the roughly fifty items, including the pair of blue and white butter boats. And after completing his inventory, Jefferson wrote the following note: "things omitted. 2 delft [a town in Holland known for its ceramic products] wash basons. 4 blankets." A year later, in response to a request from the Marquis de Marbois, secretary of the French legation to the United States, who was asking all thirteen governors for information about their states, Jefferson got cracking on a thorough inventory of Virginia. "I take every occasion which presents itself of procuring answers," he wrote to another French friend in November 1780. This was the beginning of his only full-length book, *Notes on the State of Virginia*, which he kept expanding and revising over the next several years. Besides climate, Jefferson covered a variety of topics, including boundaries, landscape, and population; the chapter on Virginia's natural history, its minerals, vegetables, and animals, was the longest, comprising about one-fourth of the text. Marbois, who didn't get much of a response from any other governor, was bowled over by what Jefferson sent to him. "I cannot express to you," the Frenchman wrote to Jefferson in March 1782, "how grateful I am for the trouble you have taken to draft detailed responses to the questions I had taken the liberty of addressing to you." For Jefferson, of course, gathering this material and doing the concomitant number crunching—according to his statistical analysis, Virginia's 1781 population of 567,614 was projected to reach 4,540,912 by 1862¾—was anything but trouble. Though containing many a trivial factoid, his treatise also presented important scientific findings. As the editor of an annotated edition, published a half century ago, has put it, Jefferson crafted "one of America's first permanent literary and intellectual landmarks."

Facing crisis after crisis, Governor Jefferson succeeded in doing little but moving the seat of government out of Williamsburg, first to Richmond and then to Charlottesville. On June 2, 1781, with the Brits coming directly after both him and the members of the legislature, he fled Monticello on horseback. He would soon join the rest of his family at his other plantation at Poplar Forest, ninety miles away. While Jefferson had already announced his retirement, his successor wouldn't be chosen until the legislature reconvened in Staunton a few days later. Since he had still technically been governor at the time of his escape, his political enemies, led by the poorly read Patrick Henry, who were bent on giving the state's new chief executive dictatorial powers, immediately seized on the appearance of impropriety. On June 12, the House ordered an investigation into Jefferson's conduct during the whole last year of his administration.

Six months later, the humiliated ex-governor had to defend himself in a public hearing against a series of charges, including whether he had abandoned his post and the citizens of Virginia. Even after he was cleared of all wrongdoing and had received a public apology from the Assembly, Jefferson remained furious. The following spring, when the freeholders of Albemarle County elected him once again to the House of Delegates, he declined to serve. On May 20, 1782, he wrote to James Monroe, then a freshman member of the state legislature, that the inquiry "had inflicted a wound on my spirit which will only be cured by the all-healing grave.... Reason and inclination unite in justifying my retirement."

Jefferson had another compelling reason for avoiding public service. His wife, Martha, who on May 8 had given birth to the couple's sixth child, Lucy Elizabeth—of the other five, only two were still alive, Martha (Patsy), born in 1772, and Mary (Polly), born in 1778—was gravely ill. Childbirth had never been easy for the frail Martha, and this time, as Jefferson quickly realized, she would not recover. For the next four months, he sat either at her bedside or at his writing desk, which had been transplanted into a small room that opened at the head of her bed. "My dear wife," he noted in his account book on September 6, 1782, "died this day at 11:45 am." His devastation was palpable. For the next three weeks, he shut himself in his bedroom. Though Patsy was still a month shy of her tenth birthday, Jefferson did not hesitate to lean on her for emotional support. Late in life, he would describe his eldest daughter as "the cherished companion of my early life and the nurse of my age." But the nursing actually began decades earlier. "I was never a moment from his side," Patsy later recalled of her whereabouts in the weeks following her mother's death. Once the distraught Jefferson summoned up the energy to leave the house, all he wanted to do was go on horseback rides with Patsy. "In those melancholy rambles," she added, "I was...a solitary witness to many a violent burst of grief." His frequent emotional outbursts must have frightened her and made *her* loss all the more excruciating. But Jefferson was too self-absorbed to be at all attentive to what the nine-year-old was experiencing.

The characterologically challenged father could not recognize his favorite daughter's emotional needs or even her separateness. For him, parental love meant teaching her how to be a good obsessive. In his first letter to Patsy, written at the end of 1783 while she was living with a family friend in Philadelphia, he recommended that the eleven-year-old adhere to the following schedule:

from 8. to 10 o'clock practice music

from 10. to 1. dance one day and draw another

from 1. to 2. draw on the day you dance, and write a letter the next day

from 3. to 4. read French

from 4. to 5. exercise yourself in music

from 5. till bedtime read English, write & c.

As part of the program, he also insisted on perfection in her appearance. "Nothing is so disgusting," ran his startling injunction, "to our sex as a want of cleanliness and delicacy in yours.... Your first work will be to dress yourself in such style, as that you may be seen by any gentleman without his being able to discover a pin amiss, or any other circumstance of neatness wanting." A few years later, the meticulous keeper of account books stressed to her the importance of "never buying anything which you have not money in your pocket to pay for." "Learn yourself," the meta-rule man added, "the habit of adhering rigorously to the rules you lay down for yourself." In Patsy, who would forever idealize him, Jefferson created the dutiful and industrious daughter whom he needed.

———

Jefferson would never get over the death of his wife. In November 1782, he wrote a friend that he was "a little emerging from the stupor of mind which has rendered me as dead to the world as she whose loss occasioned it." In an attempt to short-circuit his mourning, he jumped back into politics. In June 1783, Jefferson was one of five delegates selected by the Virginia General Assembly to serve in the new Continental Congress. On May 7, 1784, Congress appointed him a minister plenipotentiary; his assignment was to travel to Paris to assist Benjamin Franklin and John Adams in negotiating commercial treaties with European nations. To prepare himself for his new job, the data collector went into overdrive. Over the next two months, as he made the trek from Annapolis, where Congress was meeting, to Boston, from where his ship was to leave, he gathered massive amounts of economic information on each state that he passed through. His twelve-part questionnaire, which he filled out by meeting with leading merchants and public figures, covered everything from the wages of carpenters to the size of fishing vessels.

On July 5, 1784, Jefferson, accompanied by Patsy, boarded the *Ceres*, which was bound for Cowes. He entrusted his younger daughters, Polly and Lucy—the two-year-old would die of whooping cough just a few months later—to the care of an aunt back in Virginia. Traversing the Atlantic did not stop him from piling up factoids. Every day at noon, he recorded in his account book numerous measurements, including latitude and longitude, the mileage since the previous day, the temperature, and wind direction. (Two decades later, President Jefferson would know whereof he spoke when he instructed his personal secretary, Meriwether Lewis, to take "observations of latitude and longitude at all remarkable points on the [Missouri] river...with great pains and accuracy.") And during the three-week journey to England, he also interviewed the owner of the ship, the Newburyport merchant Nathaniel Tracy, to complete his Massachusetts questionnaire. As he learned from Tracy, carpenters in the Bay State were now making about $7 a day, up from $3–$6 before the war.

Father and daughter arrived in Paris on August 6. On August 30, the forty-one-year-old diplomat met for the first time with his elders on the commission, Adams and Franklin, at the latter's home in Passy. Revered by the French for his scientific knowledge and sophistication, Franklin would introduce Jefferson to the nation's leading philosophes, artists, and writers. When Philadelphia's polymath returned to America the following year, Jefferson became minister to France, a post he would hold until after the storming of the Bastille in 1789. "No one can replace him [Franklin]," Jefferson would repeatedly insist. "I am only his successor." In 1787, his slave Sally Hemings escorted his eight-year-old daughter Polly from Virginia to Paris. His two girls would both attend the Abbaye Royale de Panthemont, an exclusive convent school, where, as Jefferson was assured, "not a word is ever spoken on the subject of religion."

After a difficult first winter, when he was sidelined both by ill health and by the news of Lucy's death, this "savage of the mountains of America," as Jefferson described himself in 1785, began to acclimate to his new surroundings. Despite his lifelong antipathy toward big cities, which he later characterized as "pestilential to the morals, the health and the liberties of man," he couldn't help but adore the architecture, sculpture, music, and art that now surrounded him. Jefferson was also fascinated by Paris's technological marvels, such as its suspension bridges and gadgets; he enjoyed going to the Café Mécanique, where wine was served by dumbwaiters (as would later be the case in Monticello). The hot-air balloon enthusiast, who, before leaving Annapolis, had compiled a detailed list of recent French ascensions for a friend, rarely missed a chance to view a launch in the flesh. For the self-confessed bibliomaniac, the French capital's ubiquitous bookstalls—such as those lining the Quai des Grands-Augustins— also proved irresistible. Though Jefferson forced himself to "submit to the rule of buying only at reasonable prices," he ended up acquiring for himself about fifty feet of books a year, all of which he eventually had shipped back to Virginia. He also sent books back to several American friends—most notably, dozens on law and government to James Madison, just as his protégé was beginning to draft the Constitution. He soon found himself missing little about Virginia except for its factoids. "I thank you again and again," he wrote in September 1785 to the Scottish physician James Currie, then in Richmond, "for the details it [your last letter] contains, these being precisely of the nature I would wish.... But I can persuade nobody to believe that the small facts which they see passing daily under their eyes are precious to me at this distance; much more interesting to the heart than events of higher rank.... Continue then to give me facts, little facts."

The following September, Jefferson was, as Dumas Malone has put it, "quite swept off his supposedly well-planted feet." The new object of affection for the forty-three-year-old widower was Maria Cosway, a petite, blue-eyed, twenty-six-year-old artist, who was visiting from London where she lived with her husband, Richard Cosway, a successful portrait painter. The American ambassador first met the beautiful and musically talented Italian-born Maria—not only was she a composer, but she also played both the harpsichord and harp—on September 3, 1786, at the Halle au Blé, the domed Parisian grain market. Jefferson was accompanied by the American artist John Trumbull, who introduced him to both Cosways. Twenty years older than his wife, Richard Cosway was then in the personal employ of the Prince of Wales (later King George IV). With her family down on its luck after the death of her father, Maria had succumbed to her mother's demand to marry the socialite with the deep pockets. The vapid and mercurial Cosway had little else to offer; as numerous contemporaries noted, he had "a monkey face" and couldn't keep his hands off other women. Jefferson was instantly taken by Maria, whom he later called "the most superb thing on earth"; within minutes, he came up with an excuse to cancel his dinner engagement with the Duchess D'Anville. His long evening with the Cosways didn't end until an impromptu harp concert in the wee hours at the home of the Bohemian composer Johann Baptist Krumpholtz. "When I came home... and looked back to the morning," Jefferson later wrote Maria of their first meeting, "it seemed to have been a month gone."

For the next two weeks, Jefferson and Maria were inseparable. Either alone or in the company of others such as Maria's husband, Trumbull, William Short (Jefferson's personal secretary), or his daughter Patsy, the mutually infatuated couple played tourist, heading to one scenic attraction after another. They gallivanted to the Royal Library (today the Bibliothèque Nationale), the Louvre, Versailles, and the Théâtre-Italien, as well as to the hills along the Seine. Whether Jefferson and Maria ever consummated their love has been the source of lively debate among Jefferson scholars. While the fragmentary evidence points to little but the likelihood that they both harbored fantasies about sexual union, physical intimacy is not out of the question; after all, given her marriage of convenience, Maria felt as lonely as Jefferson, as he probably picked up quickly, and their outings took place in the city that was then widely considered the world's capital of illicit love. (Jefferson's secretary, Short, would manage to have a couple of affairs during his Parisian sojourn, including one with the young wife of Duc de La Rochefoucauld.) On September 18, Jefferson severely injured his wrist while strolling with Maria near the Champs-Élysées. Due to the intense pain, he retreated to his home for a few weeks; and though Maria intended to visit, she could never squirm away from her husband. On Friday, October 6, a still ailing Jefferson accompanied the Cosways to the town of St. Denis, where they boarded a carriage for the trip back to London.

Over the next few days, Jefferson wrote out with his left hand what Julian Boyd, an editor of his collected papers, has called "one of the notable love letters in the English language." Its form was distinctly Jeffersonian. The man who had difficulty romancing women with words (as opposed to music) declared his love in a curious 4,600-word missive, which pivots around a philosophical dialogue between his "Head" and his "Heart." As with his clumsy second proposal to Burwell, an anxious Jefferson once again pretended as if the woman of his dreams did not exist. Rather than expressing his feelings directly to Maria, he dramatized his own internal conflict. As Jefferson framed the imaginary debate, at the same time as his rational side was chastising him as "the most incorrigible of all the beings that ever sinned" for the decision to spend so much time with her, his emotional side was "rent into fragments by the force of my grief." While "Head" would have the last word, the insistence by "Heart" that he give up trying to see Maria again and turn his attention back to his male friends such as the brilliant French mathematician Nicolas de Condorcet seemed to carry the day.

All this philosophizing left Maria thoroughly confused, leading her to compose, as Boyd has put it, "a baffled...response." "How I wish I could answer," she began her first letter from London on October 30, "the Dialogue!" She reported that her heart was simultaneously both "mute" and "ready to burst with all the variety of sentiments, which a very feeling one is capable of." Not knowing what to say, she lapsed into a friendly but matter-of-fact message in her native Italian. Whatever romantic longings she had harbored for Jefferson, his bewildering words had extinguished. She returned to Paris in late August 1787 without her husband, but much to Jefferson's disappointment, he didn't get to spend much time with her. "From the mere effect of chance," Jefferson wrote to Trumbull on November 13, in what was perhaps an attempt to rationalize his hurt feelings, "she has happened to be from home several times when I have called her, and I, when she has called on me. I hope for better luck hereafter." It never came. She left Paris a month later, and they never saw each other again. The intermittent epistolary friendship, however, would continue for the rest of their lives. Maria eventually did leave her husband to start a convent school outside of Milan, where she died at the age of seventy-eight in 1838.

Just as the romance with Maria was cooling off, another woman marched into his life. On July 15, 1787, when Sally Hemings arrived with Polly at his Paris abode, the Hotel de Langeac, she was just fourteen. His slave was a half sister of his late wife; described by contemporaries as "an industrious and orderly creature in her behavior," the light-skinned and attractive Sally, with her long, straight hair, also bore a clear physical resemblance to Martha Wayles. She was the product of the union between John Wayles and Betty Hemings, a slave who became his concubine after the death of his third wife. Upon the death of John Wayles in 1773, Jefferson inherited the infant Sally. In France, she served as a lady's maid to his two daughters; Jefferson encouraged her to learn French and generously provided for her. According to his account books, he spent nearly two hundred francs in April 1789 on her clothes—a considerable amount, given that gloves cost only two francs.

The allegation that Jefferson engaged in a long-term sexual relationship with Sally, which may have begun as early as 1788, was first made public by the Scottish-born journalist James Callender, in a series of articles written for the *Richmond Recorder* in the fall of 1802. "It is well known that the man," Callender wrote of the president, "whom it delighteth the people to honor, keeps and for many years past has kept, as his concubine, one of his slaves. Her name is SALLY." Callender's reporting never carried much weight because he was known to be irascible and unstable—he died of an apparent suicide a year later—and he had an axe to grind. A former political ally of Jefferson's, Callender was miffed because the president had not appointed him postmaster in Richmond, as he had expected. In 1868, Martha's son, Thomas Jefferson Randolph, told biographer Henry Randall that Jefferson's nephew, Peter Carr, fathered Sally's children, a claim that most historians accepted for more than a century. But the entire landscape changed dramatically in 1997 with the release of *Thomas Jefferson and Sally Hemings: An American Controversy* by Annette Gordon-Reed, currently a professor of history at Harvard. Examining a wealth of sources, including Jefferson's Farm Book, in which he recorded the births of Sally's six children and detailed testimonials by two of them, Gordon-Reed argued that Jefferson was likely the father of all six. (In contrast to most of his other slaves, at Jefferson's behest, Sally, as well as her four children who reached adulthood, all lived in freedom after his death.) In 1998, *Nature* published the results of a DNA test that revealed a match between the last child, Eston Hemings, and the male Jefferson line, but not with the male Carr line. Today Gordon-Reed's position represents the scholarly consensus, although some skeptics continue to insist on alternative explanations.

In the two centuries between Callender's explosive articles and Gordon-Reed's scholarly volumes—her follow-up study, the Pulitzer Prize–winning *The Hemingses of Monticello: An American Family*, appeared in 2008—most historians, when they deigned to enter into this debate at all, cited their own idealized view of Jefferson as "proof" that the Federalist journalist must have been slinging mud. "[The charges]," asserted Dumas Malone, "are distinctly out of character, being virtually unthinkable in a man of Jefferson's moral standards and habitual conduct." Though it's impossible to know with absolute certainty, as Gordon-Reed concedes, whether Jefferson slept with his slave even once, the flip side of this long-standing assumption seems much more plausible. The choice of Sally Hemings as a mistress is entirely consistent with Jefferson's character *disorder*. For obsessives, in intimate relationships, as in everything else, control is the be-all and end-all; a genuine partnership with mutual give-and-take is anathema. In Sally, a woman thirty years his junior, whom he happened to own, Jefferson might well have found just what he was after. That was what Aaron Burr concluded, at least according to the late Gore Vidal. In his 1973 historical novel, *Burr*, the man who served as vice president during Jefferson's first term describes the submissive Sally as "exactly what Jefferson wanted a wife to be."

By the time he entered the White House in 1801—he would be the first president to be inaugurated in Washington, D.C.—Jefferson had built a formidable résumé, which included considerable experience in foreign affairs. After returning from France in September 1789, he accepted President Washington's request that he serve as secretary of state. He remained in the cabinet until his resignation in late 1793. By then, he was convinced that the president was being unduly influenced by the treasury secretary, Alexander Hamilton. According to Jefferson, Hamilton was an elitist bent on undoing the democratic reforms of the American Revolution. Eager to revive the "spirit of '76," the die-hard anti-authoritarian founded an opposition party, the Republicans. In the presidential election of 1796, Jefferson unsuccessfully opposed John Adams, Washington's successor as the leader of the Federalists. Since the vice presidency then went to whoever finished with the second most electoral votes, Jefferson had no choice but to serve in the administration of his bitter foe, whom, like Hamilton, he considered a crypto-monarchist. The hotly contested rematch, which took place between April and October 1800—each state chose its electors at a different time—didn't end until the House of Representatives declared Jefferson the victor in its thirty-sixth ballot on February 17, 1801.

Jefferson's first inaugural address, delivered on March 4, has turned out to be one of the most momentous speeches in American history, even though few in the crowd of more than 1,100, which filled the Senate chamber in the semifinished capitol building, could make out its words. The sociophobe couldn't project; his soft voice was inaudible to anyone not seated in the first few rows. Fortunately for Jefferson, in contrast to the Declaration, this text would immediately be pored over by newspaper readers across the nation. And it would be well worth the study. Laboring over every word—he cranked out three complete drafts in the two weeks allotted to him—the perfectionist had produced another masterpiece; this one inspired Americans not to break a bond with a foreign ruler, but to cement their bonds with one another. While Republicans called the end product "a Magna Carta in politics," Federalists also were unstinting in their praise. "We thought him a Virginian," one Federalist editor conceded, "and have found him an American—We thought him partisan and have found him a president."

Like other great literary achievements, his text reads today as if it were a disparate collection of famous quotations. "But every difference of opinion," declared the new president, eager to reassure an anxious nation that the transfer of power from one party to the other would be peaceful, "is not a difference of principle." In the first draft, the persnickety prose stylist had prefaced this sentiment with the phrase "but let it not be imagined that," but he cut the extraneous words in draft number two. Jefferson then uttered the statement that soon echoed around the country, "We are all Republicans, we are all Federalists." Paradoxically, he still defined the most pressing threat as the federal government, the very institution that he now headed. He declared his intention to keep it as lean as possible, promising "a wise and frugal Government, which shall restrain men from injuring one another." And before moving on to his peroration, in which he humbly accepted his demanding new post, Jefferson rallied his fellow citizens around a list of "essential principles," headed by "equal and exact justice to all men" and "the honest payment of our debts."

Attacking the national debt, which had ballooned under the Federalists, became the chief focus of his Republican administration. With the help of his able secretary of the treasury, the Swiss-born Albert Gallatin, the compulsive accountant worked tirelessly to clean up America's finances. Fully aware of the mathematical prowess of the chief executive, Gallatin asked *him* in a memo dated November 15, 1801, to "calculate what will be the annual sum wanted to pay the interest on, and pay off within eight years, a debt of $21,955,900, bearing an interest of $1,310,401.50." Since different chunks of the total were lent out at different interest rates, the problem was far from straightforward; nevertheless, an unfazed Jefferson provided the precise answer the next day: $3,277,516. He remains the only president ever to use complex logarithmic equations to crunch the national debt as well as census data. In his first State of the Union Address, which was submitted to, rather than spoken before, Congress that December, Jefferson explained that America's population was growing geometrically—as per his calculations, it was expected to double in twenty-two years—and that the "multiplications of men...educated in the love of order" meant that he could both pay down the debt and dispense with all internal taxes. And he fulfilled his promises; though to balance the nation's books, he would reduce the size of the army by half and that of the navy by nearly two-thirds.

But the president, like the farmer, did not always live within his means. In the spring of 1802, Jefferson became alarmed by the impending transfer of the

Louisiana Territory from Spain to France, which had bought back the land from its European neighbor in 1800. "This little event, of France's possessing herself of Louisiana," he wrote in April 1802, "is the embryo of a tornado." And his fears were warranted; six months after the transfer, Napoleon closed the port of New Orleans to American ships. Instead of waging war, as the Federalists advocated, Jefferson opened up America's checkbook. Though the Louisiana Purchase, which instantly doubled the size of the country, ran counter to his principles—in addition to adding $15 million to the debt, the deal implicitly chipped away at states' rights by giving the president authority not specified in the Constitution—he felt that he had no choice but "to get out of the scrape as I can." And even before the treaty was ratified by the Senate in the fall of 1803, Jefferson asked Congress to fund a trip to the Pacific that became known as the Lewis and Clark Expedition. His detailed instructions to Clark, embedded in a three-thousand-word missive dated June 20, 1803, whose numerous drafts he kept revising, included several lists of desiderata; besides weather data, his outgoing personal secretary was to gather vast amounts of information on all the Native Americans, animals, vegetables, and minerals that he came across in his travels. This investment would also pay enormous dividends. On account of this string of accomplishments, historian Joseph Ellis has lauded Jefferson's first term as "one of the two or three most uniformly successful in American presidential history."

The American people voiced a similar sentiment in 1804 when they reelected Jefferson in a landslide. He captured a staggering 73 percent of the popular vote—far more than any other presidential candidate since—which translated into 162 electoral votes; his Federalist opponent, Charles Pinckney of South Carolina, got only 14. However, in his second term, Jefferson was hamstrung by developments abroad. Hoping to stay out of the protracted war between Britain and France, Jefferson pushed through Congress the Embargo Act of 1807, which banned all international trade. "The idea of ceasing intercourse with obnoxious nations," Henry Adams has noted, "reflected his own personality in the mirror of statesmanship." Though the loner managed to get both the hated King George and Napoleon out of his face, the U.S. economy suffered terribly. Jefferson's personal life also took a turn for the worse after the death of his younger daughter, Polly, in childbirth in 1804. "My evening prospects," the heartbroken and depressed president wrote that year, alluding to his only surviving child, "now hang on the slender thread of a single life."

Fortunately for Jefferson, Martha remained much more devoted to him than to her husband, Thomas Randolph, then a congressman from Virginia, with whom she would have a total of twelve children. "The *first* and most important object with me," Martha reassured her father in 1807, "will be the dear and sacred duty of nursing and cheering your old age." After Jefferson's retirement, Martha, having already separated from the mentally unstable Randolph, would move with the children to Monticello, where she would also raise her sister's sole surviving child.

———

"Never did a prisoner," wrote the sixty-five-year-old Jefferson a couple of days before the end of his second term, "feel such relief as I shall on shaking off the shackles of power." No longer weighed down by pressing political responsibilities, the self-described "hermit of Monticello" began "enjoying a species of happiness that I never before knew, that of doing whatever hits the humor of the moment." For Jefferson, spontaneous fun meant immersion in one project after another designed to bring more order into his world. Some would be of minimal significance to posterity, but others of considerable. While he may not have been our most productive ex-president—a designation often accorded to Jimmy Carter—he may well have been our most industrious, most neat, and most devoted to the cause of organization.

Gardening was high on his agenda. For years, Jefferson had collected seeds from all over the world, which he stored in "little phials, labeled and hung on little hooks…in the neatest order," according to one visitor to Monticello, and he was eager to see what he could grow. A week after returning home from Washington, he started a massive eight-column "Kalendar" in his Garden Book, in which he tracked the hundreds of vegetables that he planted that spring and summer. (Though no subsequent "Kalendar" would be quite as long, Jefferson would compile one every year until 1825.) Applying his characteristic thoroughness, he kept experimenting and refining his methods. When the Roman broccoli which he had first sowed on April 20, 1809, "failed nearly," the recently retired president didn't give up; he tried again on May 30 and June 3, and eventually managed to transplant a total of 135 broccoli plants on July 10. "Under a total want of demand except for our family table," Jefferson wrote a friend in 1811, "I am still devoted to the garden. But though an old man, I am but a young gardener." He also laid out shrubs and filled in the flower beds that surrounded his house. While Sally's nephew, his slave Wormley, did the digging, Jefferson trailed behind with his measuring line and pruning knife in order to keep the rows properly aligned. In so doing, Jefferson was paying homage to his obsessive father, who had organized Shadwell's vegetable and flower gardens in numbered beds ordered in rows designated by letters.

In March 1815, Jefferson began labeling and organizing his books one last time. Six months earlier, after hearing that the Brits had burned down the original Library of Congress, the deeply indebted farmer had offered to sell his entire collection so that the feds could start anew. By early 1815, the deal was done; Jefferson ended up receiving $23,950 for the 6,047 volumes that, according to his measurements, occupied 855.39 square feet of wall space in bookcases that comprised a total of 676 cubic feet. While Jefferson had already updated his catalog, which subdivided Francis Bacon's three broad categories into forty-four chapters (subjects)—under Memory, for example, Civil History was chapter 1—he still needed to do some checking and rechecking. "I am now employing as many hours of every day as my strength will permit," he wrote to President Madison on March 23, "in arranging the books and putting every one in its place on the shelves and shall have them numbered correspondently." Even with the help of three grandchildren, the operation would take two months. For each book, Jefferson affixed a label that indicated both the chapter to which it belonged and its place on the shelf; in his bookcases, Jefferson had arranged the volumes both by subject and by size—the clunky folios, for example, were stacked together at the bottom. Hoping to prevent Congress from messing up his complex organizational scheme, for which he would later be feted as the "Father of American Librarianship," Jefferson used his own shelves as shipping crates. However, much to his horror, George Watterson, the Librarian of Congress, while preserving his chapter divisions, decided to organize his books alphabetically rather than by subject. Upon receiving his personal copy of Watterson's printed catalog, an enraged Jefferson took out his pen and rearranged all his books into their original order. While Watterson did not clean up his mess, several years later, Jefferson instructed his personal secretary, Nicholas Trist, to transform his marked-up catalog into a new manuscript containing his original scheme.

This compulsive reorganizer also would not hesitate to deface the Western world's most hallowed texts—the Gospels. In the summer of 1820, Jefferson vented his pique at organized religion by slicing and dicing eight Bibles—

two each in Greek, Latin, French, and English—with a razor blade. Pasting the shreds together, he created a new book with parallel passages in the four languages, which he called *The Life and Morals of Jesus of Nazareth*. This biography of Christ consisted of nothing but the texts written by the Evangelists as rearranged by Jefferson. Though his political opponents often portrayed him as an atheist, Jefferson was a devout Christian. In 1822, he would summarize his core beliefs in the following list:

1. That there is only one God, and he [is] all perfect.
2. That there is a future state of rewards and punishments.
3. That to love God with all thy heart and thy neighbor as thyself is the sum of religion.

But this creature of the Enlightenment could not stomach any counterfactual mumbo jumbo. "The Jefferson Bible," which he dubbed his "wee little book," excises all supernatural events, removing both the Annunciation and the Resurrection and every angel. While Jefferson discussed his faith with select friends and family members, he appears not to have shown this book to anyone. He viewed religion as he did most human activities—as a means not to seek interpersonal connection, but to express personal freedom. "I am of a sect by myself," he wrote in 1819, "as far as I know."

Jefferson's final retirement project has been his most enduring. Despite minor ailments like rheumatism, the still fit former president would remain in good enough health to continue his daily horseback rides until the last few weeks of his life. And in early 1819, he took on a new challenge, that of rector of a new citadel to learning chartered by the Virginia state legislature. "While you have been," Virginia senator James Barbour wrote to him in January 1825, two months before the University of Virginia held its first classes, "the ablest champion of the rights and happiness of your own generation, you have generously devoted the evening of your life to generations yet unborn." Eager to instill in America's youth "the precepts of virtue and order," Jefferson micromanaged every detail of his new creation. He designed the campus, placing at the center a large domed building, which housed the library—rather than a church—to "give it unity." He modeled the Rotunda on Andrea Palladio's Pantheon; on its two sides were several two-story pavilions alternating with one-story dormitories, all of which he numbered in his architectural drawings. He also supervised the recruiting of its first five faculty members from Europe. Throughout the summer of 1824, he spent four hours a day compiling the catalog for its library (his final tally of 6,860 volumes divided into forty-two chapters, which he estimated would cost $24,076, mirrors the numbers for the library that he had sold to the feds a decade earlier). And Jefferson also devised all the university's rules and regulations, specifying, for example, both that professors were to teach only six hours a week and that the school day was to run from 7:30 a.m. to 3:30 p.m. In order not to intrude on students, the domineering and controlling leader with the fervent antiauthoritarian streak eschewed a fixed curriculum in favor of electives. However, those who selected classes on law and government would be required to tackle his reading list, at the top of which stood the Declaration of Independence, the *Federalist Papers*, and Washington's inaugural and farewell addresses.

Shortly after Jefferson's death on July 4, 1826, a family member found in a secret drawer in his private cabinet a series of neatly labeled envelopes, which contained locks of hair and other little mementos originally belonging to his wife, Martha, and to each of the six children he had fathered with her. "They were all arranged in perfect order," observed biographer Henry Randall, "and the envelopes indicated their frequent handling." For this inveterate collector, as with his books, so with his family members—to classify and arrange was to love.

Henry Heinz outside his plant on the north side of Pittsburgh in 1907, when he was sixty-three. Heinz loved to ride as well as to collect horses. At the H. J. Heinz headquarters, he built a three-story "equine palace," which housed his company's fleet of two hundred black Percherons.

2

Marketing: Henry Heinz

Naked without His Steel Tape Measure

Home. Not well. Busy about house. Always plenty to do. Cannot well be idle and believe will rather wear out than rust out.
—Henry Heinz, Diary, December 15, 1880

It was Tuesday, May 25, 1886, and Henry J. Heinz was in Pittsburgh's Union Depot, waiting for the nine o'clock overnight train to Jersey City. The forty-one-year-old entrepreneur was about to take his family—his wife, Sallie; and their four children, Irene (fourteen), Clarence (thirteen), Howard (eight), and Clifford (two); along with his sister Mary and sister-in-law Lizzie—on a three-month European tour. Heinz could afford the extravagant vacation because business at his ten-year-old food company, F. & J. Heinz, was booming. Sales, which had started out at $44,000 ($880,000 today) in 1876, were up to nearly $500,000 ($10 million). Moreover, Heinz's expansion plans were rapidly paying dividends. Two years earlier, he had invested $20,000 ($400,000) in a factory on Pittsburgh's North Side, and Americans were now jumping at the chance to buy his newest product, bottled vinegar.

As the Heinz clan stood on the platform, they heard a couple of farewell speeches. The first came from one of the country's best-known Methodist preachers, Heinz's close friend Pittsburgh's Reverend Ezra Morgan Wood, who had delivered a sermon at President Abraham Lincoln's funeral. Afterward, an F. & J. Heinz executive read a letter signed by thirty-four employees, expressing the "earnest wish that he, his family and company...may have an enjoyable time and that a kind providence may have them all in his safe keeping during their absence and that in due time each and all of them may be returned much improved in health." As was no secret to any of Heinz's nearly five hundred employees, this trip was to be, in part, a medical vacation. With the temperamental paterfamilias battling chronic anxiety, his wife Sallie arthritis, and his eldest son Clarence asthma, the stop in Germany would be full of consultations with the cutting-edge physicians located in the family's ancestral homeland.

Four days later, the Heinz traveling party boarded the *City of Berlin*, the German steamer bound for Liverpool, some 3,100 miles away. Though removed from the pressures of his office, the five-and-a-half-footer with the sparkling blue eyes, whose curly dark hair and fluffy moustache were both starting to gray, could not relax either in his sumptuous accommodations—the two adjoining staterooms—or on deck. Instead, over the course of the eight-day journey, Heinz kept marching around on various fact-finding missions, whose results he dutifully recorded in his diary. The off-duty entrepreneur learned everything he could about Captain F. S. Land—his career at sea was already in its fourth decade—and his method of commanding his crew of eighty-two. Heinz also studied how the engine worked and set the speed. But what most interested him were the ship's statistics. The eleven-year-old paddle wheeler, which consumed 900 tons of coal every twenty-four hours, had 900 horsepower and was, he learned, 488 feet long, 44 feet wide, and 34 feet deep. And of its 422 passengers, 140 rode in steerage, 125 in intermediate, and 157 in saloon.

This was not the first or only time that a restless Heinz was seized by the impulse to quantify. "He was a man," his chauffeur would recall after his death, "who was always measuring things." Ever since adolescence, when he began working in his father's brick factory, Heinz toted a steel tape measure in his front pocket, which he would often whip out to jot down the dimensions of a doorway or some object that captured his fancy. "Every man," Heinz would insist, "should carry a tape measure with him." Of numbers, he never seemed to get enough. For Heinz, as for Jefferson, to quantify was to take charge; counting was how he kept his massive interpersonal anxiety at bay. When he visited the Rouen Cathedral in that summer of 1886, he counted all 722 steps that led up to the top of its 495-foot tower, then one of the highest in the world. In his diary, he carefully tracked his weight, which oscillated between 127 and 159 pounds, depending on his stress level—he tended to lose weight when overworked—and whether he wore his quarter-pound derby hat (a measure that he would take whenever the final tally was in danger of ending in a messy three-fourths pound). Like other obsessives such as Steve Jobs, who waged a long battle with anorexia, Heinz saw his own body as a foreign object over which he needed to exert control. And

Heinz also kept close tabs on the weight of other family members. In 1891, when both Irene and Clarence left home for college, they clocked in at 108 and 152, respectively. While Sallie's wedding weight is unknown—her husband's diary began several years after their 1869 union—the once trim Mrs. Heinz was up to 153 during that European sojourn and would balloon to 205 by the time of her death in 1894.

To date, just about every profile of Heinz turns this nervous tic inside out, using his measuring mania as proof that the tycoon was a paragon of both sanity and sagacity. E. D. McCafferty, Heinz's former secretary who published a brief life in 1923, is alluding to the various factoids that Heinz recorded on the *City of Berlin* when he argues that these "diary entries...reveal character." Of this same episode, Robert Alperts, who was handpicked by Henry Heinz II, the founder's grandson, to write the first scholarly biography a half century later, observes, "Heinz enthusiastically wrote down in his diary the statistics that one must know and record on such an occasion." (Imagine riding on an ocean liner without ready access to the ship's precise dimensions. Perish the thought!) Remarkably, even those not under the watchful eye of some Heinz heir parrot the same line. In describing the 1886 voyage to Liverpool, Quentin Skrabec Jr., author of a 2009 biography, compares Heinz's journals to those of "a scientist such as Thomas Edison."

"I like to know," Heinz would insist, "what I'm talking about. No use guessing if you can get the exact facts." But in truth, he liked meaningless factoids as much as hard data. Numbers, no matter what they measured, provided the reassurance and comfort that he could not find elsewhere—namely, in emotional connections with other human beings.

Like the Wizard of Menlo Park, Heinz was a genius, but his was a lightning-quick, impulsive intelligence, not a probing one. He was a doer rather than a thinker. An impatient man, he was constantly on the go. When he played golf, his rounds lasted just six holes. If his ride across "the big Pond," as he called it, was too smooth, he got downright uncomfortable. "We had several days of delightful motion," he once reported to his wife while traversing the Atlantic on a steamship, "which I confess broke the monotony of eating and too much merriment." Like Jefferson, he had an urgent need to keep his mind occupied at all times, even if that meant taking on stressful or demanding tasks. Unable to sit still, Heinz rarely spent twenty consecutive minutes at his desk. While Heinz also shared Jefferson's hatred of idleness, he rarely escaped into books because reading gave him a headache. In his diary, which he kept for about twenty years, Heinz mentioned only one book, *The Successful Merchant*, a biography of a nineteenth-century British grocer steeped in the principles of Methodism. ("New food for my...desires," Heinz commented upon finishing this rags-to-riches tale some five months after he started it.) And the man whose postsecondary education consisted of a few bookkeeping classes at Duff's Mercantile College in Pittsburgh was practically incapable of writing a coherent business letter. Nor did he master orthography (in contrast to his bookish wife, Sallie, who could hold her own in spelling bees).[1] On a visit to Corsica, Heinz consoled himself by noting in his diary, "Napoleon couldn't spell, either." Heinz would always distrust the college educated. In the early 1900s, as consumers began worrying about the additives that companies were tossing into ketchup, his partners would have to hire chemists behind his back.

But while Heinz's nervous temperament was incompatible with scientific discovery, it was ideally suited to building and running a business. Upon his death in 1919, "the Pickle King"—as the *New York Times* described him in its obituary—left behind the world's largest manufacturer of processed food, with annual sales exceeding $20 million ($400 million in today's dollars). By then, the H. J. Heinz Company, as the firm was renamed in 1888, employed 6,253 workers in twenty-five branch factories and was selling its products in dozens of countries. This pioneer in the art of branding had an intuitive feel for the consumer's needs and wants, and he knew how to create not only interest but also excitement in his wares. "Henry Heinz," historian Nancy Koehn of the Harvard Business School has noted, "was one of the first U.S. entrepreneurs to pursue...a consistent, innovative, and multifaceted brand-building strategy." A key part of his strategy was a revolutionary new approach to advertising. Thinking outside the box, Heinz concluded that hefty investments were essential to the long-term growth of his company. "I have contracted for more advertising matter at one time," he wrote in July 1892, "to be used inside of a year than ever before in my life at one time, over $10K. Consisting of calendars, souvenir books, stamped out pickle cards, pickle charms and spoons, and show cards for boxes. We keep our shingle and then let the public blow our horns and that counts, but we must do

---

[1] The version of the Heinz diary currently available to researchers and from which I quote in this chapter—the family won't permit access to the original manuscript—has been edited to fix his "sloppy orthography."

something to lead them to do this." That "something" would soon evolve from an afterthought to a fixture in corporate budgets, as executives around the globe tried to copy his formula for success (which eventually meant plowing a then astonishing 20 percent of sales back into advertising).

And his number fetish would be instrumental in helping him to create one of the most effective and enduring slogans in the history of advertising. For decades, Heinz searched for just the right phrase to describe his company. He thought about "pickle people" but nixed that one because "we were," he later wrote, "packing many kinds of food that could not be classed as pickles." Suddenly, in 1896, an idea came to him. While riding Manhattan's Third Avenue El, he spotted a card advertising "21 styles of shoes." Even though his firm was then selling about 60 different food products, his mind latched on to the number 57. In this case, as with his occasional self-deceptions about his weight, Heinz would throw precision out the window. "Seven…seven—there are so many illustrations," he later mused, "of the psychological influence of that figure and of its alluring significance to people of all ages and races, that '58 Varieties' or '59 Varieties' did not appeal at all to me as being equally strong." Jumping off the train, Heinz went straight to a lithography shop to have a new street-car card printed up. Within a week, the image of the green pickle with the "57 Varieties" was appearing in newspapers and billboards across the country. The CEO would later plaster "57" everywhere—on hillsides, on the Heinz Ocean Pier in Atlantic City, on Manhattan's first electric sign, lit by twelve hundred incandescent bulbs, at the corner of Twenty-Third Street and Fifth Avenue, and even near the Sphinx in Cairo. (In a comic riff on the arbitrariness of this ubiquitous magic number, the McCarthyite senator in the 1962 film *The Manchurian Candidate* shakes his bottle of Heinz ketchup before announcing that there are exactly fifty-seven Communists in the State Department.) Making no distinction between brand and self, Heinz would also equate his famous formulation with his own personal identity. In 1908, after hearing that the wife of his son Howard had given birth to his grandchild Henry J. Heinz II, the founder congratulated the couple on the arrival of "the 58th variety."

————

Heinz was more than just quirky; prone to paroxysms of anger and sudden mood swings, he was a mentally unstable man who lived close to the edge for most of his life. Madness ran rampant in the immediate family. His father waged a long battle with depression and died in an insane asylum; and of his seven siblings, several would be seriously impaired due to depression, anxiety, alcoholism, and various other psychiatric ills, including sexual addiction. Clarence, his eldest son, was a loner who went mad in his thirties. While Heinz's three other children, Irene, Howard, and Clifford, got married—the playboy Clifford three times—and built families, many of their descendants have also been scarred. As the *Los Angeles Times* reported in a 2004 feature, "alcoholism, suicide, eccentric behavior and marital instability...have plagued all three wings of the family." The society pages of mid- to late-twentieth-century newspapers are filled with stories about the crashing and burning of Heinz's heirs. One grandson—Howard's son Rust—perished in a car accident at the age of twenty-five, just a few months after an alcoholism counselor had described him as "not normal" and had recommended long-term psychiatric care at a residential facility for "his true textbook father complex." And another grandson—Irene's son John—who would die of alcoholism at fifty, was once arrested on a Manhattan street corner at 3 a.m. for beating a sixty-three-year-old stranger with a cane that contained a twenty-eight-inch dagger in its shaft.

Like Jefferson, Heinz was constantly trying to distract himself from the internal turmoil that dated back to his stressful early years. From boyhood on, this eldest child of struggling German immigrants threw himself into work and other activities, such as his counting and collecting. However, for Heinz, as opposed to Jefferson, this strategy sometimes backfired, as the constant exertion—early in his career, the entrepreneur worked seventeen-hour days—left him close to a breakdown on numerous occasions. "Am feeling feeble," the thirty-four-year-old confided to his diary on March 23, 1879, "and often think I am going into a decline caused by overwork, excitement and extreme trouble."

Two years later, he began to fear that he would lose his mind after his father officially lost his. On September 30, 1881, the family placed the chronically depressed seventy-year-old John Henry Heinz, a once successful brick manufacturer, in the Kirkbride Asylum for the Insane in Philadelphia. "[Father] is demented," Heinz noted in his diary, "and hope he may be cured. It is a hard thing to have to send him away. His mind has now been disturbed four months." (Heinz's father would never improve.) To preserve his delicate psychic equilibrium, a terrified Heinz would repeatedly turn to professional help. Just three months later, he checked himself into New York State's Dansville Sanitarium, which specialized in treating "chronic ailments, especially those arising from worry and over-work." Hydrotherapy was then the treatment of choice for most psychiatric disorders, and after a brief stay, Heinz arranged for frequent electric baths at home, which he referred to as "my cure of late."

The trip to Europe in 1886 was part of this repeated search for relief from his psychic ills, which would go on and on and on. "Not feeling at all well," a despondent Heinz noted in his journal on December 17, 1891, after having visited four Pittsburgh doctors, none of whom had a clue as to what exactly ailed him. The following week, on a visit to Philadelphia, he got his answer. "I consulted Dr. J. V. Schomaker on Walnut Street," he wrote, "who diagnoses my case as overworked nerves and rheumatism in my blood." For the last two decades of his life, Heinz would go to a German sanatorium nearly every summer for a mental tune-up, alternating between Dr. Carl von Dapper's in Bad Kissingen and Dr. Franz Dengler's in Baden-Baden. At these elegant Alpine retreats, where fellow patients included such high-flying aristos as Paul Romanov, a son of Russian Tsar Nicholas II, and Lord Chesterfield, the rest cure revolved around regulating the diet. At Bad Kissingen, under medical supervision, Heinz ingested a third of a pound of butter a day—it was draped on vegetables and stuffed in puddings. Though the scientific basis of these treatments turned out to be flimsy, the high-strung executive seemed to benefit; no doubt the constant weigh-ins boosted his mood at least a little. The thirty-year-old Howard, then a top executive in the family biz, reported to his father on May 2, 1907, "He [Professor von Noorden, a doctor at Bad Kissingen] said further that he had noticed quite a difference in your condition after you had omitted Dr. Dapper's cure in 1903 and he told me when I saw him last winter to by all means persuade you to spend some time at either Dr. Dapper's or Dr. Dengler's this year. Whatever you do let me urge you to not come home until you have had at least four weeks at some cure."

In insisting on this prescription, which the aging founder would dutifully obey, Howard was considering the welfare of his father as well as that of other family members, including himself. The demanding, hypercritical patriarch was not an easy man to be around. "Reading between the lines of his diary," the hired hagiographer Eleanor Dienstag was forced to concede in her corporate history, *In Good Company: 125 Years at the Heinz Table*, "one detects a formidable temper. It suggests he [Henry] may have been a bit of a bully." In his biography, Heinz's secretary was more blunt: "He could and did, become stirred to great angers; and no man with one experience of these willingly incurred another." As

Howard was well aware, the longer his father spent buttering himself up on the other side of the Atlantic, the longer the family back home in Pittsburgh could relish a breather from *him*. Whatever proclivities toward mental instability various family members possessed, Heinz would exacerbate. While Howard knew how to cope with his father's hectoring, that was not the case with his brother Clarence. "I was…surprised," a family friend wrote Heinz about the thirty-year-old Clarence, "at his earnestness and great desire to follow your wishes whether they were to his own liking or the contrary." In 1913, at the age of forty, Heinz's eldest son, who had not been fully compos mentis for a few years, retreated to Wisconsin, where he got round-the-clock medical attention until his death several years later. Likewise, John Given, the husband of Heinz's eldest child, Irene, also "was broken," as one biographer has put it, by his verbal assaults and had to quit the family company.

According to the Reverend John Cowan, a family friend, Heinz's spinster sister Mary, who worked as a housekeeper in his Pittsburgh mansion after his wife's death, "enjoyed two nervous breakdowns." As Cowan, hired by Heinz to write his biography, has reported, Mary would complain that "he [Henry] never could understand the strain upon her" of living with him. Heinz would come home unannounced, expecting a meal for himself as well as his dozen guests. After her return from Dowie's Sanitarium in Illinois, an anxious Mary would go back to drinking hefty doses of brandy. Heinz died, however, before he could rattle Cowan, who had been worried that his persnickety employer "would probably want to change the writing and edit it [the biography] to the last comma." Despite his protestations to the contrary—a month before his death, Heinz wrote Howard that "there never has been any *must* in my family or in the business"— the imperative mood predominated in Heinz's communications both at home and at work. To the end, the founder would remain too self-absorbed to appreciate that his impulsive behavior could adversely affect the nervous system of anyone else.

Heinz's decision to give up the reins of his company shortly after his fiftieth birthday would help him preserve his sanity. And as he became less consumed by the food biz, he turned to new obsessions. The compulsive traveler, who would visit both the Middle East and the Far East, developed "the relic *fever* bad," as his son Clarence once put it. Heinz would collect curios from all over the world such as carved ivories and timepieces, which he displayed at his massive private museum. The widower, who wouldn't remarry, loved spending hours labeling and arranging his favorite objects. By his early sixties, as the *New York Times* reported, Heinz was worth $25 million ($500 million), and though he didn't have quite as much disposable cash as his contemporaries Henry Clay Frick and Andrew Carnegie—the three "Lords of Pittsburgh" died the same year—he still emerged as one of the city's leading philanthropists. On his sixty-first birthday, Heinz wrote to Howard from London, announcing that he was "young at heart, enjoying better health than I did fifteen or twenty years ago, which ought to demonstrate that hard work never killed anyone." The regular European sanatorium and American sanitarium stints—during the Great War, when he couldn't get to Germany, he did a turn at Dr. John Kellogg's outfit in Michigan—would continue to work their magic; and though his mind became increasingly muddled, his body would remain in tip-top shape. A decade later, on his seventy-first birthday, when asked how he felt, Heinz responded by jumping over a nearby chair. His remarkable physical vitality turned out to be partly responsible for his sudden death. On May 9, 1919, an unseasonably chilly day in Pittsburgh, Heinz noticed some workmen at his company passing bricks to one another, one at a time. Climbing the ladder that led to the scaffolding, he declared, "Here, let me show you. We used to pitch them four at a time like this." He died of pneumonia five days later.

———

Though the adult Heinz would define himself by his American sensibility—"I am," he insisted, "an American in every fiber of my body and heartbeat"—the boy grew up with two German-born parents largely unfamiliar with the American way of life.

Henry Heinz's father, John Henry Heinz, hailed from Kallstadt, a town in the German region that is today known as Rheinland-Pfalz, where the family had administered vineyards and farms for centuries. (Kallstadt is also the ancestral home of another prominent American entrepreneur—Donald Trump—who is actually a close relative of the Pickle King. John Henry Heinz's mother was Charlotte Luise Trump, a sister of the Donald's great-grandfather, John Trump.) Henry Heinz's mother, Anna Margaretha Schmidt, was born in Kruspis, located some fifty miles away in Hesse; like her husband, she was also in her twenties when she emigrated to America in the early 1840s. Both his parents settled in Birmingham, a town in southwestern Pennsylvania across the Monongahela

River from Pittsburgh, where they were married in 1843. Henry, the first of the couple's eight children, was born the following October.

In 1849, the family moved to Sharpsburg, a small rural borough in O'Hara Township, five miles north of Pittsburgh, whose population then totaled about 1,400. Acquiring a kiln, John Henry Heinz became a brick maker and contractor. In 1854, he built a two-story house on a four-acre plot on the banks of the Allegheny River. One biographer has described Heinz's father as a "very uncomplaining sensitive soul, who would rather endure in silence than make a fuss." Perhaps because of John Henry Heinz's eventual decline into madness, his famous son would later say little about him. On December 23, 1891, the day his father died in the Philadelphia asylum, after noting the deranged man's final words, "*Ich bin der Doktor. Ich bin sehr krank*" ("I am the doctor. I am very sick"), Heinz added in his diary, "He was a giant in strength and very indulgent father."

Heinz, however, would take after his stern and enterprising mother. A devout Lutheran who repeatedly quoted chapter and verse of the Bible, she would make frequent demands on the children, from whom she would expect an immediate response. The mothering of the overbearing Anna came mostly in the form of mottos. Her favorites, which she would repeat time and time again, included "Labor sweetens life, idleness makes it a burden," and "Remember that the bee goes to the same flower for its honey where the spider goes for its poison" (an injunction to look on the bright side; both mottos would later grace the walls of the company's office in Pittsburgh). Forever idealizing his mother, the sixty-year-old Heinz would refer to her "Christ-like spirit." "She could handle me," Heinz recalled, "because she knew how to inspire me; because she knew what to say, when and how."

Anna Heinz's methods of persuasion included verbal and physical intimidation, a common child-rearing tool among nineteenth-century German families. While Heinz later referred to few specific early interactions with his mother, his behavior toward children offers a useful approximation of his own early experiences, as he presumably did unto others just as his mother had done unto him. In the spring of 1875, the thirty-year-old Heinz, as he acknowledged in his diary, "whipped" his fourteen-year-old brother, Jacob, for skipping school. "Would not let Irene have supper," Heinz also noted that August of the harsh disciplinary measures taken against his four-year-old daughter, "because she pouted at table....Yet all seemed well. Irene never let on about not having supper." Irene's younger brother Clarence also got roughed up as a toddler. Early in

1876, Heinz recorded the following incident, "Had to smack Clarence, but he came to me and kissed me and made up at once. Irene's example and influence lead him."

To ensure that he would get many more carrots than sticks from the anxious and overburdened Anna, the young "Harry" (as Henry was nicknamed) devised a clever strategy; he became his "mother's little helper." Feeding her large family was Anna's constant worry, and the boy pitched in by harvesting, grating, and bottling her horseradish. By performing this painstaking chore, he spared her the bruised knuckles and watery eyes. He also worked in his mother's neatly ordered garden. By the age of eight, Harry was peddling her surplus produce to neighbors in baskets. Two years later, Anna rewarded her favorite child by giving him his own three-quarters of an acre. At twelve, Harry was tilling three acres and transporting his fruits and vegetables in a cart drawn by his newly purchased horse, Old Baldy. In contrast, Harry's younger brothers, John and Peter, both of whom would end up working in the family biz, would be less successful in eluding Anna Heinz's punishments; and they would turn out very differently. Though blessed with a keen mechanical mind, John, as Harry would later complain, lacked initiative. And while Harry became a teetotaler, Peter became a chronic alcoholic, who, as one biographer has noted, "was...known for getting women pregnant out of wedlock."

The adult Heinz would formulate "Eight Important Ideas"—he couldn't resist numbering his personal tenets—that guided his business career. The first one ran, "Housewives are willing to pay someone else to take over a share of their more tedious kitchen work." Harry's addiction to making quotidian life easier for Anna Heinz would lead him to develop a whole new industry, mass-produced processed food. Thus would he also identify a new market. In the mid-nineteenth century, women preparing meals had little choice other than to slave away endlessly in the kitchen; they had few trustworthy resources outside the home to which they could turn. The condiments then sold by grocers were often laced with lead, sawdust, or even animal waste and poison, which manufacturers tried to hide by selling their wares in brown bottles. The lifelong Methodist— "Cleanliness is next to Godliness" was a tenet of the religion's founder, the Londoner John Wesley—would establish a brand known for its purity and quality. As the Rolling Stones sang in their 1966 hit, "Mother's Little Helper," "Cooking fresh food for a husband's just a drag," and about a century before "the little yellow pills" (the barbiturate Nembutal), Heinz's clear glass bottles would rush to the rescue of the world's harried housewives. In 1927, company CEO Howard Heinz explained to the Pittsburgh Chamber of Commerce that his father had started a "revolutionary" industry. "It was truly said," Heinz's son noted, "that 'women's work is never done.' Now she is no longer dependent upon her own efforts to supply her household with nourishing foods.... Who can predict what woman will accomplish in her new freedom?" Thanks to Heinz's 57-plus varieties, all women could enjoy the benefit of having an industrious little Harry by their side, and the world would never be the same.

While Anna Heinz had hoped that Harry would become a pastor, once she noticed his remarkable aptitude for business, she came around and supported his ambitious dreams. At fifteen, he dropped out of a seminary school in Sharpsburg and began working as a bookkeeper in his father's brick company. He also continued to build his fruit and vegetable business. A year later, with several employees, including two of his younger brothers and two of his younger sisters, tending his ever-expanding garden, Harry was making three deliveries a week to Pittsburgh grocers. By seventeen, Harry was earning real money—$2,400 a year ($48,000). Like Jefferson, he also loved to keep track of the temperature, and this farmer also began experimenting with various planting techniques—say, new watering regimes—to grow his crops.

By 1865, the twenty-one-year-old Harry had saved enough to buy half of his father's brick company. Three years later, confident in the managerial know-how of his new co-owner, John Heinz made a pilgrimage back to Germany to visit with relatives. During his father's absence, using money from debts to the company that had been written off as uncollectible, Harry constructed a fancy new two-story brick house for his parents that contained both bow windows and an outside balcony.

But Henry Heinz had no interest in remaining his "father's little helper." In 1869, he became his own man by forming two new partnerships. Getting out of the brick business for good—though he didn't discard his lifeline, his trusty tape measure—he started a food company with a contemporary, L. Clarence Noble. (For Heinz, business and family were always intertwined; his first son, Clarence, born in 1873, was named after Noble.) The first product in Heinz and Noble's new Anchor Brand—a name selected for its biblical meaning of hope—was Anna Heinz's recipe for bottled horseradish, which Heinz manufactured in the basement of his father's former house. That September, he also married Sarah (Sallie) Sloan Young, a Pittsburgh-born Presbyterian whose parents had come from Northern Ireland. Deeply religious like his mother, the devoted and self-sacrificing Sallie—during his lean years, she churned out butter that she sold for thirty-five cents a pound—would provide Heinz with just the kind of emotional support he needed.

As Heinz's family grew, so too did his new business venture, which Clarence Noble's younger brother, E.J., joined in 1872. Acquiring 160 acres of farmland along the Allegheny River, Heinz, Noble and Company, as the firm was now called, kept adding new products, including celery sauce and pickles. "I am now," Heinz would note in his diary a few years later, "in the pickle business." Heinz and his two partners also leased a four-story office on Second Avenue in downtown Pittsburgh, which served as both a factory and a retail outlet. Initially, even the Panic of 1873, which came on the heels of the failure of the nation's biggest bank (Jay Cooke and Company) and the ensuing stock market crash, couldn't stop the firm's steady growth. By 1875, Heinz, Noble and Company had warehouses in both St. Louis and Chicago, and its 170 employees were capable of producing 15,000 barrels of pickles and 500,000 barrels of vinegar a year. That year, with little fanfare, the company also rolled out a prototype of modern-day ketchup, based on Anna Heinz's recipe. Called catsup, this luxury version of the product hardly sold at all; Heinz wouldn't turn his attention to a mass-produced tomato paste for a couple more decades.

By early 1875, Heinz, Noble and Company was no longer immune to the effects of the nationwide recession that was driving up the unemployment rate to 14 percent. "Hard times," Heinz noted that January in his diary, "money tight." Heinz had a tougher and tougher time meeting his payroll. "I fear I shall break down," he worried on July 1, "if times don't soon change." They didn't, and he did. By early December, overrun by a series of painful boils, a devastated Heinz couldn't get out of bed. On Wednesday, December 15, 1875, when he failed to pay some creditors, he was arrested. TRIO IN A PICKLE, the *Pittsburgh Leader* headline reported the next day, HEINZ, NOBLE & CO. CHARGED WITH REMOVING THEIR GOODS TO DEFRAUD CREDITORS. The charges were false and Heinz would eventually be exonerated, but restoring his name would be a grueling process. With assets of $110,000 and liabilities of $160,000, the company had to file for bankruptcy. Heinz felt that he had let down the entire family, especially his own parents, who, at his request, had mortgaged their house. As his father and mother attempted to sell it along with all their furniture, Heinz "never went near as I could not well bear it."

On Christmas Day, with Sallie unable to stop crying, a despairing Heinz, who couldn't afford any holiday gifts, wrote in his journal, "I feel as though people were all pushing us down because we are bankrupt. Such is the world." His mother offered a prayer in the form of a printed card reminding him that "the Lord will provide," which moved him deeply. At his urging, his heirs would continue to recite its words for decades to come every Christmas. But except for the immediate family, Heinz received little support. To avoid running into familiar faces, he and Sallie decided to switch churches. "A man," he observed on December 30, "is nowhere without money." In early January, overhearing her parents talk of their misfortune, the four-year-old Irene, as an embarrassed Heinz discovered, told a family friend that she was planning to "sell one of her curls for five cents to give to Papa...[who] lost all his money."

Heinz's emotional paralysis didn't last long. On February 14, 1876, he launched the second incarnation of his food biz, the F. & J. Heinz Company. With the Noble brothers both blaming him for mismanagement, Heinz would have nothing more to do with either of them; from now on, his business would be strictly a family affair. Under the new arrangement, his wife owned half the company—Heinz himself couldn't become a partner as he wasn't yet discharged from bankruptcy—and his cousin Frederick, a recent German émigré who was an expert in modern farming techniques; his brother John; and his mother, Anna, each owned a sixth. Though Heinz would call the shots, he would officially be an employee working for the modest salary of $125 a month ($2,500). That February, a guilt-ridden Heinz compiled a new list of numbers containing the amount he owed to each of his creditors. Given that he had owned three-eighths of Heinz, Noble and Company, he felt responsible for the corresponding share of the total. Even though bankruptcy would remove any legal obligation, he—in contrast to his former partners—would insist on repayment. Heinz toted this ledger, which he labeled MO (moral obligations), in his pocket until he wiped out all his debts three years later, a full year ahead of the goal that he had set for himself.

But in the first half of 1876, Heinz continued to struggle. That February, after noting that he had come down with his tenth boil since December, he remarked in his diary, "When a person is affected they cannot read or study with a contented mind." By June, after Heinz noticed three new ones "on my seat," his boil count had doubled to twenty. Seeking a fresh start, Heinz cut his hair short and removed his side whiskers for the first time in nearly seven years. On July 15, he was forced to take another desperation measure: "Bought cheap $16 horse to help us out of pinch. He is blind."

With his back against the wall, Heinz ratcheted up his fierce ambition. This time around, he was determined not to fail. "RESOLVE," he wrote on May 28 in his diary, "TO MAKE MORE MONEY." Despite his cash-flow problems, he would soon develop bold new business practices that involved investing much more heavily in both new technology and advertising.

———

On Monday, October 23, 1876, Henry and Sallie Heinz were among the thirty thousand visitors to arrive at the Depot in Philadelphia to attend the Centennial Exposition, the World's Fair commemorating America's one hundredth birthday. More than 130,000 people a day were now filing into the fairgrounds near the station, and in the end, nearly ten million Americans—about one-fifth of the nation—would pay a visit. Officially called "The International Exhibition of Arts, Manufactures and Products of the Soil and Mine," the six-month-long extravaganza featured sixty thousand contributions from all thirty-eight states and thirty-seven foreign countries, including a new gadget called the telephone, demonstrated by Boston's Alexander Graham Bell. Taking advantage of the Pennsylvania Railroad's specially discounted tickets, the couple had made the twelve-hour trek from Pittsburgh along with Heinz's sisters, Mary and Maggie, Sallie's mother and brother, George, and their neighbor, Dr. Deetrick (who had treated Heinz a year earlier when, with bankruptcy looming, his pulse had dipped to forty).

While Sallie, like his sisters, played tourist, not so Heinz. He had some urgent business to which he needed to attend. Ever since the fair's opening on May 10, the F. & J. Heinz Company—referred to as "Heintz [sic], Noble and Co." in the official catalog because Heinz had filled out the application the previous year—had been running a small booth that featured its "pickles, vinegar, sauces and catsups." With his firm's finances then still tenuous, that was all he could afford. In contrast, that August, Heinz had managed to mount a larger stand at a regional Pittsburgh exposition where he also passed out free samples and souvenir cards. "We hear," he wrote on August 25, "people say it surpasses anything in [the] way of pickle display at [the] Centennial." Now he would get a chance to see for himself exactly what food companies, including his own, were showcasing in Philadelphia.

At the massive Agricultural Building, one of the fair's five main sites, on the banks of the Schuylkill River, Heinz was intrigued by what he found. His company's booth was situated next to those of sixty-six other American firms that also sold preserved meats, vegetables, and fruits as well as meat and vegetable extracts, all of which fell under Class 656 in the Exposition's elaborate 700-point classification system. "All the goods of this class," the fair's chronicler, John McCabe, noted, "are displayed in the most attractive manner and constitute one of the prettiest features of the agricultural exhibit." Studying his competitors—a few of which are still around in one form or another today, such as New York's Charles Gulden and Chicago's Libby, McNeill, and Libby— Heinz got ideas about new products and new marketing strategies, which he jotted down in his notebook. He also paid close attention to packaging, particularly to containers and labels. And Heinz examined the offerings of the nearly seven hundred foreign merchants in his class, in which Britain's Crosse and Blackwell—a manufacturer of pickles, preserves, and numerous sauces, including its famous chow-chow (a relish)—held the "post of honor," as McCabe would later put it. Heinz would soon translate his notes into action. Within a year, he rolled out several new varieties, including mustard and pickled tongue as well as his own highly successful chow-chow sauce—the Pennsylvania version was sweeter than the British.

In his diary after his first evening in Philadelphia, Heinz limited himself to a general impression. "I enjoyed the Exposition today very much," he wrote on October 23. "It is a wonderful affair." He commented on little else except some factoids related to a canvas that depicted the recent Paris commune, "I also saw outside the Siege of Paris, a painting 60 by 400 feet, 300 artists painted it."

Heinz went back to Pittsburgh on Thursday the twenty-sixth, leaving Sallie and the rest of the family along with Dr. Deetrick behind in Philadelphia. After they returned a few days later, Heinz needed to defuse a couple of family conflicts. One involved a possible threat to his marriage. During his absence, as Sallie informed him, Dr. Deetrick had made a pass at her. The ever-loyal Sallie told Heinz that she considered the doctor "a fool," and thus Deetrick's surprising transgression ended up bringing the couple closer together. "Sallie and I," he wrote on the twenty-ninth, "had a chat about our courtship and her old beaux, etc. . . . and about our duty to God and man." The following week, his brother John insisted on going to the fair himself. Though the request was reasonable— even his mother believed that "John had just as good a right as the rest to go"—

Heinz protested, claiming that the firm lacked the money. While John was a part owner, Heinz, then officially just a salaried employee, could still push him around. "John was determined," Heinz noted in his diary, "but did not go and all was quiet."

The overbearing Heinz did not want John, the firm's chief engineer, to wander around the Centennial Exposition by himself. However, he did insist that his brother, who had a knack for devising new ways to mass-produce the company's products, tinker with several new technological innovations that *he* had seen on display there. John had recently improved the crispness of pickles (fermented cucumbers) by changing the temperature in the industrial-sized boilers; and that fall, after upping his spending on glass bottles to $400 a month, Heinz asked John to consider various new bottle designs. In Philadelphia, Heinz had noticed a canning machine, and John also began producing tin cans for sauerkraut. "Sold first canned goods this day that I ever handled," Heinz wrote the following March. At the exposition, Heinz had also purchased a new machine that sorted pickles by size; upon his return to Pittsburgh, he assigned John the task of improving its speed.

A couple of years later, Heinz received a patent for "Improvement in Vegetable-Assorters." Thus was Heinz able to stoke the company's first wave of exponential growth by revolutionizing the way in which producers sold pickles to grocers. While pickles had been an American staple for decades, at the time, picklers still abounded; most were local operations that sold them through wholesalers. Heinz's automated sorting machine gave him an immediate edge over his many competitors; it was much faster and more reliable than conventional hand sorting. As the company noted in catalogs of that era, its patented Keystone Pickle Assorter "makes no mistakes. It never miscounts. Therefore we guarantee our pickles to be more UNIFORM IN SIZE and EXACT IN COUNT than any other brand of pickles in the market." In this instance, the number fetishist did not fudge his totals; Heinz opted to sell five different size barrels, containing from 1,000 to 3,400 pickles, and thanks to his new machine, the counts came out right every time. Once Heinz convinced grocers that this certainty would mean an extra two dollars a barrel in profits, he could barely keep up with the demand for his signature product. The clever use of such new technology—"from soil to customer" was how this obsessive referred to the control his company exercised over every step of the production process—was critical in transforming Heinz into the undisputed king of the pickle business.

After his return from Philadelphia, Heinz would also steadily beef up the budget for his advertising. Waxing increasingly creative, he would not hesitate to use his sense of humor. On Monday, November 6, 1876, this lifelong Republican would mix business and presidential politics by sending a horse-drawn carriage accompanied by three wagons to participate in a Pittsburgh parade for Rutherford B. Hayes—the teetotaler liked his stance on temperance—who was campaigning against the Democratic candidate, Samuel Tilden. While three of the signs bore the company name and trademark, the other read, TOMORROW WE WILL PICKLE TILDEN. To create his brand, Heinz insisted on uniformity and elegance in everything that he put before the public. His wagons were all painted plum red with green trimmings, and they were driven by pricey black Percherons, his specially bred French horses. In 1884, he contributed eighteen Heinz two-horse wagons to the three-and-a-half-hour-long Pittsburgh procession for the Republican presidential candidate James Blaine. The Republicans would, in turn, be good to Heinz. In 1891, the year after the congressman (and future president) William McKinley of Ohio pushed through a law raising tariffs on imported food by 50 percent, his profits doubled.

Heinz would put his heart into his marketing efforts. "Swing [Heinz] sign today across First Avenue," the tape-measure aficionado proudly noted in his diary on May 18, 1878, "18 feet long by 15 feet high, lettering...Pickles, Vinegar, Mustard....It is all made of wire and cost $40." While the denizens of Pittsburgh were initially startled by this larger-than-life advertisement, they soon accepted it. Heinz would continue to tout his products each year at the Pittsburgh exposition; and he would serve as a vice president of the civic organization that staged it for fifteen years. His varieties were like his children, and like a proud father, he couldn't stop talking them up. (After the birth of his fourth child, Clifford, he celebrated by launching "Clifford's Worcester Sauce," and a few years later, he named a brand of ketchup after his teenage son, Howard.) While Heinz could always find money for advertising, he scrimped elsewhere. In the middle of 1878, on a trip to Chicago, he plopped down only $17 for a blue suit because, as he noted, he was "trying to save." As he also acknowledged in his diary, he typically wore his suits every day for a couple of years.

Thanks to Heinz's remarkable ingenuity and drive—the smooth-talking salesman, who was not averse to staying up all night to get off orders, was constantly riding the rails to open up new markets—after just a year, the F. & J. Heinz Company was worth $14,000, up nearly fivefold. Having regained his financial footing, in the fall of 1877, a few weeks after Howard's birth, Heinz moved from Sharpsburg to a row house in downtown Pittsburgh that was close to his factory. But two years later, the neatnik would acknowledge his error and move back. "Am delighted with the change of coming to Sharpsburg," he noted in April 1879. "It seems more like living than to be stuck into the dirt in the heart of the Smoky City." Even though his business was now a smashing success, his anxiety level remained high. "My head feels dull, all over top of head and forehead," Heinz wrote that same April. "Am trying not to work too hard, but fear it is almost too late." Yet his new nervous crises would not produce boils, and he could move on to counting and measuring outgrowths of his prosperity. In early 1879, he began tallying the number of homeless men to whom he gave free meals at his firm. "I resolved to keep an account," he reported in his diary, after noting that he had served forty-three tramps and beggars in the thirty-one days of January, "and had the girl mark 1 on a piece of paper for all that were fed." The following year, he fixated on the dimensions of the iron safes that he bought both Irene and Clarence for Christmas—"twelve by nine by seven inches."

While revenues soared—in 1884, sales came to a staggering $43,000 ($860,000)—the workplace remained full of conflict. After 1880, when J. W. Ulam, one of his best employees, left to start his own pickle company, an embittered Heinz would no longer consider giving upper management positions to anyone outside the family; even so, he couldn't make peace with either of his titular bosses, his brother John and cousin Frederick. Heinz would repeatedly lash out at John for not working hard enough. Assuming that any sensible person would share his all-consuming interest in business, Heinz accused his brother of "driving more nails in my coffin than all other cares." He was incredulous that John wasn't eager to be at his post at the manufacturing division when it opened at 7 a.m. (At this stage of his career, Heinz himself typically reported for work at 9 a.m., roughly the same time as his brother.) In April 1887, in a curious attempt to "encourage Brother John," Heinz started commuting to the city on the 6 a.m. train. In response, John felt discouraged and wanted out. After Anna Heinz sided with her firstborn and put pressure on John to comply with Henry's whims, outside arbitrators stepped in and worked out the separation agreement. In 1888, Frederick also liberated himself from Henry's clutches and sold his share. H. J. Heinz and his company were now officially one and the same.

Heinz also had a tumultuous relationship with his brother Peter, who was the F. & J. Heinz Company's first "traveler" (traveling salesman). P.J., as H.J.

called him, proved to be more than capable. "He [Peter] surpasses all of our agents," Heinz noted in 1884, as his brother began selling bulk goods by wagon in Cincinnati. But despite being whisked by Heinz to temperance meetings, Peter continued to drink and chase women. In the spring of 1886, Heinz dashed off to Washington and "snatched him [Peter] away from where he was to be married. P.J. escaped." This was not actually the first time that Heinz had unhitched his brother from a wayward woman—and not even the first time in Washington. (Nine years earlier in the nation's capital, P.J. had shacked up with a divorced woman and her daughter above a saloon.) In an attempt to cure his brother's ills, Heinz sent him off to Germany that spring, where Peter soon found a potential mate, Pauline Merz, of whom the family could approve. Remarkably, after all his efforts to get Peter to keep to the straight and narrow, Heinz nearly sabotaged this union. That summer, in Wiesbaden, a few days before the wedding was to take place, the impulsive and aggrieved Heinz could not resist badmouthing the groom. As soon as he met the bride's parents, he let it rip. "I tell them plainly," Heinz wrote in his diary, "how P.J. is so that no reflections can be made." Fortunately, the Merzes were already aware of Peter's past, and the ceremony went on as planned.

After his marriage, Peter reestablished himself as a leading salesman. But while he no longer was seducing stray women, he continued to drink. In 1899, Heinz got a letter from a top company executive who stated that out "of all the cases [of alcoholism] that he has ever had in his life time, P.J. surpasses them all" and urged that "action should be taken to save our business." In the fall of 1900, after a Pinkerton detective, hired by Heinz, had followed Peter around as he went barhopping in Manhattan, his brother was forced to retire at the age of forty-nine.

———

Heinz's 1886 European trip was part medical vacation, part Protestant pilgrimage—he would sit in John Wesley's house in London and visit Martin Luther's church in Wittenberg—and part a return to his roots. In his father's hometown of Kallstadt, he would visit a myriad of uncles, aunts, cousins, nieces, and nephews, "a total of over 100 relatives," as he would dutifully count (and then recount in his journal). But business was never too far from his mind. Upon his arrival in Liverpool, Heinz systematically examined the windows of all the grocery shops and "saw no pickle displays." "I have learned little," the disappointed entrepreneur noted after his three-day visit, "in this city which I can utilize in America to advantage."

England's capital would be a different story. After taking the family to see the major sites, including the Houses of Parliament (which he described as "a beautiful structure and very large"—too large, no doubt, to measure the numbers), Buckingham Palace ("a plain structure"), and Regent's Park ("alive with people"), he enjoyed making the rounds of the pickle, glass, and vinegar factories. And then on Friday, June 18, 1886, at the end of his first week, Heinz made history. Decked out in his best tail coat (made by a British tailor in Philadelphia) and top hat, the supersalesman paid a call to Fortnum and Mason, the still-vibrant British grocer that has been catering to the royal family out of its Piccadilly Street store since 1707. Armed with a Gladstone bag containing "seven varieties of our finest and newest goods," he strode through the front door rather than through the service entrance, as was customary for English salesmen of the era. "Resisting the temptation to take out the tape measure (but the Georgian doorway was so beautifully proportioned)," as a British chronicler, attuned to his quirks, has put it, Heinz asked to see the head of grocery purchasing. Tasting the samples—the horseradish, the ketchup, and chili sauce—the head couldn't resist, stating, "I think, Mr. Heinz, we will take all of them."

"1ST SALE IN ENGLAND," reported a jubilant Heinz in his diary.

English exports initially constituted only a small fraction of his business. And the massive four-story Farrington Road Heinz headquarters, opened in 1898, hemorrhaged shillings for several years. But by 1906, led by baked beans, which Heinz himself loved to devour, English sales reached a quarter of a million dollars. Americans had first learned of beans during the Civil War, and the Heinz Company began mass-producing them in the mid-1890s. Its clever "beans and toast" campaign would forever revamp the morning meal throughout the British Empire. "At breakfast or dinner," ran a 1910 ad that circulated widely in England's northern factory belt, "see that your plate is filled with Heinz Baked Beans with Tomato Sauce. It builds up brain, body and muscle. The bean is Nature's most nourishing food." The Brits, who had once assumed that beans were meant for horses, were now largely convinced that they were the invention of a European company. In the twenty-first century, the United Kingdom still consumes more canned beans per capita than any other nation in the world.

A century before globalization, Heinz figured out that the future of his business rested on ringing up foreign sales. "I was the only one," he reflected toward the end of his life, "who had any faith in the future development of the 57 through a branch house in England." "Our market is the world," ran Heinz's "Important Idea Number Four." Between 1890 and 1915, he would take a long European trip every year but four. And by the start of the Great War, the compulsive world traveler would have agencies up and running on every continent but Antarctica. His advertising wouldn't be limited to America; countless Germans would gaze daily at his massive thirty-eight-foot-by-sixty-nine-foot sign over the Rhine River. Long before Starbucks, McDonald's, or even Coca-Cola, Heinz would reign as the most recognizable brand on earth. As Sebastian Mueller, Heinz's brother-in-law and trusty deputy for decades, once put it, Heinz products were sold wherever there were "civilized people."

In an effort to extend his global reach, Heinz kept mounting bigger and more elaborate exhibits at international expositions in both Europe and America, racking up a staggering total of fifty-five gold medals by 1904. At the 1893 Columbian Exposition in Chicago, the Heinz booth attracted such a flood of visitors that, as the *New York Times* reported, at the conclusion of this World's Fair, "it was...discovered that the gallery floor...sagged...where the pickle display of the H. J. Heinz Company stood."

But were it not for the quick thinker's quick thinking, the exquisite Heinz Pavilion in Chicago, which was made out of hand-carved oak and staffed by four beautiful women from different corners of the world, would have been a huge dud. In June 1893, a few weeks after the fair's official opening, Heinz took the family to Chicago (where their week's stay in sumptuous quarters, as he recorded in his diary, came to "$112 without food"). Heading over to the Agricultural Building, Heinz was stunned to see that almost nobody was at his exhibit. Taking an evening to diagnose the problem, Heinz realized that visitors were unwilling to hike up the forty-four steps to the second floor. As with his moment of genius on the Manhattan elevated train a few years later, Heinz concluded that the nearest lithography shop could provide a solution. He ordered small white cards that promised the bearer a free souvenir when presented at the Heinz Pavilion. These cards, which resembled baggage checks, were passed out all over the fair by a squadron of young boys. Thousands of people were now eager to parade up the stairs, where they picked up a one-and-a-quarter-inch green pickle pin, tasted his samples, and viewed his array of curios and antiquities. "A great hit," Heinz later wrote in his diary. "We hear it from all sources." By November, when fair officials noticed that the gallery had almost collapsed, despite their efforts to strengthen its foundation over the summer, Heinz had distributed a million pickle pins, causing the *Saturday Evening Post* to describe this marketing bonanza "as one of the most famous giveaways in merchandising history." It was the gift that kept on giving something back to the giver, as the potential customers who pinned the distinctive gutta-percha pickles on their shirts and blouses all became walking Heinz billboards.

The following year, in late January, a "very tired and worn" Heinz tried to soothe his "nervous stomach and head ache" by embarking on a grueling five-and-a-half-month trek across the Middle East and Europe. Accompanying the forty-nine-year-old entrepreneur were his two eldest children, Clarence and Irene, as well as Irene's close friend Myra Boyd; bothered by rheumatism, the now 205-pound Sallie wasn't feeling up to all the exertion. Heinz took his new Kodak camera, but his tape measure captured the moments that meant the most to him. "Measures over 13 feet at the base," he wrote of the Pillar of Pompey in Alexandria. After riding his camel to the Great Sphinx at Giza, he noted, "Measured some blocks 18 feet long, 6 feet thick, all in perfect condition." Of the statue of Ramesses II, the largest in Egypt, Heinz determined that the "ear measures 3 ½ feet" and "the first finger 3 feet in diameter." The Vatican provided him with lots of juicy factoids to keep track of—22 courtyards, 11,000 rooms, 23,000 windows, 10,000 statues, and 1,000 employees. "We are delighted," the serial counter wrote of his visit to St. Peter's Church, "with our climb to the top of the Dome, 715 steps." His only disappointment in Rome was his failure to gain an audience with the Pope—the rector of the American College, to whom he had written for help, couldn't pull it off. In July 1894, the curio collector and his many purchases—"six shipments and a mummy"—sailed back on the *City of Paris*, where he fraternized with Mark Twain ("medium height, say 5 feet 7 inches," Heinz noted, checking the impulse to whip out his favorite implement and record the author's exact dimensions).

Not long after Heinz's return, Sallie became gravely ill with typhoid pneumonia. On Thursday, November, 29, 1894—Thanksgiving—she died at Greenlawn, the thirty-room chateaulike estate in Pittsburgh's East End, which Heinz had recently bought and remodeled. She was fifty-one. To his eldest son, Clarence, then in Munich, a devastated Heinz could barely describe "the awfulness of what has befallen us." For obsessives, who have great difficulty connecting with others, the death of a trusted (that is, subservient) longtime spouse is particularly disorienting; the experience is akin to that of a preadolescent losing his or her mother. As he slowly recovered, Heinz was forced to rearrange his priorities. While he would never stop overseeing his company, in 1895 he handed over many management responsibilities to Sebastian Mueller. He also began immersing himself in the activities of the World Sunday School Association. "Sunday School," he later wrote, "is the world's greatest living force for character building and good citizenship." To cope with his grief, like Jefferson after the loss of his beloved Martha, Heinz stepped up his collecting and organizing. "Well, how is the Royal Kingdom?" Howard wrote to his father in the summer of 1896. "I hope you did not get any curios, but I suppose you got some, you couldn't help it." When the fourth floor of his Greenlawn mansion could no longer contain his thousands of impressive tchotchkes—among his timepieces were Lord Horatio Nelson's personal watch—he erected a private museum next to the garage and opened it to the public.

According to one Heinz hagiographer, Sallie was "the first, last and only love of his existence," a hypothesis that has rarely been questioned. But while Heinz never found a permanent replacement for Sallie, he may well have found several short-term substitutes. The devout Methodist had no stomach for adultery, which he considered grounds for dismissal from the company, but he took a thoroughly secular approach toward romance for the unattached. In 1905, in a letter to a busy and anxious Howard, then a dashing bachelor in his late twenties, Heinz asked rhetorically, "Then why not be systematic in your eating as well as your work when you are in good condition and when you are feeling poorly, let the young ladies drive away the blues?" In Pittsburgh, after fellow church-goers noticed that he was "getting sweet on Widow L.," an anonymous friend issued the following warning, "She is a very nice lady...but I know her designs on you are for money *only*, etc., etc." "Widow L." was not the only woman with whom Heinz was romantically linked. A few months before his death, while vacationing in Miami Beach, Heinz received a series of billets-doux from a Florida resident, Gussie Streeter. "I would give my life," she wrote to her "darling Mr. Heinz" after running into him briefly in the lobby of a hotel "if you would only come and talk to me as you used to....The love I have for you will last as long as I live."

Heinz didn't respond, but a staff member soon dropped Miss Streeter, about whom little else is known, a brief note, "Mr H. earnestly requests that you do not write any more letters. He is leaving Miami and will probably go to California."

Heinz didn't make it anywhere near California that year, and it appears unlikely that he ever had any intention of reviving that romance.

———

"There is Heinz and, far behind, Hunt's and Del Monte and a handful of private-label brands." Thus reported Malcolm Gladwell in his classic 2004 *New Yorker* article, "The Ketchup Conundrum," which explored why ketchup—in contrast to mustard, which comes in dozens of varieties—still comes primarily in one ("57 Varieties"). For Gladwell, the reason for this anomalous state of affairs is simple. A century ago, argues the bestselling author (as do Heinz's string of hagiographers), the founder led "a renegade band of ketchup manufacturers" that upended the establishment by making "a superior ketchup; safer, purer and better tasting." According to this conventional wisdom, Heinz, in tandem with the new Food and Drug Administration (FDA) established in 1906, worked courageously on behalf of consumers to rid the market of toxic-preservative-laced ketchup. But the full story is more complex. Far from a rebel, Heinz was already the market leader when he made the famous tweaks to his product. And he ran roughshod over the competition partly by engaging in lots of marketing flim-flam; in fact, to establish his virtual monopoly, Heinz ended up relying less on "the application of culinary science," as Gladwell maintains, than on its deliberate misapplication.

By the end of the 1880s, Heinz had designed the key accoutrements of his iconic sauce—the keystone label, the neck band, and the screw-top bottle—but the product bore little resemblance to anything we might recognize today. At its inception in 1888, the H. J. Heinz Company sold four different classes of tomato ketchup—from the luxury brand, Keystone, to the nameless "Home-Made Catsup"—in several different quantities, ranging from half-pint bottles to forty-five-gallon barrels. Price corresponded to quality and varied from about twenty-five to sixty cents a gallon. Back then, Heinz threw a lot of spices such as cayenne pepper and mace into his ketchups, all of which were thin and watery. The 1890s was both the decade that ketchup came into its own—by 1896, both the *New York Tribune* and *Scientific American* were dubbing it America's "national condiment"—and H. J. Heinz became its biggest producer. Of the total of about 150 brands, according to a 1904 survey, most had only a local or regional reach. Heinz, one of just a handful of national brands, led the market with a 20 percent share.

By 1900, food products accounted for nearly a third of all finished commodities manufactured in the United States, and calls came from consumer advocates and Congress for regulation of the industry. This "pure food movement," which Heinz soon joined, would turn the ketchup biz upside down. Its leader was Harvey W. Wiley, a charismatic chemist at the United States Department of Agriculture who in 1902 got a grant from Congress to investigate food additives and their impact on health. While corporate excesses were legion—mislabeling was common, as was the use of dangerous fillers such as sawdust—so too were Wiley's. A publicity hound, he was a zealot who vilified his enemies as "the hosts of Satan." Often loose with facts, Wiley drew press attention to his cause by devising a "Poison Squad," a group of twelve young men who served as his guinea pigs. In 1904, Wiley had his minions try sodium benzoate, a mold inhibitor then used by all ketchup manufacturers, including the H. J. Heinz Company. After several volunteers came down with various symptoms, including weight loss, fever, and a decrease in red blood cells, Wiley stopped the experiment, convinced that he had confirmed his hypothesis. Even though his study was far from scientific—Wiley used no control group, nor did he take into account whether any preexisting condition or previous test might have influenced his findings— he concluded that sodium benzoate was so harmful that it should be outlawed.

In 1905, a committee of six of Wiley's lieutenants including Sebastian Mueller, who represented the H. J. Heinz Company, went to the White House to lobby President Theodore Roosevelt. The result was the passage of the Federal Food and Drug Act a year later, which set up the FDA. In June 1907, based on the Poison Squad's test, Wiley issued a directive requiring manufacturers to limit the use of sodium benzoate to one-tenth of 1 percent and to include this information on the label. Wiley also declared his intention to impose a ban in the near future. Well aware that this was the direction in which Wiley was headed, Heinz had already been tinkering with his formula. Even though only a few years earlier at the St. Louis World's Fair, Sebastian Mueller had publicly stated that sodium benzoate was not an objectionable preservative because it was "present naturally in some fruits, and particularly our cranberry," by the fall of 1904, the H. J. Heinz Company produced one-fourth of its ketchup without preservatives, and by the end of 1905, one-half. In early 1907, Sebastian Mueller wrote to Wiley, "We have finally and fully satisfied ourselves through the results of our experiments in putting up Ketchup without a preservative, that our Ketchup may safely be sent in bottles...and will keep perfectly for a period of not less than four weeks under ordinary conditions." Thus was born the incarnation of America's national sauce that millions of people around the world have come to know and love—the thick and slow-out-of-the-bottle (or packet) ooze that we put on our favorite comfort foods.

More a triumph of marketing than of science, Heinz's new signature product would benefit his company's health much more than the consumer's. While Heinz draped himself in the mantel of purity—as he insisted, his company now used nothing but fresh tomatoes, sanitary preparation methods, and secure bottles—all was not as it appeared. As the British food writer Bee Wilson asserts in her book, *Swindled: The Dark History of Food Fraud, from Poisoned Candy to Counterfeit Coffee*, "There are considerable ironies in the way that Heinz ketchup built its empire on its status as 'pure food.'" The first involved a secret switcheroo. Despite Heinz's claims, his new manufacturing processes were not sufficient to ensure purity; he also had to substitute something for sodium benzoate. What he ended up doing was doubling the amount of both vinegar and sugar (the sweetener, which today comes in the form of high-fructose corn syrup, was necessary to avoid a bitter taste). As a result, Wilson wonders whether the "nonbezoated but sugary Heinz ketchup should qualify as a health-giving product." In the old paradigm, tomato ketchup was much more closely tied to "the thing-in-itself" (to use philosopher Immanuel Kant's term for an object's intrinsic nature)—the condiment had the consistency of a real tomato and tasted more like one, too. Another sleight of hand was Heinz's attack on his competitors, which aimed to deflect attention away from his own deceptive sales practices. While he vilified other manufacturers for using preservatives solely to keep their costs down, H. J. Heinz took to price gouging. In contrast to the benzoate users that charged from ten to twelve cents a bottle, Heinz began charging twenty-five to thirty cents a bottle. Heinz insisted that purity cost big bucks, but his added expenses actually amounted to only three or four cents a bottle. "The cost of living to the consumer for the very necessities of life," noted a contemporary critic of Heinz in the *American Food Journal*, "has been generously and directly increased, without probably the least benefit." With ketchup sales going up from 3.6 million bottles in 1904 to 6 million in 1906 and profits doubling between 1901 and 1906, Heinz was suddenly awash in cash, which he plowed back into print advertisements.

To achieve his next goal, which was to obliterate the competition, Heinz would have to take on the president. Unconvinced that benzoate was dangerous, in 1907, Theodore Roosevelt appointed a board of scientific experts, chaired by Ira Remsen, a leading chemist who headed Johns Hopkins University, to conduct further studies and render a definitive verdict. In the meantime, at the suggestion of his son Howard, then the firm's advertising manager, Heinz made a massive investment in print advertising. With his signs, Heinz had emphasized brand recognition; in his new magazine spreads, he would provide bits of information (and misinformation) designed to scare both grocers and consumers away from his competitors. "This became a national debate and the Heinz advertising aimed to influence food officials to ban benzoate," asserted historian Clayton Coppin, coauthor of *The Politics of Purity: Harvey Washington Wiley and the Origins of Federal Food Policy*. "It is far easier," Coppin explained to me, "to make your product the only legal product than it is to outcompete your rivals." Even though Heinz had no idea what the feds would eventually decide, his ads in food industry journals urged grocers to remove all benzoate ketchups from the shelves because it was "only a question of time before their sale will be prohibited." In his advertising blitz in consumer magazines such as *Collier's* and *Woman's Home Companion*, Heinz asked the rhetorical question, "Why should you use a product that has to be doctored with drugs to make it keep, when you can get food that is really pure?" As he reminded readers, their mothers never used sodium benzoate to make ketchup (but Anna Heinz and her cohorts did not have to worry about shelf life).

In January 1909, Heinz faced a major setback when the Remsen board overturned Wiley's findings. While Remsen and his four distinguished academic colleagues also did not use a control group, their testing was much more extensive than Wiley's. On his last day in office, President Roosevelt issued a food inspection decision stating that sodium benzoate is not harmful, particularly in small amounts, and this has been the law of the land ever since. But Heinz, like Wiley, was not ready to give up. Unwilling to go after the team of éminences grises directly, he came up with reasons to get rid of benzoate besides its inherent toxicity. A new Heinz ad that ran in both *Collier's* and the *Saturday Evening Post* claimed that benzoate "allows a cheapening ... of a product through the reduction of food value, employment of loose methods and too often of unfit raw materials."*(In this war of words, the pro-benzoate forces countered that vinegar and sugar were actually more effective in masking unsavory ingredients than most additives.) The H. J. Heinz Company, along with other key members of "Big Food" such as Beech-Nut and Borden's, also formed a lobbying arm, the Association for the

Promotion of Purity in Food Products. In its initial 1909 meeting at the Waldorf-Astoria Hotel in Manhattan, the organization vowed to combat "the reactionary interests...[that] have been able...to nullify some of the most important provisions of the [pure food] law." So devoted was Heinz to his purity crusade that the teetotaler looked the other way when the new group hired the controversial publicist "Poker Bill" Smith, who had recently worked for the National Wholesale Liquor Dealers Association, to fire off its press releases. Determined to deal a fatal blow to benzoate, the H. J. Heinz Company also pressured incoming president William Howard Taft to appoint Wiley secretary of agriculture; but Taft, like Roosevelt before him, remained suspicious of Wiley.

While Heinz ended up losing the benzoate battle, he won the war. By 1911, his company's share of the ketchup market would top 50 percent, and except for a few brief dips—such as in the 1960s, when Hunt and Del Monte ramped up their advertising campaigns—there it has remained for the last century.

Heinz's competitors soon stopped using sodium benzoate, but not before they made a last-ditch effort to out-Heinz Heinz. In the spring of 1909, right after Theodore Roosevelt authorized the use of sodium benzoate, the Curtice Brothers, makers of Blue Label Ketchup, a national brand that had once held 10 percent of the market, placed an ad in the *New York Times* stating that its product was "Pure and Unadulterated Containing only those ingredients Recognized and Endorsed by the U.S. Government" and that its tomatoes were "fresh from the fields—carefully washed, skins, seeds and cores removed." It was too little too late. Heinz's "Seventh Important Idea" was that government regulation would help the food-processing industry grow; and he was not disappointed when the big guys—such as the H. J. Heinz Company—received the bulk of the benefits.

———

Purity was not a just concept that Heinz stumbled upon to drive firms like the Curtice Brothers out of the ketchup biz. In an ad placed in the catalog for the 1904 St. Louis World's Fair, which talked up a dozen other Heinz varieties, he was already describing his company as a "Celebrated Pure Food Establishment." Like Steve Jobs, this germaphobe, who on a visit to Algiers lamented that "but one trip thru these dirty narrow Arab quarters will suffice for a lifetime," also worshipped at the altar of cleanliness.

This core value ran rampant throughout his North Side plant, which he began constructing in 1890 and which quickly earned the moniker "A clean spot in Pittsburgh." (This was no mean feat. "There the night is made lurid," wrote *Pittsburgh Dispatch* reporter Theodore Dreiser in 1894, "and the very atmosphere of the day darkened by the flames and the smoke.") For his headquarters, Heinz selected a vitrified brick that could withstand frequent washings; thus he could keep the building spotless inside and out. By 1910, the firm's fifty-acre campus on the banks of the Allegheny River consisted of seventeen buildings, including a three-story equine palace. Even Heinz's stables, widely considered the best commercial operation in the country, were kept spick-and-span. A series of machines fed, watered, and brushed the fleet of two hundred black draft horses, which had to be inspected by the founder himself (or Mueller, in his absence). Uniformity in measurement was of paramount importance; the horses, Heinz insisted, all had to be the same size and weight. The entrepreneur, who drew few distinctions between bipeds and quadrupeds—"A young man ought first to be a clean, wholesome animal" was another motto plastered on the office walls—treated his beloved equine charges just like his children; he would both coddle and punish. While his ailing horses could enjoy the benefits of a glass-enclosed Turkish bath, those who kicked were banished to a specially designed "jail." The stables were just as "perfectly ventilated" as the five-story Administration Building.

With cleanliness a synonym for his brand, Heinz was eager to show off his supersanitary workplace. In contrast to the benzoate users, who manufactured "the kind of food you would not care to eat if you could see it made," the H. J. Heinz Company, as its ads insisted, had nothing to hide: "Our doors are always open. The public is free to come and go at all hours." For decades, "the cleanest, largest and best-equipped Food Product establishment in the world" offered factory tours. The guides who escorted the twenty thousand visitors a year around the "Heinz Pickle Works" followed a prescribed route, using a prepared script. The stellar stables were the first stop. Then came the printing department and box factory, followed by the can factory, where, amid a loud din, workers sterilized and soldered the vessels of various Heinz varieties at breakneck speed. The tour then went from the bright and cheery "Girls' Dining Room"—60 percent of the workers were female, most of whom were Polish or Italian immigrants between the ages of fifteen and twenty-one—to the Baked Bean Building, where cans were filled at the rate of 150 per minute. And before picking up their going-away present, a Heinz pickle pin, curious onlookers got to inspect the Pickle Bottling Department, where hundreds of "Heinz girls," decked out in freshly laundered blue uniforms and spotless white hats, labeled and capped the pickle jars.

While the elegant factory incarnated efficiency, it was not quite the workers' paradise that the self-absorbed industrialist believed it to be. As with his horses, Heinz gave his "little helpers" a few choice goodies, including free manicures and noontime carriage rides. But in what mattered most, he was stingy. Piecework was common, and the majority of his "girls" made less than $6 a day at a time when $7 a day was the poverty level. "Excellent building construction, thorough cleanliness, dressing rooms, rest rooms, natatoria...Whenever they are at the service of the employees," wrote sociologist Elizabeth Beardsley Butler about the H. J. Heinz Company in 1909, "we have reason to be glad.... [But] their service is of little effect if it serves merely to obscure facts of low wages....Pleasant surroundings compensate neither for excessive work, nor a fundamental deficit in the financial basis of self-respect." (In contrast, as Butler also noted in her landmark study of Pittsburgh's working women, the men at the Heinz company did "all the responsible work" and received much more generous compensation.) Three decades before Charlie Chaplin's *Modern Times* dramatized how screwing nuts on an assembly line could lead to nuttiness, numerous "Heinz girls" had already lost their minds by placing countless cans onto labeling machines (six to eight workers were needed to keep the cans humming along in succession) or by sticking slices of pork onto rapidly moving baked beans. "Speed pressure and a low rate of pay," concluded Butler, "destroy nervous vitality, and keep the standard of life near the margin of degradation." After just two years, the typical "Heinz girl" was no longer seduced by the free ketchup and relish—the long tables in the "Girls' Dining Room" were dotted with fresh bottles that had failed inspection because of a loose cap—and had moved on.

––––––––

In early 1915, the seventy-year-old Heinz, accompanied by his son Clifford, took the SS *Great Northern* to San Francisco. En route, they sailed through the recently opened Panama Canal. The City by the Bay was hosting the Panama-Pacific International Exposition—running from February 20 to December 4, this World's Fair would attract nineteen million visitors—and the semiretired founder was eager to oversee the Heinz exhibit set up by the firm's expo manager, Mr. Foster.

Heinz's youngest child was now a thirty-one-year-old junior member of the company's board of directors with solid credentials as an equestrian—he had inherited his father's love of horses—and a playboy. Eight years earlier, Heinz had dashed up to New London, Connecticut, to wrest the recent college graduate away from a nurse with whom he had eloped. (The marriage was soon annulled.) AGED FATHER IS GRIEVED, ran the headline of the *New York Times* account of Clifford's escapade. Despite ongoing conflicts—in his diary, Heinz would express regret about the age difference between Clifford and his flings— Heinz showed more restraint with his favorite traveling companion than with other family members. And as father and son settled into their hotel on the fairgrounds, Heinz's pique toward Clifford's older brother Howard, then running the company back in Pittsburgh, was mounting, and the man who still held the title of CEO felt he had no choice but to speak his mind.

It wasn't anything about the fair that upset the founder; he was proud of the sensational Heinz tower that stood in the central crossway of the elaborate three-hundred-thousand-square-foot Palace of Food Products (originally called the Pure Food Building, it was later dubbed "Palace of the Nibbling Arts," as visitors got to taste samples as they strolled). The curio collector who headed the Pittsburgh Egyptology Association had designed a pyramid of fifty-seven canned and bottled condiments, which rose up to the heavens. "Need we say," Frank Morton Todd, the official historian of the fair, would later write of these unique building blocks, "they represent the product of Mr. Heinz of Pittsburgh, Purveyor to his Majesty the American Citizen?" And underneath this Babel-like structure, spectators could view a moving picture of Heinz workers planting tomatoes and bottling ketchup. Of these images that also displayed the latest in both farm and factory machinery, Todd would add, "Cleanliness and wholesomeness were apparent in every stage of that progress."

Howard had recently taken over as the head of the company's board of directors, and Heinz, fearing that he was becoming irrelevant, was suddenly convinced that his successor could do no right. In a six-page screed, written on March 9, 1915, from San Francisco, the founder berated Howard for not doing enough to call attention to "our splendid display" at the fair. "Our opportunity in California," he stressed, "is now." While the company had erected a thirty-foot electric sign that flashed "57" across the bay, Heinz demanded an additional $25,000 be spent on print advertising. "If my methods of advertising," Heinz railed, "have been a failure, the world at large would have made the discovery. I now insist that we act. Other men who have not the means for advertising are advertising their products....I urged this before I left home but cannot find a single advertisement in the magazines. Are you asleep?"

With his own skirt-chasing days behind him, the nearly forty-year-old Howard had evolved into a happily married father of two young sons, H. John (known as Jack) and Rust.[2] And in contrast to his brothers, the industrious industrialist had developed a knack for micromanaging both the business and his tempestuous father. Since the Great War prevented Howard from shipping Heinz back to Germany for his annual "cure," he had begun encouraging his father to make more sales trips within the United States (such as the several-month-long sojourn in San Francisco). Howard had also learned how to tune out Heinz's outbursts, a tactic that further enraged his father. "You will probably feel that I am nervous," Heinz protested in the middle of his nastygram from California. "No, I am feeling better today. The sun is shining." Addicted to control, Heinz, like other aging obsessives, was unable to pass the reins to the next generation without making a fuss.

Heinz concluded his diatribe by accusing Howard of being too domineering with his fellow board members and of spending too much time in his office. "You know you enjoy better health not at the desk," Heinz advised, "you accomplish more, the results are greater away from the desk, and yet you are determined to stay at the desk....You are working too hard at the desk." Unable to appreciate individual differences, Heinz couldn't understand why everyone did not behave exactly as he did. But in contrast to his father, who was most productive when in motion, the Yale-educated chemist had a deliberative, scientific bent. (Years later, on a visit to the Steel City, Albert Einstein would pronounce Howard Heinz "one of the two most informed and entertaining men" whom he had ever met.) While Howard appreciated the founder's seat-of-the-pants creativity, the son would implement the father's "great vision" by

---

[2] Upon Howard Heinz's death in 1941, Jack Heinz would take over the company. His firstborn was H. John Heinz III, who would become a senator from Pennsylvania; his wife, Teresa, assumed control of the Howard Heinz Endowment, the family's vast philanthropic organization, upon his death. She later married Massachusetts senator John Kerry.

more technocratic means. Howard's investments in chemical testing, for example, would produce one of the first quality-control departments run by an American corporation.

After Heinz's death four years later, company officials were surprised at what they found in his big desk, located directly across from Howard's, on the fourth floor of the Administrative Building. Inside its main drawers were various mementos along with several steel tape measures and some measurements, which no one was able to decipher.

Part Two

Secret Sex Maniacs

Dewey (front row, holding his hat) at the annual American Library Association (ALA) conference in 1899 when he was forty-seven. While Dewey irked traditionalists by supporting female advancement in the library profession, he was not a consistent champion of the feminist cause; in 1906, he was forced to resign from the ALA due to repeated instances of sexual harassment.

3

Information Technology: Melvil Dewey

The Librarian Who Worshipped Perfect Tens

> I like 10 [hours of sleep a night]. Perhaps because I believe so
> firmly in decimals, of which I have been a life-long advocate
> and active missionary. I was born December 10, 1851, the an-
> niversary of the deposit of the prototype meter in the Palace
> of the Archives in Paris. In 1872 I devised my decimal
> classification....I am so loyal to decimals as our great labor
> saver that I even like to sleep decimally.
>
> —Melvil Dewey, 1926

On the morning of Wednesday, January 5, 1887, Columbia College's new library school was set to open. But the trustees of the college, then an all-male bastion located in midtown Manhattan, wanted to shut it down before its founder, the thirty-five-year-old Melvil Dewey, Columbia's Librarian-in-Chief for the past four years, ever met the first class. As the handsome six-footer with the jet-black hair and bushy beard later recalled, he was suddenly immersed in "one of the sharpest battles of my life, for what I knew to be right."

The previous day, the chairman of Columbia's committee on buildings, Charles Silliman, had informed Dewey that he would not have access to any classrooms. The reason for the fracas? The entering class of twenty—Dewey's initial hope for ten, his favorite number, had to be scrapped—included seventeen women, and the trustees, whom Silliman represented, were reluctant to allow any "petticoats" on campus. However, this champion of women's education wasn't going to let Silliman or anyone else come between him and his lofty goals. As Dewey later wrote, he considered himself a "Moses" who was about to "lead those particular children to the promised land."

Dewey had been consumed by the idea of starting a library school for more than a decade. In an essay, "Apprenticeship of Librarians," published in 1879 in *Library Journal*, Dewey lamented, "Physicians, lawyers, preachers, yes even our cooks have special schools for special training." An admirer of Dewey's various writings on librarianship as a profession, Columbia's president, Frederick Augustus Porter Barnard, was firmly on board. "The librarian," Barnard wrote upon hiring Dewey in 1883, "is ceasing to be a mere jailer of the books, and is becoming an aggressive force in the community." That same year, in a speech at the annual American Library Association (ALA) conference in Buffalo, Dewey suggested that the school's curriculum should pivot around cataloging, bibliography, and literary methods, by which he meant classifying, arranging, and indexing. From the get-go, he envisioned training more women than men. "In much of library work," Dewey noted, "woman's quick mind and deft fingers do many things with a neatness and dispatch seldom equaled by her brothers."

In the spring of 1884, Dewey, with the help of his close friend Barnard, who dropped by his office most afternoons, got Columbia's trustees to authorize a library school; according to the original plan, the new institution was to be up and running by the fall of 1886. The one catch was that Dewey's training program had to be "self-sustaining," meaning that fees would have to cover expenses. After encountering a set of bureaucratic roadblocks, Dewey was forced to postpone its opening until the beginning of 1887.

But when Dewey publicly announced that he planned to admit women, the trustees started to push back. And as much as Dr. Barnard supported the new library school, he was losing the will to fight. In December 1886, he cautioned Dewey that Silliman's "new phase of opposition" was likely to spell doom. On January 4, after learning of Silliman's latest rebuke, the seventy-seven-year-old Columbia president tried to enlist several college officials to help Dewey. But late that afternoon, Barnard gave up, believing that the battle had been lost. Feeling faint, he called for his physician. Dewey, however, then immediately sprang into action. He sent for the janitors, whom he asked to fix up an unused storeroom over the chapel. They quickly scraped the walls and patched up the rickety furniture. Dewey also hired a truck to bring some additional chairs from his West Fifty-Sixth Street apartment.

And so opened more or less on schedule the world's first library school, Columbia's School of Library Economy (thus named, Dewey later quipped, because it forced him to get "the most possible out of the appropriations not available"). Proud of his victory over "the enemies of women," Dewey would always remember January 5, 1887, as the day that he had "kindled a fire whose light will surely be seen down through the generations."

That first year, the school's twenty students, who hailed from all over America—one even came from England—paid $50 each for four months of instruction. With his limited budget, the well-connected Dewey relied heavily on the services of twenty volunteer lecturers from around the country, including Ainsworth Spofford, the Librarian of Congress, who addressed "What to Read and When to Read and How to Read." Dewey and his assistant librarians at Columbia also taught courses for which they received no additional remuneration. Dewey emphasized technical and practical matters. In a talk entitled "Light, Heat and Ventilation," he expressed his concern that electric lights might put "freckles" on books. "Pure air" for libraries became a personal crusade. Dewey's wife, Annie, whom he had married a decade earlier, pitched in by lecturing on indexing. Despite the "super-annuated building" and the often dry subject matter, students listened with "the ferment of enthusiasm." They essentially lived in the library from early in the morning until its 10 p.m. closing time, when they still could be found combing over their lecture notes. Dewey had succeeded in imparting his missionarylike zeal to a new generation. Library work, he insisted, was not just about "shoveling" dusty books; it was really about giving every American the opportunity to pursue a lifelong education. At the end of the first term, eleven of the twenty students signed up for a second academic year during which they would attend classes for a total of seven months.

Dewey was soon flooded with a steady stream of new applicants. And in his excitement, he got a bit carried away. On the application form that he designed, he requested some curious pieces of information. Now, he didn't actually require females to submit their bust size, as generations of incredulous indexers have snickered about (such as the 1971 *Library Journal* editorial writer who, in referring to this urban legend, wondered, "Like what did you *really* have in mind, Mel baby?"). But he did ask for a few telling measurements—namely, height and weight—as well as a description of hair and eye color along with a photo. Regarding his discriminating taste in future librarians, he once remarked, "You can't polish a pumpkin."

Unbeknownst to most Americans, who are familiar with his name largely through the use of his signature achievement, the ingenious Dewey Decimal Classification (DDC) system, America's pioneering librarian had a dark side.

Dewey's desire to bring more women into the library business was rooted in part in his own out-of-control sexual desire. As one historian has noted, the library school may well have been "a Trojan horse" designed to smuggle babes onto the Columbia campus. While hard evidence for each and every one of Dewey's alleged extracurricular activities is not available, a pattern is clear and undeniable. Throughout his adult life, Dewey sought out inappropriate relationships with women. In fact, in 1906, this serial sexual harasser was forced to resign from the American Library Association, the organization that he had helped to found a generation earlier, because of his scandalous behavior. A year earlier, as four "prominent women" in the ALA charged, during a ten-day ALA-sponsored trip to Alaska following the organization's annual convention, Dewey had made unwelcome advances on several librarians. As a highly respected female member of the guild summed up the matter in 1924, "For many years women librarians have been the special prey of Mr. Dewey in a series of outrages upon decency."

Like Heinz, Dewey started out as a hyperobedient boy; as a youth, he was constantly trying to please his demanding and chronically stressed-out mother. But as an adult, Dewey would seek to turn the tables. Once he discovered that he could exercise power over women, he would insist that they do his bidding. The man who couldn't connect first charmed before attempting to dominate.

———————

Dewey's career as an organizer extraordinaire began early. By age five, Melville Louis Kossuth Dewey—his name paid homage both to the novelist Herman Melville and to the Hungarian freedom fighter Louis Kossuth—was already arranging and classifying the contents of his mother's pantry in order to improve the efficiency of the household.

The adult's abiding love of order was a direct response to his chaotic boyhood in Adams Center, a small town in western New York, located in the so-called burned-over district, the part of the state known for its Protestant fervor. "It [my home]," he wrote in his diary early in his undergraduate career at Amherst College, "was hurly-burly, scolding, etc. too much, and neither of my parents ever practiced any confidences with me." Convinced of his "own unworthiness," Melville (as he was called until he dropped the final *le* at the age of twenty-five) felt little anger about his difficult circumstances; instead he blamed himself. Straightening up his environment could help him ward off these deeply rooted feelings of shame. He spent many an afternoon cleaning up the yard, the cellar, and the woodshed as well as picking up stones, plowing the garden, and polishing his mother's sewing machine. As Melville also recorded in his diary, his early years were "as monotonous as the roar of the Niagara." Dull routines would become a lifelong addiction.

His mother, Eliza Dewey, was an imposing figure "who never feared anything." "She was," Melville later recalled, "famous as was father for being the hardest worker in town." This industrious Seventh Day Baptist handed off the bulk of the care for her fifth child and second son—whom she would refer to as "her baby" well into his thirties—to her eldest daughter, Mate, then in late adolescence. Her neglect would have long-lasting effects, as would the torrent of austere maxims and scary injunctions that flowed from her lips. "Praise to the face," she insisted, "is an open disgrace." "Don't waste" was oft repeated. Her thrift knew no bounds. After Melville became a successful adult, she would ask him to send back his old shirts, which she would then fix up for her husband, Joel Dewey, a perpetually struggling merchant.

This nineteenth-century Tiger Mother could also hold her own in mano a mano combat with feral creatures. At the age of two, Melville was grabbed by a huge dog that proceeded to rip out chunks of skin near his left eye. Hearing the screams, the local doctor hopped off his horse and tried to intercede, but to no avail. In contrast, as soon as Eliza put down her sewing and spotted the fight, she immediately wrested the toddler out of the dog's jaws.

Melville's father also deferred to the domineering woman of the house. A devout Baptist like his wife, Joel Dewey was a boot maker who ran a general store that sold everything from groceries to farm supplies. The timid shopkeeper never could refuse to let his customers—even ne'er-do-wells—buy on credit. The elder Dewey routinely accepted old cows and pigs as a substitute for cash. At thirteen, Melville began waiting on his father's customers after school. Not long after that, the avid reader—as an adolescent, he devoured all five volumes of Lord Macaulay's *History of England*—first went into the library business. (Like Jefferson, he was no fan of the novel; he called fiction the "deadly enemy of mental power.") In a corner of the store, he maintained a small collection of books, which he would rent for two cents a day. After taking a bookkeeping course, this whiz with figures, who would later win Amherst College's prestigious Walker Math Prize, did a complete inventory of his father's wares. Melville initially hoped simply to improve the store's methods. But his digging around led to the discovery of a staggering 155 promissory notes, of which 133 were no longer valid. Melville's calculations revealed that his father was actually losing money. In 1869, at the urging of his youngest child, a reluctant Joel Dewey sold the store. Melville and his parents then moved into the home of his elder brother, Manfred, a well-to-do piano salesman, in the neighboring town of Oneida.

Having attempted to fix his family's precarious finances, the grandiose seventeen-year-old turned his attention to reforming the world. Though he would soon shed his rigid Baptist beliefs, for the rest of his life he would infuse his work with evangelical zeal. The late adolescent, who never openly rebelled against his parents, began railing against "old fogies who are continually croaking 'let well enough alone.'" A technology lover, enthralled by the "elegance and speed of the steamboat and railroad," Melville sought to liberate the engines of progress. In November 1869, he settled on a cause that would occupy (and preoccupy) him for the rest of his life: "I wish to inaugurate a higher education for the masses....If the time and talent now expended at the shrine of mammon could be devoted to education what a mighty revolution would result." His work as a librarian, devoted to providing "the best reading for the largest number, at the least cost," as he later put it in the famous ALA motto, would fulfill this pledge, but in his precollege days, he had mostly tens on his mind. Given that America's haphazard system of weights and measures resulted in untold waste and confusion, the adoption of the metric system, Melville believed, could help jump-start the entire economy. "But certainly the [metric] system," he wrote in 1869, "can never be used by the people until it be learned by the people." Thus he saw it as his mission to right this wrong from the bottom up.

The very act of measuring was also dear to the young man's heart. Melville loved translating everything into numbers, including himself. On his fifteenth birthday, he began keeping a chart in which he tracked his height and weight as well as the value of all his possessions, divided into categories such as clothes, cash, and books. He updated these figures on every birthday for the next decade. In 1866, his books—including "his most essential," Webster's Dictionary, for which the twelve-year-old had shelled out $10 in 1864, nearly his entire life savings at the time—were worth $50; this amount dipped to $45 in 1870 before spiking up to $142 in 1875. In his sophomore year at Amherst, thanks to Professor Edward Hitchcock Jr., who ran the college's physical education program, he was delighted to have access to a whole new set of data. "My expiratory capacity is 273 cubic inches," he wrote in a diary entry dated December 10, 1871, "chest

38 in passive, full 39 in, arm 12.75 in, fore arm 11.25 in (all as taken by Dr. H)."
(As he also noted, he actually compiled these "birthday statistics" the night before; that year, he resorted to this "Irishy way" of keeping his diary because the
tenth fell on a Sunday.) Numerical measurements, even those that weren't expressed metrically, had a remarkable power to induce feelings of calm. "I feel
well repaid for the time spent," he observed at the end of that birthday entry,
"since these results…make me feel more safe and certain."

———

"The 900 of 020 [was]…dark before 1873."

So wrote Mary Krome, a student at the Florida State College for Women, to
Dewey in a congratulatory letter upon his eightieth birthday. Translated from the
lingo of the DDC back into English, Ms. Krome's numbers allude to Dewey's
pivotal role in moving "the history of library science" out of the dark ages.

At Amherst College, where the small-town boy began his studies in September 1870, he found his true calling. The inspiration came not from any professor
or course, but from the $12-a-month part-time job that he landed in the fall of
1872. Soon after the heavily indebted junior began keeping the account books at
the college library, he could think of little else but how to organize its thirty thousand volumes. "My heart," he wrote in March 1873, "is open to anything that is
either decimal or about libraries." That May, he cranked out a preliminary draft
of his classification scheme—a system that is used to organize libraries to this
day and was the starting point for many research projects in the PG (Pre-Google)
Era. After earning his bachelor's degree a year later, Dewey eagerly accepted a
post as the chief assistant to the college's librarian, William Montague, a foreign language professor. By May 1875, Dewey had put the entire collection in
"proper order"; by the end of that year, he had completed his forty-two-page *A
Classification and Subject Index for Cataloguing and Arranging the Books and
Pamphlets of a Library*. The following spring, Dewey shelled out a dollar to obtain copyright protection for his forthcoming book, first published later that year.

Until the Amherst junior got on the case, America's printed matter—its books
and pamphlets—were in a state of total disorder. Each of the country's roughly
one thousand libraries, whether public or academic, relied on its own idiosyncratic classification system. The books at the Amherst library were arranged
according to the shelf system, then the most common approach. Catalogers

would give each volume a number identifying the particular shelf on which it was to be placed. This method, Dewey quipped, had one advantage—librarians who already knew where a book was located could easily find it in the dark. The disadvantages were many. As the number of books grew, every few years, staff members had to spend countless hours reclassifying and rearranging the entire collection. And empty spaces on the shelves that resulted from lost or damaged books were everywhere to be seen.

In early 1873, to clean up the mess at his place of employment—he wasn't yet concerned with organizing all of America's books—Dewey embarked on a tour of fifty libraries in the northeastern United States. The protocols used elsewhere were little better. Albany's New York State Library, he was disappointed to learn, "arrange[d] the books alphabetically paying no attention to subjects." Other systems that organized books by the color of their bindings or by their size struck him as equally ridiculous. Dewey also read widely about the fledgling science of classification. He was particularly impressed with an essay by William Torrey Harris, the director of the St. Louis Public Library, which suggested arranging material alphabetically by subject. Under a relative rather than fixed location system, rather than being assigned a specific place in the library, books would be organized in relation to one another. "Of this," noted the man, who bonded more readily to abstract concepts than to other people, on February 22, 1873, "I am inclined to be a friend." But the all-consuming quest went on. "For months," he later wrote, "I dreamed day and night that there must be somewhere a satisfactory solution." One Sunday that spring, while supposedly listening to a sermon by the college's seventy-something president, the pastor William Stearns, he had his eureka moment. He would use "the simplest known symbols, the Arabic numerals as decimals...to number a classification of all human knowledge in print."

Surprisingly, the 1876 masterpiece that would turn Dewey into a household name the world over did not list him (or anyone else) as its author. The only place his name appears in the first edition of his scheme is on the copyright page. In the preface, dated June 10 (his half birthday), Dewey lays out his framework. He divides books into ten classes, which are, in turn, subdivided into ten sections and into ten divisions. As a result, all knowledge falls under one thousand headings (one thousand was also the total of the print run). For example, a geometry book was to be numbered 513—as Natural Science is Class 500, Mathematics is Section 510, and Geometry is Division 513. The main difference between this first go-round and the DDC in use today was the absence of the decimal point per se; this addition has allowed for an infinite number of categories. In the second part of the book, Dewey lists the full contents of all ten classes, devoting one page to each. And in the final third, he provides an alphabetical subject index; under G, the reader can find "Geometry, 513" right above "Geometry analytical, 516."

Dewey's work, as he concedes in the preface, wasn't entirely original: "In his varied reading, correspondence, and conversation on the subject, the author doubtless received suggestions and gained ideas which it is now impossible for him to acknowledge." But due to its inherent simplicity and logic, his system caught on immediately. The timing couldn't have been better. The public library, whose origins date back to only about 1850, was about to come into its own. In 1875, the whole country had just 257 branches, and small collections with as few as three hundred books were not uncommon. A huge time and space saver, Dewey's decimals helped to spark a spectacular growth spurt over the next quarter century; by 1900, America would be festooned with some five thousand public libraries containing more than forty million volumes.

And since the publication of the original version, twenty-two editions of the DDC system have followed. The most recent, released in 2011, which comes to more than four thousand pages, governs the arrangement of books in more than two hundred thousand libraries across nearly 150 countries. Owned by the Online Computer Library Center (OCLC), based in Dublin, Ohio, since 1988, the DDC system is not in the public domain, as is commonly assumed. It is still a major revenue engine, as the OCLC charges libraries that use it at least $500 a year. Manhattan's Library Hotel, which was inspired by the DDC—each of its ten floors corresponds to one of Dewey's categories (for example, room 800.001 features erotic literature on its shelves)—learned this lesson the hard way; in 2003, OCLC's lawyers sued the swanky rest stop for book lovers, located across the street from the New York Public Library, for triple its profits, alleging copyright infringement. The two sides subsequently reached an agreement.

It was just after 5 a.m. on April 10, 1876, and Melvil Dewey was already on the go. He had to catch the 6:15 a.m. train to Boston. After six years in sleepy Amherst, the rapid-fire talker with the high-pitched voice, who had recently deleted the *le* from his given name because he considered it "Frenchy," was off to the big city to seek fame and fortune.

While Dewey was excited to be entering the "busy world," he was also sad to be leaving "college seclusion." In Amherst, Dewey had enjoyed some relief from the loneliness and alienation that had plagued his childhood. After graduation, he boarded with Mrs. S. F. Pratt, a wealthy widow of a Turkish missionary, with whom he formed a close relationship. This mother of three young children asked him both to manage her investments and to help her with budgeting. Dewey, whose own parents had shown him little affection, referred to his landlady as "Mother." And for the first time in his life, Dewey was popular with members of the fair sex—to make their acquaintance, he rarely missed services at the local Congregational church. With dating as with decimals, Dewey could never get his fill; the peripatetic bachelor would sometimes escort home two or three different women in the same evening. In January 1875, as he noted in his characteristic shorthand, he was courting both Mary E. and "the 34-year-old girl that I lykt so much...[I]...1/2 thot of wedding." (Ever since high school, he had griped about the messiness of his native tongue—"English spelling," he once quipped, "is the wurst there is"—and he would be a lifelong advocate of simplified or phonetic spelling.) But the other 1/2 of Dewey would not budge, and no proposal was ever made to the woman more than a full decade his senior. By March 1875, Mary E. was also out of the picture—though she would pop back in a couple of years later—and Dewey was "having a good time" with both Mrs. H. and Hatty D. All told, between 1872 and 1876, Dewey romanced about twenty different women, including three Marys, three Mays, and three already-marrieds. Attachment to one woman at a time would be something to which he never could quite acclimate himself.

In an interview in Boston in early 1876, Dewey had finalized his new business venture. It was a dream come true. The publisher Edwin Ginn had signed Dewey on as a junior partner, appointing him manager of the company's new American Metric Bureau. Dewey's chief responsibility would be selling educational tools such as scales and charts designed to persuade the entire country to adopt the metric system. Dewey had long fantasized about doing away with America's "inconsistent system" of weights and measures. In a high school essay, he had argued that the metric system's "great superiority over all others consists in the fact that all its scales are purely decimal."

Dewey's last day at the Amherst library was Friday, March 31, 1876. He could

have left town then, but his fervent worship of decimals led him to delay his journey until a week from the following Monday—April 10. The man, who hated
vacations as a matter of principle, spent a few days engaging in his favorite hobbies such as horseback riding and hunting. Saturday the eighth turned out to
be a disaster. That evening, he and "Mother had a misunderstanding." "She of
course," he wrote in his diary, "had a big cry and I of course had to pacify her, all
of which was less restful than sleep would have been." Though tired, Dewey felt
better on Sunday: "We had several little crys among the family during the day
but got on very happily otherwise." That afternoon, he boosted his sagging spirits
by "talking library" at the home of his former boss, Professor Montague. But he
still couldn't shake the existential anxiety that had engulfed him. "It was a sad
day," he wrote in his diary shortly after retiring to bed at 9, "for I feared it would
be my last."

On moving day, Dewey squeezed in a four-hour stopover in Worcester, where
he thoroughly examined the wares of the new Wesson and Harrington firearms
store. Everything about guns and their construction had long fascinated Dewey,
and he posed a series of probing questions to the owner, Frank Wesson. After
an extended discussion, Dewey became convinced "he [Wesson] had the best
pocket and long range rifles on the market." As with other obsessives such as Jefferson and Lindbergh, new gadgets could leave him feeling spellbound. That
evening, the new sales rep found some temporary lodgings in Malden, a short
commute from his office at 13 Tremont Place in downtown Boston. On the
morning of the eleventh, he met with the librarian Charles Cutter of the Boston Athenaeum—Beantown was then a library mecca, and this elegant venue
was just one of its prominent shrines—to get some feedback on his new "skeme."
The meteoric rise of an American icon was now under way.

Eighteen seventy-six was to be an annus mirabilis for Dewey. Within a few
weeks, Ginn agreed to expand his job description to include both selling library
supplies and editing a new journal for librarians. As the managing editor of the
American Library Journal—to reflect its international aspirations, the adjective
was soon dropped from the title—Dewey suddenly had a huge platform. "Born
with a disposition to run things whenever I could get a chance," as Dewey noted
five decades later in his unpublished memoir, "3/4 of a Century," he immediately made the most of the opportunity. That spring, he became the prime
mover behind a national gathering of librarians at the Centennial Exhibition
in Philadelphia, thus organizing the conference that would, in turn, create the

American Library Association. Unknown to some and dismissed by others—in a line that circulated widely, an Amherst philosophy professor described Dewey to the Librarian of Congress as "a tremendous talker, and a little bit of an old maid"—he initially faced stiff opposition. Wary of the newcomer, the head of the Chicago Public Library wrote to his counterpart in Boston on May 31: "It won't pay for you and me to attend that barbecue." But Dewey was not to be deterred, promising his colleagues that they would experience "the most profitable three days of their library life." Thanks largely to Dewey's infectious enthusiasm, 103 librarians from around the country—including those head honchos from Boston and Chicago who were to become the ALA's first president and vice president, respectively—showed up at the Pennsylvania State Historical Society on October 4, 1876. Two days later, Dewey signed on as the ALA's first member and was elected both its secretary and treasurer. Librarianship, as Dewey stressed, was officially a "profession." And with his classification text now required reading for his colleagues around the country, the ALA's youngest member would soon forever change how America both organized and disseminated information.

This flurry of activity would, however, leave Dewey close to a nervous breakdown by the time he hit the quarter century mark on December 10, 1876.

———

Dewey's classification text also turned out to be the magnet that would attract his first wife. On April 18, 1876, he crossed the Charles River into Cambridge to give a lecture at Harvard "on locating books by numbers and subjects and not by numbering shelves," as the college's librarian recorded in his diary. Annie Godfrey, then the twenty-five-year-old librarian at the newly established Wellesley College, just happened to be in attendance. Three months later, Dewey sent her a proof of his book, offering "to answer any questions that may arise and...to receive any corrections or criticisms that may occur to you." They picked up the dialogue about decimals a few months later at the librarians' powwow in Philadelphia, where Annie became ALA Member No. 29. Admiring his "devotion to...[his] life work," the frumpy and slightly overweight librarian, who shared his passion for horseback riding, became the pursuer. For the next year and a half, Dewey kept her at arm's length. He cited overwork, a claim that was partly true. In late 1876, after his string of successes, Dewey felt drained and confused about what to do for an encore. He also began having trouble carrying out daily tasks. That November, a despairing and humbled Dewey, who had endured considerable criticism from his parents as a boy, begged Richard Bowker, his editor at *Library Journal*, to give him "a blowing up for my weaknesses.... It makes me shiver, but I know the final effect is good." He rebounded, but slowly. At the first annual meeting of the ALA in the fall of 1877, the overtaxed workaholic achieved little besides standardizing the size of a catalog card at 7.5×12.5 centimeters.

But the more likely reason why he put Annie on hold was that he had taken up with his former Amherst flame, Mary E. Much of the future couple's correspondence from 1877 has been burned, so the truth is hard to come by. Annie, who had an ardent suitor of her own—a hard-driving steamboat captain—didn't give up easily. She also understood her man. While she supported his grandiose ambitions, she made him promise not to work after ten. "I am going to haunt you," she wrote Dewey on December 5, 1877. "Every night when the clock strikes ten," she added, "I shall come to you in imagination...and whisper 'goodnight.'" (Dewey would take to the idea; several years later, when he became director of Columbia College's library, he would close the building at the decimal hour.) In a birthday letter posted five days later, Annie wished Dewey "many years of usefulness." They were married the following October.

In the socially prominent Annie Godfrey—her cousin was Mary Bucklin, wife of Bay State governor William Claflin, and her contacts in Cambridge included the legendary poet Henry Wadsworth Longfellow—the twenty-seven-year-old Melvil found a spouse who matched him eccentricity for eccentricity. They got to work right away on their shared goal of improving both themselves as well as the rest of humanity. Beginning in 1878—and for at least a decade after that— each month, they compiled a detailed list of "time-budgets" and "resolutions"; the latter came with a set of fines that they slapped on themselves whenever they missed the mark. Both partners were often penalized for the use of slang. Much to Dewey's delight, Annie's side of the ledger featured the following admonition, "Don't waste a minute." Dewey swore to seek "accuracy in print," but he had difficulty staying true to his word; one week, his self-rating on this scale came to a measly 48 percent. Like her husband, Annie rarely passed up the chance to turn the human experience into a number. She tracked every penny that ever left the house, every jar of fruit she ever canned, and every button she ever purchased. On the matter of writing implements, however, they didn't quite see eye to eye. While Dewey was never without five fountain pens in his vest pocket, each containing a different color of ink, Annie preferred toting pencils, color-coordinated with both her notebooks and the pockets in her customary white dresses. Perhaps as a tribute to "the lady in white," after Annie's death, the still-in-a-hurry septuagenarian would make the switch to a custom-made pencil with different colored leads on each end.

The marriage—which would produce a son, Godfrey, born in 1887—worked splendidly for Dewey; he got everything he wanted, including the freedom to come and go as he pleased. Besides the loneliness, Annie had to put up with her husband's roving eye. This penchant was perilous, because Dewey was constantly surrounded by temptation, particularly after he started the library school at Columbia. Despite mountains of incriminating evidence, Annie repeatedly stood by her man. During the 1906 sex scandal, Annie wrote a confidential letter to an ALA official declaring, "Women who have keen intuitions know by instinct that they can trust Mr. Dewey implicitly." Annie's misplaced faith in her husband may well have contributed to her ill health. She suffered from both frayed nerves and hardened arteries, for which she received all sorts of medical care, including residential treatment at Michigan's Battle Creek Sanitarium. Dewey wasn't at home when Annie—by then both exceedingly frail and totally blind—died in 1922.

During the first few years of their marriage, Dewey's career hit a snag. The core contradictions in his character were creating constant chaos. Like other obsessives, Dewey was more in love with the semblance of order—the illusion that everything was under control—than with order itself. And the man who preached patience and discipline had trouble regulating his own impulses. As Dewey acknowledged, his tendency to overextend himself was "infinitely silly"; nevertheless, he kept trying "to undertake to do 5 things at once." Likewise, despite his fierce advocacy of organizational efficiency, he was never a team player; in fact, he often alienated colleagues with his stubbornness and arrogance. A procrastinator, he couldn't pass on his copy to the *Library Journal*'s Richard Bowker on time. What's more, even his own memoranda and missives to his editor, as he admitted, were also "wholly without organization." When Bowker and publisher Frederick Leypoldt told him that some belt tightening would be needed to cope with spotty revenue, he threatened to jump ship and start a rival outlet. Startled by Dewey's wayward ways, Leypoldt's wife characterized him as "as miserable a specimen of a gabbling idiot as I ever beheld." By the end of 1880, Dewey would be dropped from the journal. In the late 1870s, he faced another setback when the business opportunity that had lured him to Boston fizzled out; he was not able to create a market for metric goods, as he had hoped. Upon his twenty-eighth birthday, seeking a fresh start, the struggling entrepreneur turned to a name change, settling on what he perceived to be the more efficient Dui.

Dui's first venture was to become the president and secretary of the Readers and Writers Economy Company, a library supply outfit. But after only a matter of months, that company was also veering toward bankruptcy, its shareholders charging him with fraud and mismanagement. As it turned out, the man who had a way with figures couldn't be counted on to keep the books; he repeatedly mixed up personal and corporate accounts. Dui claimed that the lapses were unintentional, but he was still forced to resign in late 1880. He became an emotional and physical wreck. "Hay fever took me down this year, and I suffered terrible," he wrote to Bowker, with whom he continued to work on various ALA matters, in October 1880. "For 12 hours at a time for two or three days I could not open my eyelids." While he would later proudly assert that he "never worried," he was the king of the psychosomatic symptom. Throughout his life, in addition to hay fever, he was also susceptible to colds, coughs, and "bad stomachs" as well as bronchitis, laryngitis, and asthma.

Suddenly an unemployed pariah, Dui continued to feel depressed, humiliated, and, according to one colleague, suicidal. Overwork, he conceded to a friend toward the end of 1880, "has nearly cost me my life." For the next couple of years, he scraped by as a freelance consultant for local libraries. Though down and out, Dui kept thinking big. "I feel my fingers tingle often," he told Bowker in June 1881, "to get hold of some large enterprise." His fingers worked fast. Several months later, Dui started a new company, the Library Bureau, which would sell business equipment of all sorts, including the hanging vertical file, which he invented. Over the next decade, his shares in this rapidly expanding venture, which would be folded into the Sperry Rand Corporation a century later, would make him a rich man.

The following year, Dui was visited by more good fortune. Columbia College was building a new library at the center of its Madison Avenue campus and needed a new director to organize its half-dozen independent book collections. The college's president, Frederick Augustus Porter Barnard, figured that Dui was just the man for the job. The two men had formed a bromantic bond years before, based on their shared love of tens. An important figure in the ALA—he had also been there at its creation in 1876—Barnard had known Dui for nearly a decade. The reigning president of the research group, the American Metrological Society—Dui was its secretary—Barnard was the author of the five-hundred-page magnum opus *The Metric System of Weights and Measures*, then in its third edition. This rhapsody to the *metre, litre,* and *gramme* addressed the beauty and efficiency of "units that have decimal multiples and submultiples." And if Barnard harbored any doubts about what Dui could do to spiff up Columbia's scattered and scanty collection, then ranked forty-ninth in the country and just sixth in New York City, Columbia professor John Burgess quickly put them to rest. Recently recruited from Amherst College, the political scientist showered praise on his former colleague's "fine genius for classification and convenient arrangement." Barnard had only one concern; trustees were dumbfounded by the ridiculous spelling of the job candidate's last name. (So, too, was William Poole, head of the Chicago Public Library, who joked that "Dewy" might be better, given his naïveté.) To keep his hat in the ring, Dui quickly reverted to being Dewey and promised to eschew simplified spelling in his official correspondence.

On May 7, 1883, trustees offered Dewey the job as the school's Librarian-in-Chief at a salary of $3,500 (about $80,000 today) a year. They also set aside $10,000 for the recataloging and reclassifying of Columbia's books.

Three weeks later, Dewey began work at the spanking-new English Gothic facility, built for $400,000, then a staggering sum, on Madison Avenue and Forty-Ninth Street. When he arrived, the director had only one employee—an assistant, who doubled as a janitor—and the library was open only three hours a day. For help with the pressing task of assigning decimals to its fifty thousand volumes, Dewey immediately hired six seniors from Wellesley College. This move was radical, as at the time nearly all librarians were male and Columbia was "almost as hermetically sealed to women as a monastery." Within a year, Dewey presided over a team of twenty-one employees, including five department heads and "the Wellesley Half Dozen," as his comely coterie of assistants were dubbed. Thanks to his industrious staff, Dewey soon cataloged the library's fifty thousand volumes; this massive undertaking, in turn, served as the basis for an expanded second edition of his scheme published in 1885, which officially introduced the decimal point and two new decimal places. Dewey also began beefing up the now carefully arranged collection at the hefty rate of ten thousand volumes a year.

Columbia's state-of-the-art facility became a model for academic and public libraries around the world. No other libraries—not even those at Oxford, Cambridge, Harvard, or anywhere in Germany—were in its class. As the *New York Tribune* reported, it was "the ideal of a university library...in equipment and organization." With three hundred Edison lamps allowing for evening use, Dewey could increase operating hours by a factor of ten. Patrons enjoyed a slew of modern conveniences, including trays of ice water and mail delivery. The elegant main reading room, with its fifty-eight-foot-high ceiling, could seat 160 visitors, to whom assistants could bring any volume on demand. After just one year, circulation jumped by a staggering 500 percent. Staff members were also prepared to answer queries at a reasonable fraction—1/1200—of their annual salary per hour. The transformation of the library didn't escape the notice of students. "Suddenly the place seemed to have come alive," one later recalled. "Something had happened, too, to the attendants. Brashness, alertness, service became the order of the day." Order also reigned supreme in every nook and cranny. Rubber tips placed on the oak chairs and rubber wheels affixed to book trucks eliminated noise. And Dewey managed to keep the premises spotless. To littering students, he passed out cards that read: "I picked up these pieces in the hall and infer that you threw them on the floor. My time and that of my assistants is too valuable for this work. Still we prefer to do it rather than have the building so disfigured." Eager to tidy up other libraries as well, he circulated these cards among his colleagues across the country.

Thrilled with his new hire, in May 1884 President Barnard remarked that Dewey "has been of more important service to the college than that of any other officer." That spring, the trustees bumped up his salary to $5,000—the amount doled out to full professors—and conferred upon him a new title, professor of library economy.

———

While the library school got off to a successful start in 1887, Dewey's conflict with the trustees persisted. In fact, the animosity only increased. Dewey got flak for plowing funds initially appropriated for reclassifying books back into salaries—a move he tried in order to appease his overworked staff. Trustees also objected to his annual reports touting the library school's achievements, which clocked in at fifty pages, twice the heft of those published by its already well-established law school. The Special Committee on Printing considered such marketing efforts "not in accordance with academic propriety" and a waste of precious dollars. Likewise, most of Columbia's professors, irked by the tenacity with which he collected fines for overdue books, viewed him as an arrogant nuisance. And the presence of women on campus continued to bother the trustees as well as a considerable segment of both the faculty and the alumni. Dewey's fate was sealed when his most influential and steadfast ally, President Barnard, resigned in May 1888. By the end of the year, Dewey, too, decided to step down.

But by then, Dewey had already landed a cushy new job in Albany, where he would serve as both director of the New York State Library and as secretary of the Board of Regents at the University of the State of New York.

"My whole five years at Columbia," Dewey later recalled, "were a constant struggle against the anti-Women element." While he would remain clueless about the "anti-Women element" in his own personality, he still deserves considerable credit for being a trailblazer in female education. During his Manhattan sojourn, Dewey befriended Annie Nathan Meyer, a twenty-something autodidact who bemoaned Columbia's exclusion of women. Inspired by Dewey's "vision and idealism" as well as his "purposeful punch," Meyer went on to found Barnard College, New York's first women's college, in 1889. As Dewey observed that year, Barnard "in its pre-natal days was probably discussed more in my private office in the Columbia library than anywhere else." In 1926, under President Nicholas Butler, Columbia would acknowledge its harsh treatment of Dewey, agreeing to take back the library school, which had accompanied him to Albany in 1889. As Butler noted, Dewey's "offense of having admitted women to the University without authority, was, in view of all that has happened since, ludicrous in the extreme." Dewey is also directly responsible for the sprouting of library schools—which, in the late nineteenth century, constituted a significant new avenue for professional advancement for women—all over the country. By 1893, five disciples—alumni of his programs at Columbia and Albany—had already founded similar schools in Philadelphia, Brooklyn, Amherst, Chicago, and Los Angeles. Over the next couple of decades, another ten Deweyites would also strike out on their own.

Except for the decimal system, no other achievement gave Dewey "serener satisfaction" than the invention of the modern library school. The strengths and weaknesses of this cultural institution directly reflect the two poles of his oversized personality—both the eccentricity and the genius. The persnickety pedagogue clearly loved to parade his hard-won pseudoknowledge about how to organize and take care of books, particularly in front of attentive (and attractive) women, who, as he once estimated, comprised about "nine-tenths" of his students. No detail was too minor for Dewey's "scientific" scrutiny. He even provided instruction in how to design, print, and physically apply bookplates. Such pedantry led critics to challenge the legitimacy of the enterprise from the very beginning. "A school to learn to be a librarian!" one of his contemporaries wrote. "How very odd! There'll be schools for dry goods clerks next." Over the years, many academics would continue to question whether there was, in fact, a body of serious scholarship that librarians in training needed to master; this lack of a natural research base turned out to be the major reason why fifteen library schools closed between 1978 and 1992—including the Columbia School of Library Service, as the second incarnation of Dewey's brain child was called.

But Dewey's legacy has also powered the revival of his pet idea in the form of the I-School—those graduate programs in Information Science, which have either been appended to previously existing library schools or been built from scratch in the last two decades. Since the end of the twentieth century, the field of library science, which Dewey invented in the last quarter of the nineteenth, has officially evolved into library and information studies. A forward-thinking visionary, Dewey would have approved. He was acutely aware that libraries are essentially repositories of information. A fan of new technology, he constantly tried to expand the scope of collections beyond printed matter. At the New York State Library, he began an extensive picture archive; soon he was thinking about how to include rolls for the player piano. In the 1890s, he also embraced the long-distance telephone, realizing that it would enable reference desks to respond to queries from faraway patrons. "Radio, movies and various devices," he stated in 1926, "are making short cuts to what books have been doing. Our great function... is to give to the public in the quickest and cheapest way information, inspiration and recreation on the highest plane. If a better way than the books be found, we should use it." Dewey would also have been thrilled by the development of both the online database and the e-book. After all, his decimal system was the search engine par excellence—the Google—of its day. For Dewey, faster was always better. "Mani can make muni," he once philosophized in his tweet-like prose, "but no one can make tym."

In 1889, as Dewey made the transition from an elegant Madison Avenue office in New York City to a capacious home on Albany's Madison Avenue, located just a couple of blocks from the Capitol, he was thirty-seven and balding, and his formerly thin frame was starting to fill out, as he now weighed nearly two hundred pounds. He would be busier than ever. "It was like watching a fine machine, an electric machine," observed a fellow Albany resident, who added that Dewey "worked away with a kind of furious quiet." According to a running joke, he was wont to dictate notes to two different stenographers at the same time. Heading the State Library, then in the process of being transferred to twenty rooms on the third and fourth floors on the western side of the capitol building, would prove to be the less taxing of his two demanding jobs. As secretary of the Board of Regents, the nineteen volunteers appointed by the New York State legislature to monitor the state's schools, academies, and colleges, Dewey would be jumping headfirst into the political arena. To the Albany politicos, the hard-driving pedagogue would be as welcome as "a thorn would be in a sore thumb." Unwittingly creating conflict whenever possible, the cantankerous Dewey would steadily amass a long list of enemies. As a public figure, he was now subject to constant press coverage, and the airing of his habitual shenanigans would eventually prove to be his undoing.

Dewey had landed the influential dual position on the basis of an extensive memo that he had submitted to the chairman of the search committee the previous November. His roughly ten-thousand-word missive took the form of a numbered "check list of 'things to be done,'" which featured a total of twenty bullet points (uncharacteristically, he came up with eleven for the State Library and nine for the Board of Regents rather than a perfect ten for each). The ambitious Dewey aimed high. He envisioned turning the library into a "People's University" where "any person may find information on any subject." His master plan for the Board of Regents involved greatly expanding its purview. Though some of his ideas went nowhere, he would knock off several of his key goals. "Dewey has as many crank notions as anybody outside of an asylum," the chancellor of the State University once observed, but he is "zealous, inventive and in many ways useful." As an Albany power broker, Dewey would improve the quality of both the state's public high schools (by creating higher standards for the annual Regents exams) and its professional schools (by increasing state supervision of their curricula). At the same time as he focused on the big picture, Dewey didn't neglect to get bogged down in the details. In his decade at the Board of

Regents, he personally signed all the 279,444 certificates of achievement given out to high school students. This was a bureaucrat who, as much as he preached efficiency, couldn't bear to permit the rubber stamp used by his predecessors to lighten his load.

In contrast, over at the New York State Library, Dewey turned into an expert delegator. He leaned heavily on the five members of his Columbia team whom he brought with him, particularly three nubile former students, Florence Woodworth, May Seymour, and Mary Salome Cutler. Both Woodworth, who doubled as a caretaker for his son Godfrey, and Seymour, who became his personal secretary, would move into his home. Seymour, who started out in classification at the library, would emerge as the de facto editor for every new edition of the DDC. She had the right stuff to be Dewey's right-hand woman; when unable to speak to a coworker right away, Seymour would respond decimally ("I shall be there in six and three-eighths minutes" was her stock phrase). According to eyewitnesses, both of these 24/7 acolytes were subjected to Dewey's surprise squeezes and kisses, about which they never complained. Cutler, who, unlike Woodworth and Seymour, would marry rather than remain a lifelong Dewey doter, would oversee the daily running of the library school.

But the autocratic and inflexible Dewey was tough on his employees, even those he liked. While he paid generous salaries to Woodworth and Seymour, he worked others to the bone for little more than factory wages. To finance the doubling of his staff to about a hundred employees, he ended up reducing salaries by a total of 50 percent. Dewey could also be mean-spirited. Employees were fined a half-day's pay for arriving just one-twelfth of an hour late—that is, five minutes late. Likewise, he once docked the exceedingly hardworking and loyal Woodworth—she helped Dewey plot his defense during the 1906 sex scandal— one-twelfth of her annual salary for an alleged act of "insubordination." His harsh labor practices would lead to an investigation by the state legislature in 1895. As the committee headed by Assemblyman Henry Abell was "bewildered with the astonishing rapidity with which Mr. Dewey unfurled his knowledge of the work and details" of his various departments during seven hours of testimony, as the New York Tribune reported, he was never officially charged with any wrongdoing. A decade later, Mary Salome Cutler Fairchild—as the library school's vice director was known after her marriage to Edwin Fairchild, a prominent pastor—would have a nasty falling-out with Dewey. Critiquing the curriculum as "smack[ing] of arithmetic and commerce," she promoted a deeper engagement with "culture" through broad reading. When students agreed with her and kept complaining about having to learn "minute details," Dewey hit back hard. Partly due to the stress of this confrontation, Fairchild suffered a nervous breakdown and abruptly left the library business for good.

Though Dewey's mercurial temperament often rubbed his staff and students the wrong way, he would succeed in transforming both the State Library and its affiliated library school into preeminent national institutions. By 1895, with its collection reaching half a million volumes—about four times as many as a decade earlier—the New York State Library was the fifth biggest in the nation. "The library, as the result of Mr. Dewey's work," raved the *New York Tribune*, "is one of the most scientifically arranged in the world." An average of one thousand visitors a day dropped by, including many sightseers who marveled at the exquisite Main Reading Room, with its fifty-six-foot-high ceiling and its pillars made of polished red granite. To minimize the noise caused by all the foot traffic, Dewey would put carpet on the oak parquet in the central corridors. He was an innovator who devised both the first library for the blind, which relied on raised printing rather than Braille, and the first interlibrary loan program. Dewey's traveling library system operated decimally; one thousand books deemed informative were subdivided into ten lots of one hundred each and then transported to communities all over the state in oak bookcases. In "nine cases out of ten," Dewey argued, this transient library turned out to be the first step in the building of a new branch. He also created a Children's Library by sectioning off several tables in the Main Reading Room for "little people." "Any child that is clean and orderly," Dewey noted proudly, "is treated exactly like an adult." His first decade in the state capital didn't escape the notice of New York's young governor, Theodore Roosevelt. "The New York State Library," Roosevelt observed upon taking office in 1899, "has more than doubled its efficiency within the past ten years and is an inspiration to intellectual life throughout the State." Librarians from across the country would make pilgrimages to Albany, hoping to transport some of Dewey's innovations to their home state.

Dewey prided himself on running his office at the library with a military precision. On top of his desk sat an elaborate web of tubes and electric bells along with 120 pigeonholes into which he would insert "P-slips" (notes written in shorthand on the back of catalog cards). Employees would communicate with him mostly by transmitting messages using their assigned pigeonholes. Whenever they did talk to him, they were instructed to use the "fewest possible words."

While productivity often did result—he managed to handle a staggering 555 pieces of mail every day—many of the policies and procedures didn't make sense to anyone but Dewey. Though he preached to his staff the need to tote around a memorandum pad of a prescribed size, he was known to jot things down on the backs of envelopes. Dewey would also take up valuable time trying to teach subjanitors the proper way to dust books. Likewise, he insisted that Pliny Sexton, who as a Regent was essentially one of his employers, write rather than visit him in the office, noting that they "waste 2 hours in talk over matters that could be disposed of in 2 minutes." The genial Sexton didn't protest, but he did remind Dewey in his written response that the secretary of the Board of Regents was usually the one doing all the gabbing.

The lonely and alienated boy from Adams Center set up a workplace that minimized interpersonal contact in the name of efficiency. His employees grumbled, accusing him of "stirring up things and making changes all the while." But there was little they could do to protest. The Regents, with the notable exception of Sexton, also began to resent him, and they, in contrast, had some clout. In 1899, after numerous skirmishes, Dewey resigned from his position as secretary to the University of the State of New York, agreeing to devote himself full-time to the library for the same salary. That year, the *Brooklyn Eagle* captured both the good and the bad wrought by his eccentricities, describing him as "a bright man of singular energy, marvelous intellectual fecundity" who nevertheless had a "queering personality" that often put him "on the defensive with many state officers."

The frantic pace at which Dewey worked throughout his Albany years—whether manning two jobs or one—exacerbated his chronic stress-related symptoms. To maintain his mental equilibrium, this fitness enthusiast latched on to the bicycle. Upon his arrival in the capital, Dewey was eager to switch from the saddle horse, which he considered too expensive. He first experimented with the high-wheel bicycle then in vogue, but quickly gave up, concluding "that my neck was too valuable to risk." After giving the tricycle a try, he moved on to the "safety" bicycle, which had just come on the market. It was love at first sight. Basking in "the priceless value of the new exercise," he became consumed with buying "the latest and best pattern whenever improvements are made." Since the new invention was consistent with his favorite motto, "save time and helth," he arranged for bulk purchases; he began selling "the librarian's horse" to his staff and students on the installment plan. He would later deny the rumors swirling around the state capital that he made a hefty profit from these transactions.

With hay fever bothering both him and his wife more than ever, the couple stepped up their efforts to find a permanent summer getaway. The aim wasn't to build just a cozy summer cottage for the family of three, but to create a model community, an aspiration that both had long shared. After completing the requisite ten-year search, in 1893 the Deweys settled on a small town in the Adirondacks that they renamed Lake Placid (the other two finalists were situated in the White Mountains of New Hampshire and the Green Mountains of Vermont). That spring, Dewey bought a ten-acre plot near the village's Main Street, upon which he intended to build a clubhouse. But he soon changed course. Instead he acquired an already built fifteen-bedroom house named Bonnie Blink. Several months later, he scooped up several smaller houses spread out over one hundred acres adjacent to his main clubhouse.

By 1895, the Lake Placid Club, as the Deweys' "cooperativ summer home" became known, was up and running. The couple sought to sign up members with needs similar to their own, noting that the club was designed primarily for "the overworkt or convalescent needing special building up for the coming year's work." This resort for the very, very nervous—to borrow a line from comic Mel Brooks, who called the asylum in his 1977 film *High Anxiety* "the Institute for the Very, *Very* Nervous"—featured numerous golf courses and tennis courts as well as inviting hiking trails; however, it lacked some standard amenities found in most hotels. While the club housed three unabridged dictionaries, it had no bar, cigar stand, or stock ticker. To ensure the equanimity of its guests, Dewey also forbade gambling and "partizan politics." As explained in the 250-page handbook published in 1901, which described its operations and customs, tens were everywhere:

- the physical plant consisted of 10 square miles of woods, farms, and lakes
- annual fee = $10 (Dewey initially sought 100 members)
- lifetime membership = $1,000
- no music, dancing, or other amusements after 10 p.m.; this period of "entire quiet" lasted 10 hours, until 8 a.m.
- its 3 libraries each contained "over 1000 carefully chosen volumes"
- while the club was open from June 1 to November 1, the prime summer season ran from July 10 to September 10, during which room rates went up by 100 percent

- discount tickets offered by the club for 500 miles of travel on the New York Central Railroad sold for $10
- in its first 5 years, "the club grew tenfold"

Like Jefferson, he was also constantly thinking about building new additions to his home, though he was just a would-be architect. As one biographer has put it, Dewey "haunted every structural effort with his personal presence day or night, equipt with his perpetual companion, a six-foot measuring stick, each foot divided into tenths."

His stewardship of the Lake Placid Club, however, would jeopardize his position as the state's top librarian. Once the press got wind that he was away from Albany for five months a year, he was vilified. That charge he could fend off with the following testimonial from Herbert Putnam, the Librarian of Congress: "Mr. Dewey eats, drinks, sleeps and talks library and library work throughout the 24 hours, the week, the month and the year." But another scandal—involving race, not sex—that emerged at about the same time provoked outrage that he could not contain. In January 1905, upon discovering that the club excluded Jews from membership, influential Jewish leaders circulated a petition to Andrew Draper, state commissioner of education, demanding Dewey's ouster. As the dozens of signers maintained, what Dewey chose to do on club grounds was his business, but money from the state's coffers shouldn't be used to pay a state official who held such prejudice. Dewey countered that he "despised it [prejudice]" and wasn't directly involved in formulating this particular club policy. This defense didn't wash with the public. The comments by one Manhattan rabbi, published in the New York Tribune that month, captured the sentiments of many: "Such a distinction will not do. One cannot play Dr. Jekyll and Mr. Hyde.... The fact remains that the State Librarian...has been the manager of an organization which puts the gravest affront possible on the entire Jewish community."

Dewey's anti-Semitism was closely tied to his love of order, the reigning social order. While he had Jewish friends, he realized that certain powerful members of the upper crust didn't like to mingle with Jews and other minorities; and fearing their disapproval—and the attendant loss of membership in his club—he chose not to make any special exceptions. "No one shall be received," ran the discriminatory clause in the club catalog, "as member or guest, against whom there is physical, moral, social or race objection." In this case, Dewey's obsessionality was fully in synch with that of his times. This is precisely the argument that *Harper's Weekly* used in February 1905 in a spirited editorial defending Dewey's exclusionary practices at Lake Placid: "Experience has taught that Jews destroy the popularity of clubs and summer hotels where their presence is conspicuous. Non-Jews don't like the general run of Jews as companions." In explaining this predilection, the magazine stated that "average Jewish manners are different from the average manners of non-Jews" and also alluded to the concern that more socializing between the races—it referred to Jews as "Asians"—might lead to more intermarriages, adding that an "important purpose of organized society is the promotion of marriage." But as usual, Dewey projected his flaws onto others. To a friend, he made the case that Draper, the New York State official entrusted with deciding his fate, was emotionally unstable and in cahoots "with the Jews for my overthrow." That fall, he was forced to submit his resignation as both the New York State librarian and the head of the library school.

The following year, Dewey suffered another body blow when he was ostracized from the American Library Association. His womanizing had finally caught up with him. In 1905, with his career on the line, the press savaging him as a bigot, and his wife sequestered at the Battle Creek Sanitarium, Dewey kept propositioning women left and right. For those who, like Dewey, turn to sexual gratification largely to numb emotional pain, acute stress can often be a trigger for an increase in promiscuity. That May, he tried to put the moves on Adelaide Hasse, a New York City librarian, then beginning a massive index of government documents. Offering to help the thirty-seven-year-old bachelorette publish her work, the fifty-four-year-old Dewey invited her for an extended visit, writing that "I have horses and an auto and will give you a lot better air than you breathe in great and wicked Gotham." Hasse did come to Albany, but didn't stay for the weekend, as originally planned. After one long drive, she "ran away so suddenly," as her disappointed host later put it. While Hasse was alarmed by Dewey's "obnoxious personal traits," she discouraged the ALA from taking any action against him. Two months later, right after the 1905 ALA convention in Portland, Oregon, Dewey went on that fateful ten-day ALA-sponsored trip to Alaska, where he apparently lost all ability to control his sexual impulses. And in contrast to Hasse, the outraged female librarians on the Alaska trip demanded that the ALA take a stand. The following June, with two librarians threatening to resign if Dewey appeared at the 1906 ALA conference set for Narragansett Pier, Rhode Island, James Canfield, Columbia's librarian, urged Dewey not to attend lest he "precipitate a crisis which none of us could control." While Dewey reluctantly agreed, he just didn't get it, writing Canfield that "I...had so much trust in women. Pure women would understand my ways."

For the next couple of decades, Dewey's relationship with the ALA remained frosty. In 1907, upon learning that a librarian had suggested erecting a statue to "M.D.," Edwin Anderson, his successor at the New York State Library, blasted this notion as "a serious blow to decency." In 1915, Mary Wright Plummer, the head of the library school at the New York Public Library, then also serving a term as ALA president, remarked, "There is no demand on the part of librarians for Mr. D's presence....I shall never, as long as I am a member of the profession, consent to meet him." This ALA founder and two-time president—he was elected to one-year terms in both 1890 and 1892—wouldn't be officially reha-bilitated until 1926, when he gave a notable address at the fiftieth-anniversary meeting.

Leaving his Madison Avenue home in Albany, Dewey began living in Lake Placid full-time. With no mountains of books to slap decimals on for the first time in decades, he focused his attention on his club and its numbers. "We have," he wrote to his longtime friend, the publisher Richard Bowker, in 1909, "spent $313,000 on improvements since I resigned at Albany. That means a good deal....We try in these various things to put into the working out of this idea as much energy and skill as we would into organizing a library. We have today over 650 guests, are taking in about $3000 daily for their expenses." He managed Lake Placid just like the State Library. The key members of his Albany staff, such as May Seymour, the editor of the DDC, moved along with him. In 1907, he hired Katharine Sharp, another former student, then directing the library school at the University of Illinois; she became the club's "Social Organizer." He kept expanding its activities and programs, which would eventually include concerts by top-notch musicians, conferences run by leading scholars, and a school for boys. By 1920, the club featured a forest theater with seating for one thousand people, one hundred private cottages, and ten golf courses (he was finishing up five new ones to go with the five already built). That year, he could boast that members and guests hailed from forty-six states and twenty-six nations, and that the total number of visitors exceeded a substantial multiple of ten: "Over 10,000 come....Already sum improvements that hav had more than national influence has started here....mor and mor the Club will be a rekogniyzed center for... educating the publik."

Dewey also took the innovative step of keeping the club open year-round. The eight members who stayed on in the one heated residence that first winter season in 1905 entertained themselves by snowshoeing, tobogganing, ice skating, and cross-country skiing. By 1921, Dewey had added a speed-skating track and a ski jump. Soon Lake Placid was stacking up well against such international hot spots as St. Moritz in the Swiss Alps. By the end of the decade, the town, which still had fewer than four thousand residents, won the right to host the III Winter Olympics and the first on American soil. Since the club never did change its discriminatory ways, Jewish groups protested to Governor Franklin D. Roosevelt about the use of state funds to build a bobsled track. The ever combative Dewey relished this battle (which ended in a compromise whereby the new facility would be built in the neighboring town of North Elba rather than on club property). "This nu Jew attak," he wrote to his club colleagues, "will giv us much valuabl publisiti....their attak helps to show *why* our members have always declined to admit them."

While Dewey was again rationalizing his bigotry, his prediction turned out to be correct. With Lake Placid still dotted with signs reading NO JEWS OR DOGS ALLOWED, Roosevelt opened the games in February 1932. The club then went into a steady decline before closing soon after the XIII Winter Olympics held in 1980 (famous for the so-called Miracle on Ice, the surprise victory of the Americans over the Soviets in hockey). Today Lake Placid remains America's oldest continuously operating ski resort.

———

On Tuesday, May 27, 1913, Dewey was in Manhattan to give a speech at the Aldine Club on Twenty-Third Street and Fifth Avenue. The Lake Placid resident was a frequent rider on the sleeper train that his club ran to New York City every night at 10 p.m. The event was the monthly dinner meeting of the Efficiency Society, a group that Dewey had helped to establish a year earlier. This collection of business leaders, engineers, and educators was dedicated to doing for the American office what Frederick W. Taylor's scientific management had done for the American factory. But that was not quite how it worked out. In the end, most of the reforms proposed by the committee of ten that ran the show would have less to do with a Marxist nightmare—Communist radicals such as Vladimir Lenin often railed against the dehumanization of the worker caused by

Taylor's mechanization—than with a Marx Brothers routine (though Dewey and his nine brethren weren't trying to be funny).

Dinner was at 6:30, and Dewey, the first speaker of the night, began his talk before some three hundred Efficiency Society members and guests shortly after eight. "In keeping with its name," the *New York Times* reported the next day, "the society 'got down to business' by eliminating long introductions of speakers."

Since his ignominious exit from the library world in 1906, Dewey had rebranded himself as a management consultant focused on organizing organizations. He had the street cred. After all, Frederick Taylor himself had cited the decimal system as an early influence on his industrial system of classification. In 1912, Dewey published a forty-page book chapter, "Office Efficiency," which began thus: "Man goes from barbarism to civilization by lerning [*sic*] to do things better, quicker, more easily or cheaply." He was trying to transfer his various library innovations, which he dubbed the "spirit of 76"—a phrase also used by Jefferson to refer to the American Revolution—to the workplace. But his recommendations—such as using the decimal system for filing everyday correspondence—often bordered on the ridiculous. Dewey was a steadfast advocate of the paper clip—of the large steel spring, not the brass horseshoe variety—which he believed could eliminate "the few seconds spent in unfurling or uncreasing a paper." He also insisted that desks should have windows at the left and that roll tops should be verboten as they "tempt to disorder." This level of detail—along with his immersion in such mundane matters as dust management—would scare off many executives from organizing their offices à la Dewey. But his linguistic innovations held more promise. As he also argued, simplified spelling combined with tighter prose could save corporate America considerable time and labor.

Language was to be the focal point of Dewey's after-dinner speech. He began by mentioning that he used to spell his name with an extra *le* before his own conversion forty years ago. According to Dewey's estimate, 15 percent of the energy spent on typewriting machines was wasted. "Language," he stressed, "is a machine for accomplishing results. It is meant to convey the thought of the writer to the mind of the reader and the simplest way in which this can be done is the best way. We use needless words and false motions." Dewey gave a host of examples. He preferred "buyer" to "purchasing agent," "many" to "a large number of," and "invite" to "extend an invitation to."

Over the next few years, Dewey devoted more and more energy to the efficiency movement. That fall, he hosted a meeting of the society at Lake Placid at which his wife presided over a session for the ladies on "Home Economics." This expert on how to set a table insisted that silverware should always be placed "one inch from the edge of the table." The following year, Dewey became chairman of a "Languaj Committee." In January 1915, with the Efficiency Society struggling—despite the moniker, it was poorly managed, and the expense of maintaining its requisite ten clerks was creating a $200 hole every month—he was elected president. Dewey also couldn't live up to the imposing title he now held. One afternoon during the Great War, he received word that a colleague from the Efficiency Society was about to visit him at work. Realizing that his office "was worse than a bear's den," he was forced to squirrel away his loose papers in a clothes basket, which was, in turn, hidden in a closet. (It would take a week for a secretary to unpack and organize the material in the basket.) In 1918, Dewey merged his outfit with the National Institute of Efficiency. But the new Washington, D.C.–based National Efficiency Society, which Dewey ran out of New York City, soon faltered. Dewey wasn't able to collect enough $10 annual dues payments from America's executives and engineers. By the early 1920s, this incarnation, whose motto defined efficiency as "the ratio of achievement to effort," was, as Dewey was forced to acknowledge, "not ded, but sleeping quyt soundli."

However, unlike Dewey the management consultant, Dewey the "languaj" maven wasn't just waved offstage. Several of his simplified spellings have been incorporated into the lexicon; *catalog*, like his first name, has done well without its vestigial last two letters, and New Yorkers now have their state thruway. Moreover, his celebration of the streamlined sentence has carried the day. Dewey's ideas about prose would soon be echoed by his fellow upstate New Yorker, Cornell English professor William Strunk Jr., who, in 1918, completed the first draft of what has since become known as *The Elements of Style*—in its original form, this guide to word usage was passed out just to Cornell students. In fact, the governing maxim of this classic text, "Omit needless words," closely parallels the takeaway from Dewey's 1913 speech at the Aldine Club. (The book was later transformed into a megaseller when rewritten by the *New Yorker*'s E. B. White, who had studied with Strunk at Cornell, for a fortieth-anniversary edition in 1959.)

Friday, November 25, 1927—25 N 27 in Deweyese—found the nearly seventy-eight-year-old Dewey in his office. He had an important letter to write.

Dewey was then in Florida with his second wife, Emily Beal, an administrator at the Lake Placid Club since 1916, whom he had married two years after Annie's death. After being sidelined with the flu for six weeks in the winter of 1925, Dewey decided to spend his remaining winters down south. He later explained, "6 fizicians told me that I was taking my lyf in my hands to try...to waste the vytaliti necesari to combat our northern cold." But once again, a modest, private escape wouldn't be sufficient; Dewey immediately began planning another cooperative community. In early 1927, he bought three thousand acres in the town of Lake Stearns in south-central Florida, which he got the state legislature to rename Lake Placid. On November 1, 1927, he opened a southern branch of his retreat headquartered in the spruced-up former Hotel Stearns, to which he gave a new moniker, "Club Loj."

Dewey was eager to thank Anne Colony, an assistant at the Lake Placid in the Adirondacks, for recommending his new stenographer, an attractive thirty-something redhead from Boston who had once worked as a secretary for Bishop Howard Robbins, the dean at Manhattan's St. John the Divine Cathedral. Thus began his note of gratitude:

> *Dear Anne: After a 2 week trial I report on your...selection of my companion and potential boss. I...wish I had bought her by the pound instead of the piece when the dainty little flapper got off the train. I told her she was better looking than I expected and would tell her later how good I thought her....We conclude that you did a very good job for she is certainly a great improvement on the ½ dozen other candidates we experimented with.*

Without skipping a beat, Dewey continued dictating:

> *As she is writing this herself I don't dare say anything too complimentary for fear I would turn her bad while still young but she really is a mighty good girl. Thank you for finding her for me.*

When exposed to the decimal man's lechery, the women in his inner circle were used to looking the other way. The following week, a reassuring Colony responded: "Your letter about DH pleased me very much and confirmed my judgment of her."

With such an inauspicious beginning, the relationship with DH was destined to end disastrously. Dewey's boundary violations soon moved beyond the verbal to his standard repertory of hugs and kisses. In one incident in the summer of 1929 at the other Lake Placid, he embraced her in front of his wife. Rather than insisting that Dewey stop right away, his wife became an enabler; she allowed her husband to shift the onus onto DH. Under the arrangement the couple worked out, his secretary was supposed to tell Mrs. Dewey if she was ever troubled by his "unconventional" behavior, and only then would he agree to curb his excesses. Not long afterward, DH left his employ, and the Deweys forgot about her.

But three months after her departure, DH's lawyer sent Dewey a letter requesting $50,000 in damages for an alleged sexual "attack." His former employee may have had character issues of her own, so it's hard to determine whether his standard assortment of unwelcome hugs and kisses ever actually devolved into rape. Dewey claimed that DH had once confessed to him that she was prone to lashing out both verbally and physically—that she was a biter and scratcher. Dewey's conclusion that DH was "unbalanst" and suffered from "impulses symtums" could have been true; on the other hand, he may well have been attempting yet again to blame someone else for his own out-of-control behavior. Upon learning that Dean Robbins sided with DH, he wrote his lawyer, T. Harvey Ferris, that the cleric may be "a strong Puritan and honestly somewhat shocked that a man of high ideals should kiss a secretary, but he surely knows it has been done in thousands of cases and is too big a man to distort this into criminal intent." (It's unclear both how Dewey came up with this particular multiple of ten and exactly how many of these other cases involved him.) With Robbins willing to testify on behalf of DH, whose dream team of three savvy lawyers included a seasoned Tammany Hall politician, Dewey was in big trouble. Realizing the gravity of the situation, Ferris informed him, "This is no gentleman's game." In February 1930, Ferris negotiated a settlement, which Dewey quickly accepted. While admitting no wrongdoing, Dewey agreed to fork over to DH a total of $2,147.66 for lost salary and legal fees. His bill from Ferris came to another $435.51, a third of which went to Pinkerton detectives who had been hired to dig up dirt on DH and her lawyers.

By 1930, Dewey also faced a host of financial problems. The Florida Lake Placid was not doing well. Dewey had hoped that the other Lake Placid—which by then had grown to ten thousand acres—could be counted on to bail it out, but the board of the sister club balked. As the Great Depression worsened, so did Dewey's woes. The following year, occupancy at the original Lake Placid was down by 15 percent, and the one in Florida was barely surviving. That winter, just two guests signed up for its two hundred places, and the Deweys were having trouble meeting their payroll. Amid the stress and uncertainty, on December 10, 1931, Dewey penned a birthday letter, which he sent out to "a fu" friends across the country. "Today," he wrote, "starts my 9th decade." He didn't yet feel old; old age, he believed, "has kept about 10 years ahead of me." Calling himself an "80 year-old machine," he declared that "I am bizi and hapi...because my mind is skoold not to wori." He was proud that he could still throw himself into his work and "get qualiti and quantiti results." He then went on to list some of those numbers. The DDC, he noted, was now in "96% of public libraries and 89% of collej libraries."

Over the next few days, Dewey was feted. The former head of the alumni association of his library school sent a bound volume of letters from one hundred colleagues across the country who hailed his achievements. He received one hundred congratulatory telegrams from forty countries. The ex-president of the Florida Library Association also drove a small group of librarians over "100 myls" to pay him a visit.

Dewey felt compelled to note these various multiples of ten in a postscript to his birthday letter, in which he also expressed his hope to "retyr at 100." Having finished jotting down his thoughts, he added: "For 60 years known as leading apostl of decimals, 10 seems to pursue me for even my 8 paje letr has grown to the mistik 10."

Dewey died suddenly of a cerebral hemorrhage half a month later—just one and a half months before American skater Irving Jaffee nabbed the gold medal in the ten-thousand-meter race at the Lake Placid Olympics.

Kinsey poses alongside his cabinets full of sexual histories. With him are his three coauthors on *Sexual Behavior in the Human Female*, Clyde Martin (standing in back), Paul Gebhard (the man with a moustache), and Wardell Pomeroy (facing away from the camera). According to Gebhard, Kinsey encouraged "interstaff sex." While Gebhard had a steamy affair with Martin's wife, Kinsey would have sex with both Pomeroy and Martin, with whom he also fell in love. And Martin, in turn, was also a regular sex partner of Kinsey's wife, Clara.

4

Sexuality: Alfred Kinsey

The Rabid Orgasm Counter

> There is, moreover, a reality involved in any such summation of orgasms, for all orgasms appear to be physiologically similar quantities, whether they are derived from masturbatory, heterosexual, homosexual, or other sorts of activity.... For most females and males... the sum total of such orgasms may constitute a significant entity in the life of an individual.
>
> — Alfred Kinsey et al., *Sexual Behavior in the Human Female* (1953)

On the morning of Thursday, June 22, 1916, a day before his twenty-second birthday, Alfred Kinsey was slated to do one of the things that came naturally to him — deliver a lecture. The future academic, who, that fall, would begin graduate study in biology at Harvard — where he would also develop his penchant for bow ties, rumpled suits, and scuffed loafers — was about to give a valedictory address at the Bowdoin College commencement. The tall, blond, and blue-eyed psychology major was one of four seniors to receive this honor (and one of only two to graduate magna cum laude). Like Melvil Dewey a generation earlier, this straight-A man had also found his calling in a part-time classification gig that he stumbled upon as a junior; rather than organizing the books in Amherst's library, Kinsey organized the plant and animal specimens in Bowdoin's biology museum. Since arriving in Brunswick, Maine, two years earlier, the junior transfer had spent most of his waking hours — at least sixteen hours a week on both zoology and psychology, and four hours on biology — in laboratories and classrooms. His superlative scholarship dazzled his professors; the Harvard-educated zoologist Alfred Gross, a fixture at Maine's premier liberal arts institution for more than a generation, would later call Kinsey his best student ever. But his classmates weren't sure quite what to make of the loner who kept more than twenty types of snakes in his dorm room. According to the *Bowdoin Bugle*, the college yearbook, Kinsey was a "dignified non-committal individual who stalked about the campus with little to say to anyone. On entering his room, one never knows whether Mr. Kinsey or a large able-bodied snake is going to greet him."

Though shy in most social settings, Kinsey was not nervous. The outgoing president of the college's Debating Council, he had won numerous awards for his excellence as a public speaker. In front of an audience, Kinsey felt more comfortable than he did just about anywhere else. He liked being the person in charge—and much preferred monologuing to dialoguing—and he also feasted on the attention. But on this occasion, despite his self-confident manner and his facility with words, Kinsey would embarrass himself; in fact, with his ill-conceived remarks, he would inadvertently add a touch of levity to the solemn occasion.

For most of graduation week, the mood had been somber, as the carnage then taking place in Europe was on everyone's mind. In his baccalaureate sermon delivered the previous Sunday, Bowdoin president William DeWitt Hyde noted that "the great war has made impossible the isolation of the United States" and stressed the importance of "military preparedness." Additionally, the night before commencement, at the end of a performance of Shakespeare's *As You Like It*, fifty members of the class of 1911, back in Brunswick for their fifth reunion, terrified the audience by darting around campus clad in Ku Klux Klan uniforms. (Since the release of the movie *The Birth of a Nation* the previous February, the KKK was undergoing a boomlet in the virulently anti-Catholic Maine.)

After the first student speaker finished his talk on the "morbidly tragic personality" of Edgar Allan Poe, all eyes turned to Kinsey. Pointing to another part of the rustic campus, he began, "I owned a friend in a gray squirrel, yonder."

Much to the surprise of his classmates and their families, Kinsey's farewell address, entitled, "Art and Science—Companions," was to focus on his star-crossed liaison with a rodent.

"We met first by chance. When I threw an acorn at him, he perched on an upper limb and scolded in a dozen ways. He coughed and choked with invective; he mispronounced all he said. But my squirrel and I found, as time went on, that our paths were often to cross. We talked; we confided our troubles. Each was a mystery to the other, but we were friends."

The philosophical points that Kinsey was trying to make about the relation between art and science were muddled. "Art, the guardian of beauty...had taken [my squirrel] out of a disorderly superabundance of things, had made it a unit," he declared. "Science, seeking a different end, individualizes the squirrel in a different way."

But what did come through loud and clear was that this academic superstar did not yet know the ABCs of how to connect with any other sentient being. "Great truths of trust and fear, of troubles and delights, of delightful peculiarities, of friendship, I learned from my squirrel, the individual of beauty. And when, one morning, I found that the car had struck the life from the gray thing, I felt the loss of a particularly personal possession I had cherished. I was glad for the laws it had taught, glad for the love it had inspired." For Kinsey, his favorite squirrel was less an animal that had met its own tragic end than an object that he had lost. The socially obtuse scholar-in-the-making was thus on full display; Kinsey was indeed prone to forgetting that other creatures existed independently of himself.

Born into a family that neither understood nor appreciated him, Kinsey had always had trouble connecting. In his high school yearbook, he rendered his assessment of both his parents and all humankind by citing a line from *Hamlet*, "Man delights not me; no, nor woman either." And neither Kinsey's mother nor his father, a hard-driving engineering professor who had recently disowned the late adolescent for pursuing a career in some other field besides engineering, attended the graduation. Instead of becoming a connector, Kinsey became a collector—a not uncommon move for loners with a similar early history. As the late art historian Werner Muensterberger argues in his landmark work, *Collecting: An Unruly Passion* (1994), children who can't or won't "grasp and cling" to their parents often turn to objects as "symbolic substitutes" for human contact.

But Kinsey, unlike Jefferson or Heinz, was no ordinary collector. He was, concluded Wardell Pomeroy, a clinical psychologist who coauthored both of his bestselling sex surveys, "perhaps the most unusual one this nation of collectors has ever seen." As a child, Kinsey started with stamps before moving on to pancake disks—the CDs of the early 1900s—of classical music. "If your collection is larger, even a shade larger than any other like it in the world," the adult Kinsey philosophized, "that greatly increases your happiness." At Harvard, he would focus on an insect—the gall wasp—and he gathered some five million specimens during his two decades as a field biologist. In his home in Bloomington, where

Kinsey settled after obtaining his first teaching job at Indiana University in 1920, he mounted his extensive knife and sword collection on a wall in an upstairs bedroom.

And in the late 1930s, Kinsey would start a collection that would change the course of American history. Turning from biology to sexology, he began compiling sex histories of thousands of men and women, fact-filled documents that pivoted around mountains of raw orgasm data. As he noted in *Sexual Behavior in the Human Female* (1953), before marriage, the average American female experienced a total of 223, just one-seventh of the corresponding figure for males, which he had reported in his first survey, *Sexual Behavior in the Human Male* (1948). And at his new place of employment, Indiana University's Institute for Sex Research, which he set up in 1947, he also amassed the world's largest collection of sex books. The Dewey Decimal Classification System, this iconoclast decided, would not do, so he devised his own. Kinsey placed brown tape at the bottom of the spines upon which he wrote in white ink one of his thirty designations—say, FM for modern fiction and AN for anthropology. He also stashed away in the institute every erotic artifact and factoid he could lay his hands on, including ceramic art from Peru, bathroom graffiti, and some 5,200 penis measurements. This chase consumed him right up until his death. "It is a shame," he noted in 1956, after gathering his final two sex histories—Numbers 7984 and 7985—"there comes a time that you have to work up data and publish it instead of continuing the gathering. Frankly, I very much enjoy the gathering."

The magic formula that produced America's pioneering sexologist was a mania for collecting, counting, and organizing, fueled by a trinity of sexual perversions, namely exhibitionism, voyeurism, and sadomasochism. Thanks to Kinsey, S/M—the shorthand he invented—has entered the everyday lexicon. "In sex research," as Paul Gebhard, the now ninety-something anthropologist who coauthored the female volume, explained to me not long ago, "perversions come in handy. They are the name of the game." After all, the preeminent early-twentieth-century German sexologist Hans Magnus Hirschfeld was a transvestite, and Havelock Ellis, his British counterpart, suffered from undinism (he was turned on by the sight of women urinating). Besides these perversions, Kinsey's personal tastes also veered toward gay sex, which he tried hard to keep under wraps until his midthirties, and frequent action of all sorts. Such was the makeup of this sex maniac, who, "by getting people to think and talk about sex," as Bill

Condon, writer and director of the 2004 biopic *Kinsey*, has put it, "had a staggering effect on the culture." The "Sexual Revolution" of the 1960s is unthinkable
without the big assist from the Indiana University orgasm counter. "[Hugh]
Hefner," wrote a biographer of *Playboy*'s founder, "recognized Kinsey as the in-
controvertible word of the new God based on the new holy writ—demonstrable
evidence."

But while Kinsey's obsessions and compulsions jump-started his scholarly success, they also ended up killing him. In August 1956, just three years after the
release of his much-anticipated female volume—the "mistress piece" that would
be the companion to his "masterpiece," as the *Indianapolis Star* put it—he died
a broken man. He was just sixty-two.

Kinsey's sudden demise was not entirely due to his own self-destructive bent.
A changing of the political winds also played a role. In the summer of 1954,
a conservative backlash succeeded in convincing the Rockefeller Foundation,
which had underwritten his research for a decade, to cut off his funding. A
year earlier, Billy Graham had led the charge with an influential sermon, "The
Bible and Dr. Kinsey," which was soon transformed into a widely circulating
booklet. Of the recently published female volume, the reverend warned, "It is
impossible to estimate the damage this book will do to the already deteriorating
morals of America." With McCarthyism in full swing, in the fall of 1953, Carroll
Reece, a Republican from Tennessee, also launched a congressional investigation into nonprofit foundations in order to tell "the story of how Communists
and socialists are financed in the United States." While the Reece Committee
elicited some fierce opposition—the *New York Post* would dub its report "a man-
ifesto of Neanderthals"—its high-profile activities exerted enormous influence.
A worried Dean Rusk—the future secretary of state then headed the Rockefeller
Foundation—soon concluded that he had no choice but to dump his most controversial investigator.

But Kinsey's life was already spinning out of control before these politically
motivated attacks ever got under way. In June 1953, he collapsed from nervous
exhaustion and was forced to check himself into a hospital. Visiting Kinsey at
his bedside, Edgar Anderson, who had attended graduate school with him at
Harvard, was startled to see "his face lined, slowed down by drugs." A chronic
insomniac, Kinsey was by then a walking pharmacy who, just to keep chugging
along at all, had to take powerful sedatives at night and both tranquilizers and
amphetamines during the day.

As he neared sixty, his many eccentricities were leading not to productivity but to paralysis. Emotionally spent, he often felt tired and listless. He also began struggling with impotence; this was a particularly vexing development for some-one who measured out his life not "with coffee spoons," as did many of his contemporaries—to cite a line from T. S. Eliot's 1915 poem, "The Love Song of J. Alfred Prufrock"—but with orgasm numbers. In contrast, throughout his first decade and a half in the sex business, Kinsey had maintained a frantic pace. As his wife, Clara McMillen—known as Mac—complained to *Life* in 1948, "I hardly ever see him at night any more since he took up sex." While Mac, whom he had married in 1921 and with whom he raised three children, was ostensi-bly referring to his scientific concerns, her comment also applies to his active pursuit of his numerous sexual fantasies. By the mid-1940s, Kinsey, who had once enjoyed a satisfying sex life with Mac, slept in his own bedroom, as he pre-ferred experimenting with other "sexual outlets," to borrow the central concept from his reports, in which he identified five royal roads to the orgasm besides heterosexual sex—masturbation, nocturnal emissions, heterosexual petting, ho-mosexual sex, and animal contacts. According to Paul Gebhard, who took his sex history, Kinsey then rated himself as a 4 on his famous scale (with 0 being ex-clusively heterosexual and 6 being exclusively homosexual). He ended up with several steady male partners, whom he had first met while conducting their his-tories. He also participated in orgies in his home, which featured both male staff members and their wives; those shenanigans, which he initiated, were about the only occasions when he was still intimate with Mac.

And he did not shy away from the risky and the kinky. In 1938, Kinsey began frequenting "tea rooms" (public urinals), where he could indulge in as much anonymous gay sex as he wished. A decade later, when fame disqualified him from these encounters, he lamented with a smile the loss of "a lot of valuable re-search opportunities." Perhaps to compensate, in the late 1940s, Kinsey became addicted to a sadomasochistic masturbatory ritual, whereby he would stick a swiz-zle stick up his urethra and tie a rope around his scrotum, according to Kinsey biographer James Jones, who also claimed that Kinsey had first experimented with this technique as an adolescent. As the years went on, to achieve his requi-site thrill, he would continually up the ante—that is, inflict an ever-increasing amount of pain on himself. As an exhibitionist proud of his "very large genitalia," to quote a collaborator who got a good view, Kinsey had himself filmed while masturbating, though in a slight bow to modesty, his head did not appear on camera. The voyeur within also watched intently as his full-time photographer, William Dellenback, would, at his behest, shoot some of the other sexual goings-on in his attic, including S/M sessions between gays and dozens of other men and women engaging in masturbation. With the highly responsive women who were capable of lightning-quick orgasms, Kinsey got in a little extra action in between takes. Ever the dutiful wife, Mac—which also stood for "Mrs. Alfred C."— passed around cookies and persimmon pudding to the naked participants as they attempted to relax after the filming.

A subject in one of those filmed S/M marathons was the even more sexually hyperactive Samuel Steward, an English professor at Chicago's DePaul University, who emerged as Kinsey's close friend (but not lover). In Kinsey, with whom he spent about seven hundred hours between 1949 and 1956, Steward found "an ideal father...who listened and sympathized." For Steward, later a celebrated tattoo artist, as for many gay men of his generation, Kinsey provided an existential anchor. By presenting homosexuality as a relatively common "outlet"— according to his data, about 10 percent of men were more or less exclusively homosexual—Kinsey offered hope of a more tolerant future, something that has been realized in recent initiatives such as gay marriage laws and the ban on discrimination against gays in the military. Steward's history took Kinsey a remarkable five hours to record—ninety minutes was typical—because he had had several hundred sex partners. "The thing that amazed him most of all," observed Steward, "was that...I was a 'recordkeeper.'" Becoming an "unofficial collaborator," Steward shared his "Stud File," which featured three-by-five index cards on each lover.

Though Kinsey never revealed much about his private life to Steward, this fellow obsessive could sense the inner turmoil, which struck him as particularly acute in those final few years. "But had he...controlled the demon within," mused Steward, "he would not have been Dr. Kinsey."

Behind the adult sex doctor's inner torment was a lonely child's terror. During his first decade, Alfred was racked by a string of serious illnesses, including rheumatic fever and typhoid fever, and was often bedridden; on a couple of occasions, the boy, who missed as much school as he attended, was close to death. And then, just as the high school student started gravitating toward an academic pursuit that he loved—field biology—he came smack up against another nearly lethal enemy—his tyrannical superfather.

The first child of Alfred Seguine Kinsey and Sarah Ann Charles was born in Hoboken, New Jersey, on June 23, 1894. Alfred Charles had two siblings, Mildred, born in 1896, and Robert, born in 1908. A night-school graduate of Manhattan's Cooper Institute (today Cooper Union), Alfred Seguine taught shop practice at Hoboken's pillar of higher education, the Stevens Institute of Technology. Promoted from instructor to professor in 1908, Alfred Seguine followed in the path blazed by Stevens's star alumnus, Frederick W. Taylor, "the father of scientific management" and author of the definitive treatise on shop management, with whom he networked. To avoid confusion with his hated father, who eventually published a series of engineering textbooks, Prok—an abbreviation of Professor Kinsey, this was the nickname by which he would be known once he got to Indiana—would later sign all his correspondence "Alfred C."

The overbearing paterfamilias was a zealous Methodist who foisted his religion on the family; on Sundays, the children had no choice but to join him and do triple duty—attend Sunday school, morning services, and evening prayer. The opinionated and petulant Alfred Seguine, who frequently invoked the specter of a vengeful God, rubbed just about everyone he ever came across the wrong way. On account of his obliviousness to the feelings of others, Alfred Seguine has been described by Stevens alums as "a pompous ass" and "the great I man"—crunching the numbers, students proved their hypothesis that he used the first person singular far more frequently than any other faculty member. While Alfred's mother was not a menacing presence, the boy could not connect with her, either. Having received only four years of schooling, Sarah Kinsey was withdrawn and passive; she readily accepted the role the reigning bully assigned to her—that of cook and maid. Forced to make ends meet on a shoestring budget, she would often dispatch her firstborn to beg local merchants to extend the family's credit—an errand that left him feeling humiliated. Alfred Charles always resented her for not doing more to stand up to his father. Little good did the compliance do her; after nearly forty years of marriage, Alfred Seguine would demand a divorce and marry a much younger woman.

Until 1904, when Alfred Seguine's finances improved enough to afford a move to the white-collar community of South Orange, the family lived in a series of cold-water tenement flats near the Stevens campus on Fifth Street. While

Hoboken, when first laid out in 1804, was a summer retreat from Manhattan, by the late nineteenth century it was a densely populated factory town. Between 1860 and 1900, its mostly working-class population, which was teeming with immigrants from Germany, Ireland, and Italy, shot up from 10,000 to 65,000. With soot, filth, and garbage everywhere, children were routinely endangered. In August 1898, the *New York Evening Journal* ran an article headlined RAT BITES BABY IN ITS BED, which detailed the woes of Mrs. John Kloepping, the distraught mother of an eight-month-old daughter, who lived on Eighth Street—just a few blocks from the Kinseys. She was forced to abandon her rat-infested apartment in the middle of the night.

Kinsey would always hate Hoboken and everything associated with it. Years later, when he became an avid horticulturist, he would exclude the few flowers that grew there—marigolds, zinnias, and wisteria—from his garden. As an adult, he could not stomach potatoes, a mainstay of the dinners served up by his parents.

With Hoboken's unsanitary conditions largely to blame for the medical afflictions that nearly killed the boy, the man emerged as a neatnik. After meals, the adult Kinsey had a habit of systematically picking up all the crumbs scattered on the table with his fingertips and then placing them back on his plate. In his research trips—first as a field biologist and then as a sexologist— Prok, who always took a cold bath or shower first thing in the morning, would insist that his assistants do the same. When he lacked empirical evidence—say, he spotted a dry towel or had not heard the hum of the water—he would not hesitate to badger them into submission by emitting an abrupt "You smell!" To acquit himself of this dreaded duty, his colleague Paul Gebhard would turn on the shower while he shaved. The Hoboken native would also constantly monitor the cleanliness in his office. Thirty years into his tenure at I.U., Kinsey fired off an angry missive to a campus administrator about his frustration with "the worst janitor service that I have ever seen." Likewise, when visiting members of his staff at their desks, he would not hesitate to straighten their pencils and line up their papers.

In the ten-room house that his father rented in the Melville Woods section of South Orange (a leafy suburb of New York City), the young Alfred got a new lease on life. No longer was he hemmed in. He slept above his parents in his own room in the attic. His health woes behind him, the adolescent delighted in exploring the undeveloped hills adjacent to the garden, which he helped to maintain on the family's one-eighth-acre plot of land. While Alfred was not able to cultivate human friendships, he did bond with plants and animals. During long hikes, he collected many botanical specimens, particularly pressed leaves and ferns. He also enjoyed bird-watching. And like Gregor Samsa, the alienated protagonist of Franz Kafka's *The Metamorphosis*, who sought escape from the clutches of his oppressive parents by turning into a bug, Alfred turned to bugs, with whom he began a lifelong love affair. His favorites were caterpillars, mosquitoes, beetles, and ants. At the YMCA camps, which he began attending every summer from the age of fourteen, he was known as the resident "bugologist." By high school, the budding naturalist was also sticking his nose in a book every chance he could get. He emerged as the class valedictorian, who, according to a prophecy contained in his Columbia High yearbook, was destined to emerge as "a second Darwin." Summing up Kinsey's persona, his classmate Hazel Balch later recalled that he was the go-to guy "if you wanted to talk bugs maybe, but he didn't have fun." Though Alfred was handsome—nearly six feet, he was fit and lean with golden-blond hair, which he kept neatly trimmed—his nerdiness and aloofness squelched much interest from the fairer sex. "He wasn't," stressed Balch, "the type who appealed to girls." And even if the shy Alfred had sent some sparks flying, his father would not have allowed him to date. In the strict rules laid down by Alfred Seguine, a mover and shaker in South Orange's Methodist community, attending dances—even the prom—was verboten.

Nearly all of the young man's relationships with bipeds pivoted around pedagogy. At his father's behest, Alfred taught Sunday school classes and took on a leadership role in the Boy Scouts of America. In 1913, he became one of the nation's first hundred Eagle Scouts, an honor still reserved for an elite minority. By then, Alfred was also imparting his love of nature as a counselor at Kamp Kiamesha in the Kittatinny Mountains in western New Jersey. In the musical realm, he was both mentor and mentee. An enthusiastic pianist who possessed the diligence to practice his favorite classical compositions for hours on end, Alfred gave lessons to younger children to pay for his own instruction. The most important figure in his South Orange days turned out to be Natalie Roeth, his high school biology teacher. As the head of the biology club, she led students on trips around the countryside where they searched for plant and animal specimens. Alfred was eager to show her his new discoveries. He would always remember the time he tracked down Dutchman's breeches, a small white flower whose seeds were spread by ants. For the rest of his life, Kinsey would correspond regularly with Miss Roeth. Not long after the male volume appeared, Kinsey wrote to thank her for doing "more than anyone else at the very crucial age to turn me to science." As much as he respected the scholarly acumen of this graduate of Mount Holyoke College, he cherished her nurturing of his developing mind even more. This maternal surrogate was the one person in his youth who valued his unique sensibility.

Master and pupil would be Kinsey's only template for human connection. And after completing his doctorate at Harvard, he was never again the novice. In nearly all his subsequent relationships—even with Mac, his three surviving children, Anne, Joan, and Bruce (his first child, David, died of a thyroid problem at the age of three), university colleagues, neighbors, and coworkers—Kinsey presented himself as the scientific expert who at any moment would break out into "a little lecture." "He was a teacher—always," recalled his elder daughter, Anne. This was Kinsey's way of regulating his nearly crippling interpersonal anxiety and staying in control. This scion of two self-absorbed parents never learned how to be himself in the presence of others. However, Kinsey could easily become someone else.

Paradoxically, this lack of a core identity served him well when it came time to collect sex histories. "The con approach was deliberately cultivated by him," observed his informant, Samuel Steward, "so that he could win the trust of the person being interviewed; in like manner, he took up smoking and drinking (very, very gingerly) to put his interviewees at ease. . . . [He had a] talent for talking to the most uneducated hustlers and prostitutes in their own language, no matter how coarse." Late in life, the man who could not relate to others as equals found comfort in the companionship of young children. "Our birthdays were two days apart," Reed Martin, the son of Clyde Martin, the chief number cruncher on both Kinsey reports, told me in a phone interview, "and we celebrated them together. When I turned eight in June of 1954, he bought me a toy train set, and he helped me set up the track in my house. He was always asking me, 'What are you thinking?' I felt close to Prok, who was my good friend."

After giving the valedictory address at his Columbia High graduation in June 1912, Alfred Charles stayed put. Alfred Seguine had mapped out his son's future, and his namesake had no choice but to follow orders. The following September, the eighteen-year-old began pursuing a mechanical engineering degree at the Stevens Institute, the only college to which he was allowed to apply. For the next two years, he commuted with his father to Hoboken on train rides that must have sizzled with tension. The star student rebelled by nearly flunking out; in the spring semester of his freshman year, he got a 46 in Descriptive Geometry. That year, the only course in which his grade exceeded 90 was shop management, which he took from "the great I man" himself. But after completing his sophomore year, Kinsey made a gutsy move. Without telling his father, he abruptly withdrew from Stevens and began to make plans to attend Bowdoin College in Maine.

In his application to graduate school, submitted during his final year in college, Kinsey offered an explanation of why he transferred from Stevens to Bowdoin. "I had started at Stevens," he would confide in Harvard's secretary of graduate education, "only because my father wisht [sic] it. After two years work there I was convinced and finally convinced my father that I could not be interested enough in engineering to make it a life work. Finally he gave his consent, and I changed to Bowdoin to major in biology in which I have been interested for nine years." But this version of the family drama smoothed over the truth. In fact, a wounded and outraged Alfred Seguine did not come around; instead he bullied his son by refusing to support his education any longer. But by the middle of the summer of 1914, the determined youngster patched together a couple of scholarships, which enabled him to attend this exclusive private college. That September, armed with a single parting gift from his father—a $25 suit—Kinsey trekked off to Maine to build a life of his own. Thus was born both the man and the compulsive risk taker who would continue to take on established authorities. Except for a few brief visits, he would have little to do with either parent again.

As soon as he arrived at Bowdoin, Kinsey began to thrive. He went there for the two top-notch biology profs, and they did not disappoint. In his first week, he bonded with Dr. Alfred Gross during an ornithology hike. "He knew his birds thoroughly," observed the much-impressed Gross, who soon gave Kinsey free run of his house to practice the piano. The next semester, Gross's colleague, Dr. Manton Copeland, who also possessed a newly minted Harvard Ph.D., offered Kinsey that perfect part-time job at the college's biology museum. Nothing could have thrilled Kinsey more than the painstaking task of labeling and putting in cases its massive collection of plant and animal specimens.

———

On Sunday, October 12, 1919, Kinsey was back in South Orange to gather his belongings. Having just raced through Harvard's Bussey Institute—a now-defunct wing of the university, which once housed its graduate program in applied biology—in three years to obtain his Sc.D., he was about to begin his career as a research scientist.

The recipient of a postdoctoral research fellowship from Harvard, Kinsey was getting ready to travel across America in pursuit of what would emerge as his all-time favorite bug—the gall wasp. (A gall is the abnormal growth on trees or bushes in which the wasp's eggs grow; it's produced in response to a poison secreted by this tiny insect, which is typically the size of a small ant.) In his 250-page dissertation, "Life Histories of American Cynipidae," based on his examination of thousands of gall wasps in the Northeast, Kinsey had identified sixteen new species, but he was far from satisfied. Seeking to live up to the nickname bestowed on him at Harvard—"Get a million Kinsey"—he aimed to break still more new ground by tracking down hundreds of thousands of additional specimens in the South and West. "I have taken some time to prepare, as completely as possible, the details of equipment, etc. for my trip," he wrote that day to his advisor, the world-renowned Harvard entomologist and classification expert William Morton Wheeler. "And I anticipate that, in consequence, my time will be very largely free for actual collecting." The expert organizer had indeed thought of everything; he set up an elaborate protocol whereby he would send ahead his suitcase by train, thus allowing him to carry only the necessary provisions in his backpack. Signing off, Kinsey added, "I shall think very often of the Bussey and of the good friendships there!" Who exactly Kinsey was referring to here is hard to determine. While Wheeler considered Kinsey's recently submitted thesis "a remarkably fine piece of work," he had hardly ever spent any time with his star pupil. As at Bowdoin, Kinsey had led a monastic existence, spending much more time in the company of animals than people. In three years, he had made exactly one friend, Edgar Anderson, who did not arrive until his last semester. While the future director of the Missouri Botanical Garden could not help but notice Kinsey's "almost professional perfectionism," he enjoyed picking the brain of his older colleague on natural history expeditions.

On Monday, October 13, the same day the discovery of America was celebrated in various pockets of the country—the national holiday was not on the books until 1937—this Christopher Columbus of the insect world set off. A week and a half later, Kinsey sent Wheeler an update from Big Stone Gap, a small town on the western edge of Virginia: "Collecting has begun very satisfactorily." Having already traveled through southern New Jersey and eastern Virginia, he had begun shipping galls back to Boston in carefully packed crates. "I am having," he added, "a very profitable time in seeing these new sorts of country. The birds are very interesting, the mountains being full of birds in migration. I am becoming acquainted with many new plants." For the natural history geek, this was as close to heaven as one could get. Over the next ten months, Kinsey would travel a total of eighteen thousand miles—twenty-five hundred on foot—in thirty-six states. The compulsive counter kept track of all the numbers, especially the most critical one—his final haul of galls, which came to an even three hundred thousand. In May, during a brief break from his isolation—hiking mostly in the mountains, he often did not see another soul for several days—Kinsey met his father, then on the college lecture circuit, in Columbus, Ohio. Alfred Seguine passed on an urgent message from Wheeler notifying Kinsey that Indiana University was interested in hiring him as an assistant professor of zoology. That August, following a month in Boston in which he reconnected with his abandoned galls, the twenty-six-year-old moved to Bloomington to take up the relatively well-paying $2,000-a-year job ($75,000 today), which came with another $800 to tend to his tiny companions. "I am more and more satisfied," he wrote to Natalie Roeth, as he settled into his basement office in I.U.'s Biology Hall, "that no other occupation in this world could give me the pleasure that this job of bug hunting is giving. I shall never cease to thank you for leading me into it!"

Hooked, Kinsey did everything he could to assure himself a steady supply of the dopamine rush provided by his bug of choice. Year after year, he kept collecting, organizing, examining—he took twenty-eight microscopic measurements—and labeling his gall wasps. Aided by a few research assistants and a light teaching load, he soon amassed "quantities never dreamed of by any previous investigator," according to Edgar Anderson, who was floored by the exactitude with which he conducted his research. "Each insect was glued to a snippet of stiff paper and impaled on a steel pin. Minute paper labels...were affixed to the same pin and thousands upon thousands of these exquisitely prepared specimens were pinned in insect-proof boxes." Using India ink, Kinsey's staff recorded in his own specially developed lettering style a slew of data for each insect such as species, place and date of collection, and sex (the females were infinitesimally bigger). When properly crafted, these tiny labels—no more than three-eighths of an inch by five-eighths—often left the boss "beam[ing]...[with] pleasure," as one former student recalled. With all this data to crunch, Kinsey began publishing up a storm. In the 1920s, he came out with a half dozen major papers, which were followed by a six-hundred-page doorstop, *The Gall Wasp Genus Cynips: A Study in the Origin of Species* (1930). As the title indicates, Kinsey, whose belief system by then had shifted from Methodism to Darwinism, emphasized the theoretical implications of his findings. Having identified fifty new species, many of which he named after himself—we now have gall wasps such as Advene Kinsey and Anda Kinsey—he offered a series of speculations about the nature of evolution itself. As usual, he bragged about his numbers, noting that since 1917 he had traveled thirty-two thousand miles and had managed to label seventeen thousand wasps.

After finishing a magnum opus, many researchers take a minute to catch their breath, but not Kinsey. Doing without his galls—his raison d'être—for any length of time was unthinkable. On January 30, 1930, just as his first bug book was about to be published, the soon-to-be thirty-six-year-old typed a memo, "Major Research Problems," in which he listed thirteen additional studies that he wished to complete. Next to each, he estimated in pencil the number of years it was likely to take; the total came to thirty. Thus, as he noted at the bottom of the page, he was unofficially booked until the age of sixty-six. The two most ambitious projects were a book on the biology of gall wasps, which he anticipated would take four years, and a three-volume critique of taxonomy [the science of classification]—a six-year job. He went to work right away on the former, which would eventually take him, accompanied by several graduate students, to Arizona, Mexico, and Guatemala in both 1931 and 1935. As with his traveling fellowship from Harvard, he planned these extended field trips with a military precision. To collect his galls, he insisted on specially sewn cloth bags because "they are much stronger, take up less room and may be more securely tied at the top than paper bags." In 1936, Kinsey published a follow-up book, *The Origin of Higher Categories in Cynips*. Like its predecessor, it elicited a half dozen good reviews by specialists but was ignored by the larger scientific community. Eager to make a mark, Kinsey worked at a feverish pace, churning out nine more papers for leading entomology journals over the next two years.

But Kinsey never did write that megatome on taxonomy, as by the late 1930s his attention had turned from crawling critters to climaxes. Surprisingly, though his object of study was now radically different, his overall approach remained the same. Kinsey said as much in the introduction to his male report, where he explained how his sexual research "was born out of the senior author's long-time experience with a problem in insect taxonomy. The transfer from insect to human material is not illogical." For Kinsey, distinguishing between different species of gall wasps was no different from distinguishing between different types of human sexual behavior. Repeatedly referring to the "human animal" in his two reports, this sexologist would attempt to erase the distinctions between human beings and all other animals. In his framework, human sexuality, like the mating patterns of insects, is severed from any relational context; both men and women are biologically driven orgasm machines pump-primed to get their next fix.

Just as Kinsey experienced little love during his childhood and adolescence — except perhaps for the occasional furtive glance exchanged with a squirrel or a snake — there is little love in his surveys. This glaring absence led renowned Columbia University English professor Lionel Trilling to note in his review of the first survey that the chapter on human-animal contacts "is, oddly, the only chapter in the book which hints that sex may be touched with tenderness." Likewise, anthropologist Margaret Mead complained in 1948 that Kinsey "suggests no way of choosing between a woman and a sheep." "Because of their convenient size," sheep actually figure prominently at the end of the male volume, where he flashed his data about sex between men and animals. "What is there to prevent," Kinsey asked innocently, "insects of one species from mating with insects of another species?...Why should mammals mate only with mammals of their own kind?" As he relayed to an America in equal parts stunned and titillated, according to his research, about 17 percent of farm boys experience orgasm as a result of sex with an animal. Noting that besides sheep, "practically every other type of mammal that has ever been kept on a farm enters into the record," he also reported that vaginal coitus is the "most frequent technique," though fellatio and anal intercourse are not uncommon. The female volume would contain an analogous chapter where he reported that 0.4% of adult women achieved an orgasm as a result of contact with an animal — dogs and cats were the favored partners. Kinsey tracked down a "shy" sixty-eight-year-old widow who had engaged in weekly sex with her dog, named Tony, for eight years. While this caninophile was an outlier, she wasn't the record setter; one woman in his sample reached orgasm about nine hundred times via animal contacts. With coitus rarely doable, these women, Kinsey reported, tended to be on the receiving end of oral sex.

Upon arriving in Bloomington in the summer of 1920, Kinsey made sure that his whole life revolved around bugs. Nothing else mattered, even when it came to selecting a wife. While the assistant professor of zoology, as the authors of the two major Kinsey biographies both argue, had experienced frequent homosexual fantasies since adolescence, in his midtwenties, the only path to success he could envision was as a conventional family man. Clara McMillen, I.U.'s top undergraduate chemistry major, whom he had first met during his interview the previous April, proved irresistible mate material. She had all the requisite qualifications. As a child, she had chased butterflies and moths; so devoted was this Brookville, Indiana, girl to insects that she had once paid for a newspaper ad in the hope of expanding her caterpillar collection. And the dark-eyed tomboy, who did not care for makeup, liked to go on nature walks. While Clara pursued the still shy but handsome Kinsey, she initially worried about their compatibility, considering him "too churchy." His tone-deaf gifts that first Christmas—hiking boots, a compass, and a hunting knife—also led her to have some second thoughts.

But in February 1921, after a courtship of less than two months, the couple was engaged. At their wedding a few months later at the Brookville home of Mac's grandparents, Kinsey did not have a single friend (human or animal) in attendance. Of his bride, an elated Kinsey rhapsodized to Miss Roeth, "She is a very brilliant scholar.... She knows the birds better than I do, knows the flowers and the trees, etc., is a capable hiker and camper, a champion swimmer.... So you see I am even more certainly headed into a life with the open." And to the outdoors they went on their honeymoon. With his permanent hiking partner often lagging far behind, Kinsey marched to the top of the White Mountains of New Hampshire. At his insistence, they took a fire warden's trail that, as a terrified Clara—a Midwesterner who had never been near any patch of earth much steeper than a pancake—later put it, "went straight up." As they recuperated in their tent at night, the professor lectured on plants and animals and taught her how to cuddle a gentle grass snake. From the get-go, their marriage was a ménage à trois. Long before Kinsey's sexual escapades, Clara would have to learn how to coexist with a mistress. "I always realized," she acknowledged later, "that his work would come first. You can't ask a man to give up what is the driving force of his life because he is your husband."

With the easygoing Clara becoming the eternal student of Kinseyana—she cut short her own promising academic career after just a semester of graduate school—the early years of their marriage worked out just as Kinsey drew them up. "He wanted a helpmate and that's what he got," recalled Paul Gebhard. "He felt it was the wife's job to keep the house tidy, raise the children, serve healthy, nutritious meals on time, and that was about it." Practical, resourceful, and kind, Clara evolved into a nurturing mother and an efficient household manager. She also became the "greatest of cooks," according to Glenway Wescott—the novelist was a longtime friend and occasional sex partner of Kinsey—who once noted that "if Alfred were not the hardest-worker of men, he would be the fattest." To be fair to Kinsey, though his need for control was extreme, his ideas about how the sexes should divvy up the labor were not all that out of step with his times. And to his credit, despite occasional outbursts of temper, he did not become a tyrant like his father. Doing his best to treat both his wife and children with respect, he aimed to resolve family conflict through dialogue rather than diktat. While delegating most of the child care to Clara, Kinsey did pitch in, taking charge of the nightly baths—as a neatnik, this was a temptation that he could not resist—and bedtime stories. But he drafted the children into the bug business, taking them along with Clara on several extended research trips. One year, Kinsey sent out Christmas cards featuring a picture of his son Bruce toting bags of galls.

And thus might Kinsey have carried on to the end of his days—as a conventional mid-twentieth-century father and husband, dedicating his life to entomology. But Clara changed him dramatically. Her steady affection brought out parts of his personality that had been forced to remain in hiding, such as his sensuality, heretofore largely confined to piano playing. A virgin at the time of his marriage, as was his bride, Kinsey soon found that he thoroughly enjoyed sex. This new pastime, however, initially required work. During their honeymoon up in the mountains, the future sex doctor and his wife never did succeed in making whoopee; and it was not for a lack of trying. Terrified and confused, the Kinseys ignored the glitch for a few months until a Bloomington doctor discovered that Mac's hymen was unusually thick. This rare physiological disorder, in combination with Kinsey's inordinately sized member, had made consummating the marriage impossible. After some minor surgery on Mac, all systems were go. To ensure against any such humiliations in the future, Kinsey started to immerse himself in the scientific literature on sex such as the work of Havelock Ellis. The couple worked to polish their lovemaking techniques and experimented with various coital positions—the man on bottom was their favorite. Kinsey soon became master of everything to do with his own sex life. He even developed his own special form of birth control, which involved sterilizing condoms with a certain percentage of alcohol so that they could be used time and time again.

Though Kinsey continued to revere cleanliness and control as much as ever, he also began to appreciate the unruly. This turn in his aesthetic sensibility found expression in the two-story house that he built in the Vinegar Hill neighborhood, then on the outskirts of Bloomington, in 1926. While the former engineering student hired a local firm headed by Charles Pike as the contractor, Kinsey both drew up the blueprints himself and supervised every detail of the construction, as Thomas Jefferson did with his house at Monticello. As Pike's workmen began to lay the overburned bricks — to keep expenses down, they used discards from a local kiln — in a symmetrical fashion, Kinsey suddenly stopped them. The emerging exhibitionist, who liked to prance around naked in front of his children, insisted on an au naturel domicile that featured both misaligned bricks and excess mortar hanging out every which way. This distinctive exterior attracted the attention of neighbors, who were evenly divided between fans and skeptics. Inside the rooms had an adobe look, as Mac washed the brown walls with tea (which she believed would help preserve them). To make sure that all family members could get cleaned up on the double, particularly in those steamy Bloomington summers, Kinsey installed an extra shower, which looked like a telephone booth, in the basement, as Consuelo Lopez-Morillas, who moved into the house after Clara's death, explained to me.

Buying up a few adjacent lots, Kinsey also created a decidedly disorderly garden. "Straight is the line of duty but curved the line of beauty" was its credo. Built in the English style, it included a lily pond and rock gardens. The passionate horticulturalist sprinkled in a wide variety of plants and flowers around native and nursery-bred trees. Gardening became both his preferred form of exercise as well as his favorite hobby. But Kinsey could never entirely divorce work from pleasure, acknowledging that his beloved irises "do provide material for scientific study." And study them he did. The collector extraordinaire collected more than 250 different species and summarized his findings in a review article for the *Bulletin of the American Iris Society*. "Instead of just simply having a diverse garden, a damn good second-rate garden," Paul Gebhard later recalled, "[he had to] have the very best iris collection in the whole Midwest." Kinsey returned to his notion about the need to merge art and science that he had first spoken of in his garbled college valedictory decades earlier. "Gardens," he remarked in that scholarly article, "must be made with some respect for...art." Kinsey worked hard to perfect his earthly paradise, repeatedly tearing up and rebuilding sections of turf. He went at it regularly in the summer months, whiling away many early mornings and most Sundays. The preeminent "bugologist" had no trouble putting in long hours, as he was immune to insect bites. Wearing nothing but a skimpy flesh-colored pair of shorts ("a loincloth type of thing," as his daughter Joan put it) and one shoe on his right foot so that he could do the spading, he startled neighbors and passersby, who assumed that he was not wearing any clothes at all.

Kinsey also combined his idiosyncratic mix of the sensual and the scholarly in a unique form of entertainment that he hosted on Sunday nights in his living room: the musicale. In the late 1920s, he started collecting 78 rpm records—within a decade, he had more than a thousand—and he liked to play his favorite selections for friends. He was drawn to conservative—tonal—composers such as Jean Sibelius. These carefully choreographed gatherings were an act of rebellion against Alfred Seguine, who had once ordered Kinsey's aunt out of the Hoboken home for playing the piano on the Sabbath. At precisely eight o'clock, the piano player turned music critic began with an introductory lecture. For the next two hours, as he mixed in compositions and more commentary, the guests, who sat in preassigned hardback chairs arranged in a semicircle facing the master, were expected to listen in absolute silence. "You could be expelled from the group," one attendee recalled, "if you squeaked." But he played the music loud because he wanted to draw attention to the details. At ten o'clock on the dot, Mac would pass out the refreshments—persimmon pudding and iced water—and conver-sation was briefly permitted. Twenty minutes later, Kinsey would return to the turntable and put his special cactus needle—he would count the number of times he used it—on the final piece, which was some kind of lighter fare. At ten thirty, he would usher everyone out the door.

After several years of marriage, Kinsey officially transformed Mac from his mate into his mother. She provided him with what he had never had as a boy, a secure emotional base. But rather than responding in kind, Kinsey made use of his newfound self-confidence to go scouting for new sexual partners. On his research trips, he no longer was interested in communing solely with bugs; he began hitting on his male grad students. His first major crush was on Ralph Voris, who, as Kinsey later confided to Gebhard, became the second great love of his life. A handsome small-town boy from Oklahoma, Voris, who first went gall col-lecting with Kinsey in 1925, completed his doctorate at I.U. in 1928. A brilliant entomologist who became the reigning expert on the staphylinid beetle, Voris could, as Kinsey once noted gleefully, "sit all day beside an uninhabited pile of dung until it came alive with bugs."

"He was in love with Voris," recalled a colleague, "from day one." While eyewitness accounts are missing, most Kinseyologists assume that the two insect mavens boosted each other's orgasm counts on those nights when they shared the same tent or hotel room. The intimate friends communicated about everything from classification to coital positions. They also swapped sex histories. After leaving Bloomington, Voris, who was also married, took up a teaching position at Southwest Missouri State College in Springfield. In frequent letters, Kinsey shared his innermost thoughts and aspirations with Voris, whom he affectionately dubbed "Mr. Man." But except for a few isolated days every year or two—on research trips, at academic conferences, and at their respective homes in Bloomington and Springfield—Kinsey saw little of Voris between his graduation and his sudden death in 1940. Not as smitten as his mentor, Voris was often fending off Kinsey's invitations. Unable to stare the truth in the face, Kinsey settled on a scientific explanation for the infrequency of their trysts, lamenting to his former star student that "your bugs and mine do not always live in the same places." The torch would never be extinguished, as Kinsey kept a picture of Voris on his desk for the rest of his life.

With Voris proving elusive, Kinsey became sexually interested in the research assistants whom he took on field trips. Letting his inner exhibitionist out, he had no hesitation about walking around naked in front of a student, whom he might ask to take his picture as he bathed in the river. He regaled his crew with smutty chatter. "He would just bring it [sex] up right out of the blue," recalled Homer T. Rainwater, an I.U. graduate student who accompanied Kinsey on his 1934 expedition to Arkansas and Missouri. While Rainwater was a little startled when Kinsey started prying into the details of his marital relations, he was floored when Prok expatiated about the wonders of masturbation. Asked if Prok ever initiated group masturbation sessions, Rainwater responded, "No, he didn't go that far. He almost did, but didn't." But on other occasions, Kinsey was not able to show similar restraint. The following year on his jaunt to Mexico and Guatemala, not long after enlightening grad student Osmond Breland about his theory of "explosions"—according to Kinsey, ejaculations were produced by a closed plumbing system of sorts—he and Breland engaged in a threesome with an unsuspecting undergrad. By the mid-1930s, a pattern had been set; travel became a means to gratify his limitless sexual curiosity and desire. And by the end of the decade, as his scientific orgasm counting began, Kinsey would spend more and more time away from Bloomington. While Mac continued to play the good soldier, she did privately lament that marriage to Prok meant "being alone a lot."

———

In early 1938, Kinsey was feeling restless. While fellow entomologists acknowledged that he had no peer in gall research, their numbers were few and their influence negligible. And since I.U. did not attract top-flight graduate students, nationally, the ambitious academic was still a relative nobody. Kinsey was relieved that the university's longtime president William Bryan, whom he detested as a stodgy Victorian, had finally retired, but he harbored doubts about his thirty-five-year-old replacement, the former dean of I.U.'s Business School, Herman Wells. "Wells [is] not too long on scholarship," Kinsey confided to Voris that March. "I am not yet certain that I want to fix my future here. If it comes out right in this shuffle, I.U. will be a good place to stay; if it is screwed up as soon things threaten to be, I shall be in the market for another job. Someplace where there is...a graduate program that allows a better ground for taxonomic...studies." Kinsey ended up staying put, as a dream assignment suddenly came his way. That spring, I.U. students petitioned the new president to update the university's ossified one-hour "hygiene" class, which, rather than educating students about sex, celebrated Victorian mystifications. Wells turned to Kinsey, who relished the chance to turn his hobby—combing through the sexological literature—into a scholarly sideline. Heading a committee of seven tenured professors, who hailed from a variety of disciplines including law, sociology, medicine, psychology, and history, Kinsey systematically designed a "Marriage Course," which was first offered to I.U. seniors in June 1938.

"Marriage Course" was a euphemism for "Sex Course," because any sex outside of marriage was then still considered socially taboo, if not criminal. In the late 1930s, all states had sodomy laws on the books, under which homosexuality as well as anal and oral sex—even between spouses—could be punishable by a lengthy prison sentence. Kinsey was taking his cue from the leading sex manual of the day, *Ideal Marriage: Its Physiology and Technique* by the Dutch gynecologist Theodoor van de Velde. (While the 1930 American edition of this graphic how-to manual, which the Catholic Church immediately placed on its index of banned books, contained a note from the publisher limiting its sale to medical professionals, after World War II it would sell nearly half a million copies.) Citing experts on love from the Latin poet Ovid to the German philosopher Friedrich Nietzsche, van de Velde called marriage "sacred to the believing Christian." "If there are varieties," ran an aphorism from the French novelist Honoré de Balzac that summed up the Dutchman's angle, "between one erotic occasion and another, a man can always enjoy happiness with one and the same woman." Emphasizing physiology rather than psychology, van de Velde addressed his step-by-step guide to orgasmic bliss to "the husband who wants to be more than a blunderer." In van de Velde, who insisted that the genitals be touched only with "perfectly clean hands," Kinsey found a kindred spirit. The gynecologist who had helped him to perfect his own technique between the sheets would forever shape Kinsey's thinking. A decade and a half later, in ads for the female volume placed in the *New York Times*, Kinsey included the following question, "Do you realize that many authorities believe that reading the book can strengthen the individual's family life?" Like van de Velde, Kinsey would present himself as an ardent defender of marriage when offering his steamy suggestions, but privately he felt otherwise. He once described the rise of romantic love in the Renaissance as "the worst thing that ever happened to Western humanity." For Kinsey, as for Dewey, Lindbergh, and other obsessives with runaway sexual impulses, purely monogamous relationships were akin to a prison sentence.

Of the twelve lectures in that initial version of "Kinsey's course in connubial calisthenics," as the I.U. students dubbed it, Prok delivered three. In the opener, he sketched his biological view of society, which obliterated nearly all distinctions between humans and infrahumans. Just as the French students would argue a generation later that "we are all German Jews," this sexual revolutionary made his case that we are all insects. For Kinsey, sex alone was the glue that organized animal societies of all stripes. "The anthropoid [ape] family breaks up," he insisted, "as soon as the sexual attraction wanes." Identifying the breast as a sex organ, he also argued that mother love in humans was motivated by the "sexual response" elicited by "the feeding babe." In other words, for Kinsey, women were interested in the welfare of their children largely because they saw them as a source of sexual gratification. (At the time, little was known about oxytocin, the so-called bonding hormone, but the very concept of nonsexual bonding would never register with him.) In the second lecture, using several slides of penises and vaginas, he covered everything students might want to know about human anatomy and physiology—and then some. Here, he leaned heavily on van de Velde's manual, which had also broken down the sex act into its component parts with an analytic detachment, as if the issue at hand were how to rev up an automobile engine. "Intercourse," Kinsey declared matter-of-factly, "consists of a series of physiological reactions which are as mechanical as the blinking of an eyelid."

In his final lecture on individual variation, Kinsey put forth his unique take on human sexuality. "There are only three kinds of sexual abnormalities," he maintained, "abstinence, celibacy, and delayed marriage." This bold statement encapsulates what would be both the upside and the downside of Kinsey's oeuvre. As a crusader against conventional morality and punitive sex laws, Prok aimed to get both the church and the government out of the bedroom. And his twin tomes would ultimately help to convince most Americans that what consenting adults do behind closed doors is nobody else's business; by the early 1960s, those age-old sodomy laws started tumbling down. However, the monomaniacal Kinsey would also go overboard, arguing that sexual perversions per se do not exist. For example, he would always insist that more sex—no matter what the consequences—is always better. He once defined a nymphomaniac "as someone who has more sex than you do." Antipsychological to the core, Prok would attempt to normalize the behavior of sex addicts like himself. To Kinsey, the idea that anyone—but men in particular—might not be eager to rack up orgasms every which way was nearly unthinkable. "To most males," he later noted in the female volume, "the desire for variety in sexual activity seems as reasonable as the desire for variety in the books that one reads."

All of a sudden, the man who formerly had had trouble connecting with anyone found himself with legions of fans. I.U. students could not get enough of Kinsey. In the fall of 1938, enrollment in the noncredit class doubled to two hundred; two years later, it would be up to four hundred. "To me the behavior of the penis was already awe inspiring, now it seems even more wonderful," noted an entranced I.U. coed on one of the many course evaluations that gave an emphatic thumbs-up to his use of slides. About a third of those attending "the course on legalized frigging," as his former student Breland described it, met with Prok in his office for private conferences. No longer did Kinsey have to traipse around campsites to dredge up some research assistant whom he could instruct in the fine art of masturbation; now undergrads came to him in droves, begging for information about all his favorite topics, including homosexuality. After counseling these anxious and guilt-ridden I.U. students, he asked them to return the favor by filling out detailed questionnaires about their sex lives. Having devoured just about everything scholars had written about sex, Kinsey was surprised to discover that little was known about what people actually did in the bedroom. While he was not yet sure that he had found an entirely new line of work, his inquiring mind wanted some answers. By the end of 1938, he had collected his first sixty-two sex histories.

Over the next several months, Kinsey revised his research protocol, switching to face-to-face interviews. In contrast to his original paper-and-pencil instrument with its two hundred items covering the major sexual outlets, including animal contacts, the oral interview contained at least 300 items and up to 521. To record those orgasm frequencies, Kinsey invented his own secret code, which was a quirky combination of abbreviations and mathematical signs. This shorthand allowed him to jot down the responses quickly on a single sheet divided into twenty-four squares and to ensure that the data would remain confidential. In Kinseyese, the same letter could refer to several different things. While M could mean "masturbation," "mother," "Methodist," or "masochist," S could signify "single" or "sadist." Years later, when traveling with his staff, Kinsey would enjoy bantering in his own private language, saying, for example, "My history today liked Go better than Z, but Ag with an H really made him er" (*My history today liked genital-oral contact better than that with animals, but anal-genital with a homosexual really turned him on*). The man who could not connect in social settings proved remarkably adept as an interviewer. The quest for orgasm numbers brought out his often-hidden compassionate side. Sympathetic to the fears and concerns of his subjects, he rarely failed to establish rapport. He knew just when to slow down and when to push forward. If a subject grew up in a rural area or liked experimentation, he would be inclined to skip, "Have you ever had sex with an animal?" and jump right to "When was the first time you had sex with an animal?"

By the middle of 1939, having finalized his new mode of collecting data after first trying it out on his pliable wife (he would wait a bit before taking the sex histories of his three children), Kinsey was literally off and running. That June, he hit the road to widen his sample to include other types of subjects, namely, prostitutes and urban homosexuals, in whom he took an abiding interest. On July 8, he shared his excitement with Voris: "I have just come back from the trip to Chicago—that we talked of last Xmas—safe and sound—with 8 histories the like of which is in no published study. Again—wish I could summarize for you or show you the detailed histories." Kinsey would go back to Chicago once a month for the rest of the year. By October, as he reported to Voris, he had compiled a total of 570 histories, 120 of which were *H* (homosexual). He was also proud to have interviewed 40 prostitutes—both male and female—who together had serviced some 12,000 clients. "You can figure the average," he told Voris. "Several with 2000 and 3000 each." Kinsey was getting his hands on all the factoids that he had ever dreamed of. At the end of each interview, he asked his subjects to take four penis measurements—size and circumference in both a flaccid and an erect state—and then mail in the results. To the procrastinators, he followed up with a polite and efficient reminder note ("Will you send us the measurements which we need to complete your history?"). These additional tidbits became a standard part of his inventory. A decade later, after giving his sex history, Glenway Wescott noted in his journal, "I had to measure my poor penis in its two states and both domains for Dr. K and…have got my sense of humor back."

Kinsey's grueling schedule did not allow him a second to reflect or feel—which was, of course, just the way he wanted it. In the summer of 1939, in addition to administering the Marriage Course and collecting his sex histories, he was still doing what he was hired to do: study insects and teach biology—his two classes met for five hours a day. "This has been," he wrote Voris that July, "the busiest six months that I have ever spent. I have measured some thousands of bugs." And his personal life was becoming more chaotic than ever, as he no longer made any attempt to curb his voracious sexual appetite. During his Chicago sojourns, the exhilarated scholar began to participate as well as observe. That was when he started visiting "tea rooms." In 1939, back in Bloomington, he also initiated an affair with Clyde Martin, the handsome I.U. undergrad whom he had hired that spring to crunch his rapidly expanding mass of orgasm numbers. Having taken Martin's history, Kinsey knew that this shy, lonely scholarship student, less than half his age, was not averse to gay sex. Martin, as Gebhard has stated, was to become the third and final love of his life. But Martin, like Voris, was not as enamored of Kinsey. Perhaps to get his boss to simmer down, Martin asked for permission to sleep with Mac. Kinsey agreed to serve as the go-between, and soon Martin and Mac were also having regular trysts in Kinsey's own bedroom. Boss and employee continued to have sex for a couple more years. After Martin squirmed out of the sexual liaison, the bullying did not end. "Martin was really servile," another staff member recalled, "and Kinsey demanded that he be." The complex relationship between Kinsey and Martin—who married his wife, Alice, in Kinsey's garden in 1942 and mined the sex data until he left the Kinsey Institute in 1960—was the impetus for T. C. Boyle's moving roman à clef, *The Inner Circle*. When I asked Boyle what motivated him to write about the Kinsey-Martin dyad—while Kinsey appears under his own name, the assistant is called John Milk—the author responded, "While Kinsey had a progressive agenda, he also had an overweening ego. What attracts me to such a guru is how he can make use of and drain his subordinates."

With the sex research becoming all-consuming, Kinsey was forced to prioritize. He wrote Voris on March 29, 1940, "I am going to have to make some drastic reorganization of the gall wasp work in order to concentrate on the study of the [sex] material we now have." For this order aficionado, *reorganization* was a euphemism for "abandonment." As a bugologist, he was more or less done. That fall, Kinsey also said good-bye to the Marriage Course. Despite its popularity, "the smut session," as the stodgy dean of I.U.'s School of Medicine called it, never was without opponents. Chief among them was Dr. Thurman Rice, a key member of Indiana's Board of Health. A few weeks after meeting with Kinsey on campus in 1939, Rice wrote to express his concern that a particular slide depicting coitus was too graphic, "I have been married for nearly thirty years, and have given the subject real objective study. The picture is too good." A year later, Rice was joined by a chorus of other voices, including several profs at the med school and a local interdenominational association of preachers, who pressured Wells to either dump Kinsey or modify the course. The fair-minded I.U. president, who had declared at his inauguration a couple of years earlier that "authority must be derived from reason," liked and respected Kinsey and was emerging as a steadfast supporter of his controversial work. (Rumors have persisted that the lifelong bachelor, who had a penchant for hiring handsome undergrads as houseboys, may have been gay, but no evidence of his sexual orientation has ever been found.) Wells offered his trusted friend a choice between the course or the research. While Kinsey was outraged by his detractors—comparing himself to Galileo, he felt the unenlightened were branding him a heretic—he did not mind having more time to do what he loved above all. After a visit during this transitional phase of Kinsey's career, Edgar Anderson could tell that Kinsey was "settling down into... [his] real life work." The friend who knew him the longest wrote, "One would never have believed that all sides of you could have found a project big enough to need them all." Anderson identified a handful of Kinseys who would work together to produce the groundbreaking sex reports—"the Scotch Presbyterian reformer," "the scientific fanatic with his zeal for masses of neat data in orderly boxes and drawers," "the monographer," "the naturalist," and "the camp counselor." And Anderson did not even know about the secret sex maniac who was driving the ship.

———————

In the fall of 1940, the forty-six-year-old biologist forged ahead by turning back the clock nearly a quarter century. "Get a million [gall wasps] Kinsey" was now "Get 10,000 [sex histories] Kinsey" (a figure that he repeatedly upped as the decade wore on). "For more than twenty years," he wrote then to a friend, "I have worked on individual variations in the population of insects....The unearthing of the facts in Human Sexual Behavior proves a much more difficult and much more dangerous undertaking; but the very difficulty is one of the things that leads me on." Once again, Kinsey would scour "the length of the continent in the most remote desert and mountainous areas" to find his prey. In 1941, working up to fourteen hours a day, he spent 106 days on the road and took forty trips to penal institutions. His persistence soon attracted the attention of donors. That year, he received his first grant of $1,600 from the National Research Council's Committee for Research in Problems of Sex (CRPS), which was funded by the Rockefeller Foundation. The following year, he got $7,500. In December 1942, the top three CRPS scientists came to Bloomington. Over the next decade, these site visits would emerge as a key element in Kinsey's ongoing PR campaign. He would have little trouble wowing academics (and later journalists) by showing them the nuts and bolts of the research, such as his interview techniques, his coded records, and his orderly files. And to give his visitors a firsthand feel for the project (as well as to gain control over them by learning their secrets), this voyeur would routinely take their sex histories. During these nonstop charm offensives, Kinsey would remain glued to his guests for as many as fifteen hours a day—he would sometimes even follow them into the bathroom. After meeting with Kinsey, the three scientific heavyweights all left with a "very favorable" impression of his survey, though one, a world-famous endocrinologist, could not help but notice that their host was a tad unbalanced: "[Kinsey] thought about his work every waking hour...[he was] the most intense person I ever knew outside of an institution for psychiatry. He was absolutely wound up." But Kinsey achieved his goal. In 1943, his grant was bumped up to $23,000, and by 1947 it would reach $40,000.

In early 1946, soon after his team had collected the ten thousandth history, Kinsey settled down to write the male volume. He cut back on his travels and put the kibosh on his teaching career. The project would take two years to complete. He pounded out all the words himself, though he solicited feedback from his two top lieutenants, Gebhard and Pomeroy. And his statistician, Clyde Martin, was in charge of charts and graphs. Kinsey's obsessive touches were all over the manuscript, the first chunk of which he submitted to his publisher, W. B. Saunders, in the spring of 1947. He double-checked Martin's graphs to make sure the width and length of the lines were just right. He stunned his editor, Helen Dietz, by using a ruler to fix the jagged marks that she had placed on the left-hand side of the pages to indicate to the typesetter that a smaller font was to be used. "When I commented on his unusual care," Dietz later recalled, "he looked at me in gentle rebuke and assured me that everything worth doing was worth doing precisely and carefully." Kinsey also flooded Dietz with questions about such concerns as the quality of the manuscript paper and the type of pencil he should use to make corrections on the finished manuscript. In the summer of 1947, Kinsey began seducing—metaphorically speaking, as he was eager to present himself to the public as a well-adjusted family man—the newspaper and magazine journalists who made the pilgrimage to Bloomington. Due to his superb public relations efforts, Saunders, which specialized in medical texts, boosted the initial print run from ten thousand to one hundred thousand copies.

Published on January 5, 1948, the book was an instant hit. Kinsey was suddenly "America's Most-Talked-About Male," according to the influential journalist Vance Packard, later the author of the classic book on the advertising industry, *The Hidden Persuaders*. *Life* compared him to his hero: "To find another scientific book which even approaches this, it probably is necessary to go back to Darwin's *On the Origin of Species*." Likewise, *Science Illustrated* raved, "His encyclopedic work is being hailed as one of the great sociological labors of our age, a frame of factual reference in a field which up to now has been disorganized, chaotic and filled with dangerous misinformation." According to the serial counter himself, about 95 percent of the articles in the popular press were positive. At Kinsey's behest, George Gallup conducted a poll to track the public response, which indicated that 78 percent of Americans considered his report "a good thing," as opposed to 10 percent who disapproved. In May, after the book hit Number 1 on the *New York Times* bestseller list, an excited Kinsey wrote to a colleague, "When I can get enough sleep, I realize that this has been a handsome reception to our work." (For the man who sexualized everything, *handsome* was a favorite descriptor.) By June, 150,000 copies had been sold, and contracts had been signed for British, Swedish, French, and Italian editions. That December, actress Mae West, who would later describe herself in *Cosmopolitan* as a kindred spirit when it came to "observing [and] investigating" sex, sent Kinsey a telegram, inviting him to her suite at Manhattan's Warwick Hotel. He declined, as he had little interest in bantering with celebrities; and he would never develop a knack for small talk.

While the public adored him, many academics were lukewarm. As a biologist who was encroaching on the turf then patrolled by psychoanalysts, psychologists, and sociologists, Kinsey met with considerable criticism in the professional reviews that came out over the next few years. (Ever the collector, Kinsey asked an assistant to type the most scathing barbs on three-by-five cards.) In a twelve-page piece published in *Psychosomatic Medicine* in 1948, the psychoanalyst Lawrence Kubie, while lauding Kinsey's "colossal undertaking," attacked him for various reasons, including his failure to understand the fallibility of human memory and his lack of attention to psychological factors. Kinsey responded with outrage. The self-absorbed former bugologist saw everything in Manichean terms; other people were either for him or against him. Convinced that he was unmasking millennia of religious cant about sexuality, Kinsey had assumed that the entire scientific community would automatically offer enthusiastic support. "If Kubie's review is scientific," he told a colleague, "then I have never had any contact with science." In contrast, his sponsors at the Rockefeller Foundation sniffed out Kubie for what he really was, a Freudian wounded that Kinsey's survey did not pay sufficient homage to analytic tenets, and they paid little attention to his critique. A much more serious threat to Kinsey's continued funding—he was then hard at work on the female volume—came in the form of Warren Weaver, the head of the natural sciences division at the Rockefeller Foundation. Unlike Kubie, this former math prof at the University of Wisconsin had no sympathy for what Kinsey was trying to do. Moreover, Weaver was a renowned expert in statistics, the area in which the male volume was the most vulnerable. Though Kinsey loved to count, like Heinz, he could at times be surprisingly imprecise with his numbers. He sometimes labeled a single case as "the average."

Even worse for Kinsey, his bête noire was cut from the same characterological cloth. As Weaver later noted in his autobiography, he also took "too much delight in precision." Beset by his own set of compulsions, Weaver could not mount a flight of stairs without counting every step. A collector by nature, Weaver amassed 160 different versions of *Alice's Adventures in Wonderland* published in forty-two languages and wrote a scholarly monograph on the translations. A major figure in twentieth-century science who coined the term "molecular genetics" in 1938, Weaver was interested in applying statistical theory to all branches of science. Aghast that Kinsey did not have a trained statistician on board—Clyde Martin lacked a Ph.D.—Weaver wrote the president of the Rockefeller Foundation in 1951 that "I know of no evidence that Kinsey understands the underlying statistical character of his work." Weaver argued that his sex histories did not constitute a random sample and that his data thus could not claim to be representative. In that same memo, Weaver also expressed his disgust that Kinsey was using foundation dollars to collect erotic books and pay for a "full-time pornographer," an allusion to William Dellenback, the photographer whom Kinsey had hired.

To placate this éminence grise, the head honchos at the Rockefeller Foundation asked the American Statistical Association (ASA) to convene a statistical advisory panel to evaluate the male volume. Weaver himself looked over the shoulders of the three preeminent academics who completed the first draft of their report at the end of 1951. Its findings were balanced, as these number crunchers, unlike Weaver, were sensitive to the immense challenges that Kinsey faced. Declaring that "our overall impression is...favorable," the ASA panel noted that Kinsey's sexological survey was "superior" to what came before, but involved "many problems of measurement and sampling, for some of which there appear...to be no satisfactory solutions." (This conclusion resonates with the reigning consensus among contemporary sex researchers that while survey data are often messy, they still can provide some useful baselines.) As the ASA report argued, Kinsey's sample of 5,300 males was not random—certain groups such as prisoners and Indiana residents were overrepresented—but it would have been impossible to come up with a sample that was truly representative of the American population as a whole. Published three years later as a 338-page book, *Statistical Problems of the Kinsey Report* captures the essence of the matter. Kinsey's data were not quite as definitive as he often insisted, but merely constituted, as he conceded in his introduction, "a first step in the accumulation of a body of scientific fact." Weaver, however, was not satisfied, since he had hoped that the

ASA findings would destroy Kinsey. Remaining on the offensive, Weaver wrote to a colleague that he objected "strenuously to the direct and implied interpretations which one finds throughout his two books." But Kinsey had weathered the storm, and not much damage was done to his reputation.

———

Like Steve Jobs a half century later, this control freak would also master the product launch. On Thursday, August 20, 1953, at precisely 7:00 a.m. on both coasts and 6:30 a.m. Central Standard Time, Kinsey suddenly commandeered the national conversation. That was when the ironclad press embargo on his second survey, *Sexual Behavior in the Human Female*, was lifted. Despite its eight hundred pages of dense, humorless prose and the steep eight-dollar tab (more than twice the cost of a typical hardback), this report on the sex lives of 5,900 American women would rise to the top of the bestseller list even faster than the male volume, of which 250,000 copies priced at "sex-fifty" had already been sold. On "K-Day in the U.S.A.," as the occasion was dubbed by journalists, dozens of major newspapers jumped at the chance to summarize Kinsey's findings on the front page. Several weeks later, after the biologist had graced the pages of some thirty mass-circulation magazines, one New York woman quipped, "I wonder what angle *Popular Mechanics* will use." For the rest of 1953, Kinsey was one of the most talked about personages in America, right up there with President Dwight Eisenhower and England's newly crowned Elizabeth II. Hollywood stars also combed through his latest opus and formulated opinions. Acknowledging that she belonged to the 50 percent of women who, according to Kinsey, slept in the nude, actress Zsa Zsa Gabor questioned whether the text was lively enough, complaining, "The whole thing is too scientific."

While *U.S. News and World Report* speculated that a "slick press agent, hired by Kinsey, was behind the build-up," this super micromanager had orchestrated this flurry of publicity all by his lonesome. That spring, Kinsey had invited thirty journalists to attend—in groups of ten—four days of seminars in Bloomington on the forthcoming female volume. No galleys were sent out; the book had to be read on-site. Kinsey carefully organized the program, which, besides lectures, lunches, and a tour, also included lots of late-night frank, scientific sex talk with him. All reporters signed an agreement stipulating that they wouldn't publish their stories, which could contain no more than five thousand words, until

K-Day. He also obtained the right to review the final drafts for factual errors. Over the summer, Kinsey continued to stay on top of every detail. He monitored the list of review copies, which would not be sent out until late August, and all the advertising and promotional copy. He also increased the security measures in his office, burning the trash in the wastebaskets and putting the janitors under surveillance.

In late August, just as the press frenzy was at its peak, Prok himself was nowhere to be found. While his office announced that he was away on vacation, the workaholic hardly ever thought of anything besides the sex business; and to him, days off were anathema. In fact, Kinsey was ensconced in his refuge at California's San Quentin State Prison, where he was busy interviewing prisoners about their sexual practices. As he told the warden, "This is the last place anyone will look for me." Having completed two groundbreaking books, he was not interested in resting on his laurels. He was just warming up. Noting that "sex is here to stay," Kinsey was determined to publish at least seven more volumes covering such topics as sexual adjustment in prison populations, the legal aspects of sex behavior, prostitution, and the heterosexual-homosexual balance. To knock off these items on his checklist, Kinsey estimated that his team needed to collect a total of 100,000 sex histories, about 85,000 more than they then had on hand.

But Kinsey never published another word on sex. Just a year after "K-Day," with the congressional committee, led by Republican Carroll Reece, having completed its public hearings on "subversion" in nonprofits, the Rockefeller Foundation's Dean Rusk officially caved in, issuing a press release stating that Kinsey was now "in a position to obtain support from other sources." His two surveys had been profitable, but Kinsey, as Rusk knew well, actually had no other means of funding at the ready.

The loss of both dollars and prestige proved devastating. With his nerves frayed and his heart, which he called his "stubborn organ," failing—due to the bout with rheumatic fever in childhood, it had always been weak—Kinsey was close to suicidal despair. "If I can't work," he repeatedly told friends in his final years, "I would rather die." He forced himself to court potential benefactors, but he was ill suited to the task. While he could talk up his research, he "talked down to people," as Glenway Wescott later recalled. His efforts were nearly all in vain. In an effort to boost his spirits, in the fall of 1955, Kinsey went on a seven-week trip to a half dozen European countries. During this "vacation," the sixty-one-year-old scientist did little but collect information about sex. Portugal was a disappointment because, as he wrote in his journal, "Didn't get much on sex here." In London, accompanied by Mac, he hung out at Piccadilly Circus on a Saturday night between 8 p.m. and 3 a.m. to do a crucial count—his tally of both male and female prostitutes came to about one thousand. In Copenhagen, Kinsey met with an archivist who possessed the manuscripts of Hans Christian Andersen to verify his hypothesis that the fairy-tale writer was a closeted homosexual (a view now shared by most Andersen biographers). "The world simply must learn," Kinsey observed after examining the evidence, "that persons with homosexual histories and exclusively homosexual histories have been… important."

Kinsey had long worked to expose the disparity between the public and private. "I expect extramarital coitus," the emerging sex researcher had written to Clyde Martin in 1940, "is in 80 percent of the really successful businessman's history….God, what a gap between social front and reality!" In an America burdened by rigid sexual norms, Kinsey was eager to prove that he was not the only alpha male who liked sex with other men or who racked up big orgasm numbers. However, he was also convinced that no one had the right to do unto him as he had done unto others; he felt entitled to his own secrets long after he was gone. When told by a friend that someone would probably write his biography, he protested, "Nonsense! The progress of science depends upon knowledge. It has nothing to do with personalities." But this anti-introspective man could never acknowledge that for him, as for his predecessors in sexology such as Havelock Ellis, validation for his particular sexual tastes was a primary driver behind the scholarly oeuvre.

After suffering a heart attack on June 1, 1956, Kinsey was hospitalized for a week. Even though the prognosis was grim—his heart was enlarged and he was experiencing constant fibrillation—he refused to slow down, as his doctors advised. That summer, despite his weakened state, he continued to give lectures. In July, he spoke about sex education at a conference of high school biology teachers that met in Bloomington. Without notes, Kinsey gave a performance that was, as a colleague later put it, "of a well-nigh somnambulistic perfection in its concentratedness, directness, plainness, and phrasing." A month later, Clara drove an ashen Kinsey to Purdue University in Lafayette to deliver an address before the National Deans Association, in which he managed to weave in a characteristic insult, noting that men engage in less sex as they age and "then they become deans."

On August 18, Kinsey asked Indiana University president Herman Wells to come to his home to discuss some business matters related to his Institute for Sex Research. After meeting with the out-of-breath Kinsey, who was lying in bed propped up on pillows, Wells pulled Clara outside and told her to insist that her husband stop working. "No, it is impossible to do it," she responded. "He went to Purdue last week when he shouldn't have, and there is nothing you or I can do. He is just—this is his obsession."

A week later, Kinsey died of pneumonia.

Lindbergh with his wife, Anne Morrow, in 1930, when he was at the height of his fame. In a wife, the Lone Eagle sought a copilot, and some of the couple's happiest times together were spent in the air.

5

Aviation: Charles Lindbergh

At Home in Flight

A pilot doesn't feel at home in a plane until he's flown it for
thousands of miles. At first it's like moving into a new house.
—Charles Lindbergh, *The Spirit of St. Louis* (1953)

On Monday, February 21, 1916, the fourteen-year-old Charles Augustus Lindbergh was excused from school. The tenth grader had something more important to do than attend his classes at Sidwell Friends—the exclusive private
school, then located on I Street in northwest Washington, D.C. (and which,
over the past century, has educated numerous presidential offspring, including
the two Obama girls). At ten o'clock that morning, the adolescent had an ap-
pointment at the White House with the president of the United States, Woodrow
Wilson.

The future international celebrity, who would often meet with heads of state
after becoming the first pilot to cross the Atlantic in 1927, had not yet done
anything of note. He was tagging along with his father, Charles August Lindbergh, called "C.A." by the family, a fifth-term representative from Minnesota's
Sixth Congressional District. To pass on some gifts from a Native American—a
few velvet pillows for Mr. Wilson and a pair of moccasins for Mrs. Wilson—the
Republican congressman had managed to book a minute of the president's time.

This was not the first time that the young Charles would see a president in
the flesh. At Union Station, the boy, who by the late 1930s would himself be
considered presidential timber (and whose hypothetical defeat of FDR in the
election of 1940 Philip Roth explored in his 2004 novel, *The Plot Against America*), had once spotted Theodore Roosevelt sitting in the backseat of a limousine.
In Rock Creek Park, he had stumbled upon William Howard Taft taking a stroll

behind his horse-drawn carriage. "In Washington," as Lindbergh later recalled in his Pulitzer Prize–winning autobiography, *The Spirit of St. Louis* (published on September 14, 1953, the same day as Kinsey's female survey), "one lived with famous figures, saw history in the making."

Home was then a Washington, D.C., boardinghouse where he shared a bedroom with his mother, Evangeline; his father maintained a separate residence. Though his parents could not stand each other, they could not divorce on account of the congressman's political career. The young Charles was constantly shuttling from one temporary way station to the next; over the next few years, he would attend four other high schools. From his birth until the fall of 1920, when he started college, he would live at nearly two dozen different addresses.

At nine thirty, the Native American, a man named Mr. Lyons, appeared, and off the trio went to the White House.

A half hour later, looking over at Congressman Lindbergh, President Wilson stated, "The gifts are beautiful. I am delighted to receive them. Mrs. Wilson will also be pleased."

At that moment, C. A. Lindbergh introduced his son.

"How are you?" asked the president, as he shook the adolescent's hand.

"Very well, thank you," responded Charles.

And that was it. President Wilson got back to thinking about the nation's affairs; that evening, he would confer with three top congressional leaders on how to handle the "Lusitania Crisis," the foreign policy mess that had resulted from the sinking of a British ship by a German submarine a year earlier and was about to lead to U.S. involvement in the Great War.

After Charles returned to the boardinghouse, his mother peppered him with questions about the events of the day. When asked how he felt about meeting the president, the normally reticent boy blurted out, "It didn't faze me any because the president is just a man, even if he is president."

————

Being just a man would not satisfy Charles Augustus Lindbergh; from boyhood on, he wanted to be a superman. For this fiercely ambitious loner, who, as his father once put it, never had much interest in "things on earth," the presidency would not be a lofty enough goal. To chase his dreams, he would head for the heavens. "The very fact of flying," he once wrote, "denied old concepts of impossibility." For his extraordinary derring-do, he succeeded in becoming the most famous person on the planet in the late 1920s and early 1930s.

As a pilot flying during an age when there was no air traffic to control, Lindbergh would enjoy hovering alone over the world like God himself. "I lived on a higher plane than the skeptics on the ground," he once observed. "In flying, I tasted a wine of the gods of which they could know nothing." A fawning press corps would agree that the svelte, six-foot, three-inch, blond and blue-eyed aviator possessed divine powers. "Lindbergh is no ordinary man," observed the *Sunday Express* after his historic achievement. "He is the stuff heroes are made of. He defied death and…dazzles the world."

Lindbergh would never stop attempting larger-than-life deeds. Soon after returning from Paris, he became determined to conquer time itself. "If a man could learn to fly," he wondered, "why could he not learn to live forever?" Throughout the 1930s, Lindbergh worked closely with Dr. Alexis Carrel, a physician who had won the Nobel Prize in Medicine in 1912, on various scientific experiments in the hope of making his dream of eternal life a reality.

And in the 1950s, he began engaging in sexual exploits that few mere mortals could even contemplate. To follow his outsized libido, this father of six children with Anne Morrow—the couple's first, Charles Augustus Jr., murdered at the age of twenty months in the "crime of the century" in 1932, was followed by Jon, Land, Anne, Scott, and Reeve—would disappear from his family for months at a time. Taking on a Superman-like alias, Careu Kent, he started three new European families. Unbeknownst to his wife (and to A. Scott Berg, who penned the Pulitzer Prize–winning 1998 biography authorized by her), for the last two decades of his life, Lindbergh would regularly visit his three German mistresses, with whom he would sire a total of seven more children, on "love trips" to Europe. "Only an obsessive-compulsive person like my father could have managed to keep these three families secret," his youngest child, the writer Reeve Lindbergh, told me. And he of the preternatural sexual appetite also squeezed in his fun. In the 1960s, Lindbergh also arranged trysts all over the world with his steady American girlfriend, a blonde and blue-eyed Pan Am stewardess forty years his junior. Moreover, during his trips to Africa and Asia on behalf of environmental nonprofits such as the World Wildlife Fund, the sexagenarian had numerous flings with young locals. "When I was a teenager, my grandfather used to tell us [the family] that he would sleep with the oldest woman in the tribe whenever he went to Kenya," Kristina Lindbergh, his eldest grandchild, said to me in a recent interview. "We didn't think much of it at the time. Given what we know now, I wouldn't be surprised if we have some more relatives."

Like Kinsey, Lindbergh viewed sex in purely mechanistic terms. For this high-flier, women were machines whose services he could use every now and then, rather than fellow human beings with whom he could build intimate relationships. This pattern had roots in his boyhood, when, to escape loneliness, he gravitated not toward bugs, as did Kinsey, but toward the inanimate. At ten, he became infatuated with the "new member of the family," the Model T that his mother christened "Maria" (pronounced "Mariah"). A year later, though his feet could still barely reach the gas pedal, the boy was already a more able driver than either parent. "Maria," he later mused, "brought modern science to our home, and nothing else attracted me as much." In 1914, he used it to chauffeur C.A. during his congressional campaign. "While I wanted very much to have my father win," Lindbergh later recalled, "my primary interest [was]...to be with him and drive Maria." Charles and "Maria" were inseparable; he often sat beside her, making notes in a logbook he kept about her performance. In his senior year of high school in his native Minnesota, he ogled not girls but the latest gadgets in the local hardware store window. At the University of Wisconsin, the painfully shy engineering student "preferred to ride my motorcycle...[than to take on] the additional problem of women." And in *We*, the bestselling quickie book completed after his return from Paris, he told the love story between him and his plane. "*The Spirit of St. Louis*," he wrote, "is...like a living creature, gliding along smoothly, happily.... We shared our experiences together, each feeling beauty, life, and death as keenly, each dependent on the other's loyalty. We have made this flight across the ocean, not *I* or *it*."

After the socially awkward aviator became a celebrity, he finally turned his attention to what he called "my girl-meeting project." For the world's most eligible bachelor, looking for the perfect wife resembled designing an exquisite new machine. "The physical characteristics I wanted in a woman," he later wrote, "were not difficult to describe—good health, good form, good sight and hearing. Such qualities could be outlined like the specifications for an airplane. I wanted to marry a girl who liked flying."

In October 1928, at the age of twenty-six, he went out on his first date, which naturally took place in the air. A year earlier, President Calvin Coolidge had introduced him to the American ambassador to Mexico, Dwight Morrow. Now Lindbergh took his daughter Anne for a spin around Long Island in a small, open-cockpit biplane. Anne passed the test with flying colors; she had no trouble steering and gave every indication that she would evolve into an exceptional copilot (which she, in fact, did). A few days later, Lindbergh invited her on a less consequential "ground date." While driving her home, he proposed. Stunned, Anne initially demurred, responding, "You must be kidding! You don't know me."

"Oh, I do know you," the smitten aviator protested. (In the decades to come, his motor would continue to rev up quickly.) Then, without further ado, came the requisite flying lessons; the wedding took place in May 1929. "At first, my mother believed his awkwardness was rooted in his Midwestern simplicity," Reeve Lindbergh explained to me.

In the early years of the marriage, Anne's rivals were of the mechanized variety. In March 1933, on the first anniversary of the kidnapping of Charles Jr. and right after the birth of Jon, with Anne at his side, Lindbergh took off on a nine-month trip around the world. Repeatedly ignoring and humiliating his wife—in front of a friend who was putting them up for the night, he once dragged her to bed by the ear—he was more interested in spending quality time with his specially designed Lockheed Sirius, *Tingmissartoq* (Eskimo for "he who flies like a big bird"), than with her. For the engineering geek, one of the highlights of this expedition was the night in Scotland that he spent fixing the plane's broken cable during a cold rainstorm.

Lindbergh and his wife would live in houses in beautiful settings all over the world—in suburban New Jersey and Connecticut, England, France, Switzerland, and Hawaii—but he rarely stayed home. After the birth of each of their children, he took to the air, leaving his family for a long trip. In fact, Lindbergh spent more hours in some of the Jennys—the World War I–era planes that he flew in the early 1920s—than in some of those homes. "Charles," a family friend has stated, "was only interested in houses so that he'd have a place to 'park' Anne and the children." By the 1950s, when his piloting days were over, he took to flying around the globe in "tourist class"—he received a nominal consulting fee from Pan Am for conducting inspections—to escape from his various human entanglements. As if he were still flying on a monoplane like *The Spirit of St. Louis*, he liked to travel light. Refusing to check any baggage, he would carry a trench coat draped around his briefcase, which contained just two nylon wash-and-wear shirts along with two pairs of trousers, underwear, and socks.

But while Lindbergh's severe interpersonal anxiety would wreak havoc on his family—in the 1950s, Anne, confused and infuriated by her husband's erratic behavior and prolonged absences, went into a deep depression for which she sought psychoanalytic relief—it turned out to be essential in cementing his legend. Before Lindbergh, pilots were reluctant to try to win the $25,000 prize offered by hotelier Raymond Orteig for the first nonstop flight from New York to Paris without a copilot, as they worried about their ability to man flight controls for more than thirty hours. In contrast, Lindbergh was more nervous about sitting that long in close proximity to another human being. "By flying alone," he wrote in *The Spirit of St. Louis*, "I've gained in...freedom. My movements weren't restricted by someone else's temperament, health or knowledge....I've not been enmeshed in petty quarreling and heavy organizational problems." For Lindbergh, human relationships would always be synonymous with Sturm und Drang. But by removing from his plane the weight of what he considered nonessentials, such as another passenger as well as a radio, the Lone Eagle increased its fuel capacity. As it turned out, the "two-ton flying gas tank" was exactly what "Lucky Lindy" needed to survive—the two-man crews were crashing left and right—and to march directly into the history books.

———

A couple of months after the minute with President Wilson, C. A. Lindbergh pulled his son out of school again. The congressman was seeking the Republican nomination for senator, and he needed his trusty chauffeur to drive him to his speeches during the spring campaign.

Catching the train in Washington on Saturday, April 22, 1916, father and son arrived in Minneapolis at 7 a.m. on Monday the twenty-fourth. Their first order of business was to pick up the family's new car, having recently sold off Charles's beloved Maria, which, due to its hand crank, was no longer state-of-the-art. At his son's suggestion, C.A. decided to purchase a self-starting Saxon Six. When they arrived at the Saxon store, the salesman, as Charles recorded in his diary, "took me to a side street and taught me to run the car. The Saxon he said was the best car he ever rode in." Over the next several weeks, Charles drove his father, who ran on an antiwar platform, some three thousand miles around the state. In the primary held on June 19, C.A. Lindbergh, who had decided to give up his House seat, suffered a crushing defeat, finishing a distant fourth. He would throw his hat into the ring a few more times—running in a gubernatorial primary in 1918 and another Senate primary in 1923—but he never came close to holding elective office again. After a series of business ventures failed, he was reduced to living in flophouses. "I am at my rope's end," he wrote to Charles in 1921, "for I can sell nothing." When he died of a brain tumor in 1924, he was nearly destitute.

This was not the first time that a Lindbergh's political career ended in despair. C. A. Lindbergh's father, Ola Mansson, born in 1808 in Skåne, a province in southern Sweden, had served a dozen years in the Swedish Parliament before being caught embezzling money from the Bank of Sweden. Just as Mansson lost his seat in Parliament, his wife—and the mother of his eight children—discovered that he had taken up with a mistress nearly thirty years his junior. The product of this illicit liaison, C.A. was born in Stockholm in 1858. The following year, abandoning his Swedish family, Mansson immigrated with his lover and infant son to America. After settling on a Minnesota farm and renaming himself August Lindbergh (an amalgam of the Swedish words for "linden tree" and "mountain"), he would father five more children with his common-law wife. Though Charles Lindbergh, like his father, would never learn all the details about August Lindbergh's checkered history, he would follow in his footsteps. He, too, would establish families on both sides of the Atlantic (though the aviator would start by siring children in America rather than in Europe). And in 1958, exactly a century after the birth of C.A., a German woman slightly more than half Charles Lindbergh's age would bring into the world the first of his seven illegitimate European children.

After finishing law school at the University of Michigan in 1883, C. A. Lindbergh settled in Little Falls, Minnesota, a small town on the Mississippi River located in the middle of the state. The six-footer with the dimpled chin—a feature shared by his son—was considered by many to be "the handsomest man in Little Falls." In 1887, C.A., who had built a thriving law practice as well as an extensive real estate business, married Mary LaFond, an attractive young woman born on the Minnesota frontier who was the daughter of his landlord. She died a decade later, leaving him with two daughters, Lillian and Eva. In 1900, the forty-two-year-old widower began wooing Evangeline Lodge Land, a twenty-four-year-old graduate of the University of Michigan. The daughter of Charles Land, a Detroit dentist and inventor, and Evangeline Lodge, this chemistry major, once known as "the most beautiful girl at Ann Arbor," had just arrived in Little Falls to take up a position as a schoolteacher. While Evangeline Land was bright, she was subject to violent mood swings. Rage attacks would alternate with periods of extreme detachment, for which she would later earn the nickname "Stone Face." Of her erratic behavior, her stepdaughter Eva would once muse, "Only insanity explains it." As Charles later put it, his mother had a "flashy Irish temper" and was "often unpredictable." A case in point: in December 1900, Evangeline refused to teach in her drafty fifth-floor classroom and moved some laboratory equipment downstairs. When the superintendent told her that to do so was to violate school regulations, she walked out on the spot, never to return. Not long after tying the knot in March 1901, C.A. and Evangeline, along with the two daughters from his first marriage, moved into a new three-story, thirteen-room house on a 120-acre estate in Little Falls. Charles, the couple's only child, was born in February 1902.

Charles Lindbergh's earliest memory was of a devastating trauma. On the morning of August 6, 1905, Lindholm Manor, as Evangeline dubbed the "dream house" that C.A. had built for her, suddenly caught fire. After being rushed down the steps, Charles saw a huge cloud of smoke; his nurse told him not to look back. "Where is my father—my mother?" the terrified three-year-old then yelled to her. "What will happen to my toys?" While no one perished, his family was never the same. C.A. built a new house upon the same foundation, but the next iteration was just one and a half stories. Gone were the cook, maid, and nurse who had slept in the servants' quarters on the third floor of the old house. Having recently moved out of the master bedroom, C.A. was no longer willing to invest much in the marriage.

While Lindbergh's father was more stable than his mother, his old man was also no joy to be around. Before her wedding, Evangeline had wondered if C.A. might be "a bit too sharp-witted," and these concerns turned out to be well grounded. Described by contemporaries as "austere," "severe," and "eccentric," and by one biographer as "sadistic," C.A. could not stop denigrating his nearest and dearest. "I do not tell people when I am pleased," he once wrote to his daughter Eva. "I tell them when I am not pleased." Not averse to slapping his wife, C.A. once slimed her as "a bloodsucker" within earshot of the boy, whom he would repeatedly berate with epithets such as "fool." And like his father (and his son), C.A. was a womanizer. At times, Evangeline's fury nearly devolved into violence. She once grabbed a gun and held it to her husband's head, threatening to shoot. After C.A. was elected to Congress in 1906, the couple worked out their informal separation agreement. "I would rather be dead a hundred times [than live with her]," C.A. once wrote to his daughter Eva. In order for Charles to maintain some kind of relationship with his father, he would attend school in Washington and go back to the Minnesota farm only in the summer.

While Charles would later insist that he had enjoyed an idyllic Tom Sawyer–like childhood, his early behavior suggests the presence of deep emotional wounds. With his two high-maintenance parents engaged in a perpetual cold war, the boy kept looking for order and comfort wherever he could find it. For emotional sustenance, he turned to nature. In the rebuilt Minnesota house, Charles developed a fondness for the screened-in sleeping porch in the back that overlooked the roaring Mississippi River. A decade and a half before hopping into his first plane, he had already found a home in the sky. He often slept on a cot in this "bedroom," even in the Minnesota winter. "I was," noted the aviator years later, "in close contact with sun, wind, rain, and stars." Like other hard-core collectors such as Kinsey, he also learned to bond with things rather than people. "As a boy," he later wrote, "I had collected about everything—stones, butterflies, coins, turtles, cigarette cards, cigar bands, stamps, tin cans, lead pipe, and burned-out electric-light bulbs, among other items." During his first two decades, Lindbergh's favorite flesh-and-blood companions were the family's farm dogs—such as Tody, a dachshund-stretch mongrel, and Spot, a brown-and-white hunting dog—who doubled as his bedmates. He formed few friendships with peers; his mother would have to pay neighborhood boys to play with him. In Washington, his classmates nicknamed the socially obtuse loner "Cheese" (his name sounded like the particularly smelly Dutch Limburger). Obsessed with self-reliance, C.A. tried to convince Charles that he was not missing much. "I have one thing that I take pride in above all others," C.A. would write to his teenage son, "and that is that you are able to buck the world alone and independent if it was necessary. I love that quality in a person, and especially in you, because it was hardly forced upon you." But little did the self-absorbed C.A. realize that Charles could not have done otherwise. Adhering to this paternal injunction, Charles Lindbergh would forever view his lack of connection with fellow human beings as an asset to celebrate rather than a source of anguish to mourn. And in solitude, he would always exult.

With his father out of Congress, in the fall of 1917 Charles began his senior year of high school in Little Falls. His father also returned to Minnesota, but he continued to live under a separate roof. The emotionally needy Evangeline now treated Charles as if he were her husband and confidant rather than her son. At fifteen, he ran the household. The precocious Mr. Fix-It threw himself into both winterizing and mechanizing the farm. He built a well in the basement for which he did all the plumbing himself. He also constructed a concrete duck pond, which he named "Moo Pond" after the Ojibway term for "dirt"—the neat-nik was keenly aware that "a duck pond would almost always be dirty"—as well as a suspension bridge out of barbed wire. He began breeding a variety of animals including Guernsey cattle, Shropshire sheep, and Toulouse geese, which he sold in Minneapolis. The small farm became one of the most high-tech affairs in the area. Charles ordered a three-wheeled tractor from LaCrosse, which he assembled himself, and installed a souped-up Empire Milking Machine, which he also marketed to other farmers. Charles preferred managing the farm to attending his classes; only physics and mechanical drawing were of any interest. Unwilling to do any homework, he nearly flunked out. "I was," he later recalled, "rescued by World War I." In early 1918, with food in short supply, the principal announced that students could get academic credit for farmwork. That final semester, Charles made only one more trip to school—to pick up his diploma on June 5. After the armistice was signed in November 1918, he gradually turned the farm back over to tenants and started thinking about college. "It was a difficult and rather heartbreaking procedure giving up the stock and machinery," he later wrote. Like Kinsey, as an adolescent Lindbergh had developed close ties to his farm's animals and gadgets, but not to his parents or to any other human beings.

In the fall of 1920, Lindbergh jumped on his motorcycle—a twin-cylinder Excelsior—and drove the 350 miles to Madison, Wisconsin. He selected the University of Wisconsin less for its impressive engineering school than for the lakes near campus. As he later explained, "I could not be happy living long away from water." Psychologically fused with her son, Evangeline could not abide the thought of losing her longtime roommate; she had already taken the train to Madison to find them an apartment. This unusual living arrangement had the neighbors whispering about what had brought the apparently unmarried middle-aged woman and the dashing college student together. Once again, Lindbergh refused to do even the minimum to stay afloat academically. He barely passed most classes, and he failed English. On a freshman essay, "An Ideal Student," in which he preached the "fundamentals of hygiene," his instructor gave him an F, commenting, "Again, some excellent touches, but marred by an irritating profusion of mechanical errors. Please arrange for a conference at once." (He ignored the request.) Extracurricular activities—the ROTC program and the rifle and pistol teams—were all that he cared about. "I was on academic probation when I entered my sophomore year," he later wrote. "So I decided to leave the university before I received official notification to do so."

In March 1922, he fled to Lincoln, Nebraska, to begin flying school. Reacting like a jilted lover, his mother was nearly speechless. "*Il est très difficile*," she wrote to him in her broken French—though college-educated, she was no foreign language whiz—right after his departure, "*de viver* [*sic*] [live] *dans cet 'flat' mais très necessaire. Il est aussi très difficile d'exprimer mes sentiments* so I'll not try to." Evangeline, who began inundating (and embarrassing) her son with daily letters, would not let go easily. "There has been no word from you for 2 weeks and 2 days," she stated a few years later in a missive, in which she threatened a visit unless he wrote back right away, "and you have not written me for 2 weeks and 5 days—exact reckoning." Only by taking to the air would Lindbergh manage to gain his freedom from his overbearing mother.

For the next couple of years, he eked out a living as a stunt pilot, entertaining the public in more than seven hundred barnstorming flights. In March 1924, to get his hands on higher-performing planes, the technophile enlisted in the U.S. Army. In the flight training program in San Antonio, Texas, Lindbergh was in his element. "Military training," he later recalled, "taught me precision and the perfection of flying techniques." Relishing his courses in aerodynamics, meteorology, and bombing methods, the college dropout metamorphosed into a stellar student. "For the first time in my experience," he later wrote, "school and life became both rationally and emotionally connected." The following March, Lindbergh graduated first in his class—he had been one of 104 entering students—and received his commission as a second lieutenant in the Air Service Reserve Corps.

But in the Army, "Slim," as the 145-pound cadet was called, still could not make a friend. His main way to connect with others was to choreograph practical jokes, and he specialized not in the harmless—say, dropping toothpaste into a snoring mouth—but in the sadistic. To unnerve a soldier sleeping in the buff, who boasted about nights with prostitutes in San Antonio's "Spick Town"—such racist vernacular was common in the 1920s—Lindbergh devised a startling contrapasso. "I suggested," he noted proudly more than forty years after the fact, "that we paint the penis green." And he did not stop there. To ensure a rude awakening, Lindbergh also had the erect member lassoed with some string, which he then hooked up to the ceiling while another soldier tugged on it from outside the barracks.

After moving to St. Louis in the fall of 1925 to run airmail routes for the Robertson Aircraft Corporation, this envious virgin, too shy to get anywhere near a nubile woman, was still taunting fellow pilots who pursued sexual adventures. Lindbergh would not allow a roommate, Phil Love, to talk on the phone to his girlfriend—he would make a racket by crashing pots and pans—and every time Love went out on a date, Lindbergh would stick frogs or lizards in his bed. And he almost killed another roommate, Bud Gurney, who, after a night on the town, took a couple of gulps from a water jug into which Lindbergh had poured kerosene. In his last few months in St. Louis, "Slim" lived alone, as no one would dare room with him anymore.

"I'll organize a flight to Paris!"

Lindbergh later recalled in his memoir that the idea first came to him in September 1926, as he was high up in the moonlit sky, en route from Peoria to Chicago.

Five months earlier, Robertson's chief pilot had inaugurated its airmail route—the second in the nation—which went from St. Louis to Chicago via Springfield and Peoria. On the afternoon of April 15, 1926, a crowd of a couple hundred had given Lindbergh (along with the two pilots whom he had hired to work under him) a grand send-off, which was widely covered by the press. "We pilots…all felt," he later wrote, "that we were taking part in an event which pointed the way toward a new and marvelous era." But within a few months, the monotony of the task—the contract called for five round-trips a week between St. Louis and Chicago—was leaving him feeling apathetic and restless. He and his team had mastered the challenge of boring through the night sky, completing more than 99 percent of their scheduled flights.

As he looked down at the lights on farmhouses on the outskirts of Peoria, Lindbergh kept turning over in his mind the crash in New York a few days earlier of a Paris-bound flight piloted by the Frenchman René Fonck, which had killed two of his three crew members. Fonck's three-engine Sikorsky biplane, he was certain, had been doomed by its weight. As he approached Ottawa, Illinois—about ninety miles from Chicago—he began fantasizing about a sexy new biplane, the Wright-Bellanca, and its efficiency. "In a Bellanca filled with fuel tanks," he speculated from the cockpit of his old World War I Army plane, "I could fly on all night like the moon."

Getting up at daybreak the next morning, Lindbergh flew back to St. Louis. As soon as he returned to his boardinghouse near Lambert Field, located in farmland ten miles northwest of the business district, he thought through the steps that he would have to take to get to Paris. So he took out a pad and began making lists.

For Lindbergh, travel and list making were already intimately connected. A few years earlier, he had compiled an exhaustive set of lists documenting all the trips he had taken as a child, which he then plotted on a massive map of the United States, color-coordinated by his means of transportation. In 1913, he and his mother had boarded the *Colon*, a second-class boat, which took them to Panama. Besides the train treks to Washington and Detroit (where he visited his grandparents), he also recorded various automobile excursions, such as a forty-day slog with his mother to California — he did the driving — in the Saxon Six in 1916.

For his new venture, he came up with seven lists: "Action," "Advantages," "Results," "Co-operation," "Equipment," "Maps," and "Landmarks."

The lists reveal the nature of the man, who was all about practicality and efficiency. Each of the numbered points below the headings contained just a few words. "Action" was the longest list, with eight, which included such items as "2. Propaganda" (publicity), "3. Backers," and "8. Advertising." Having managed the family farm, the twenty-four-year-old was already well versed in the ways of the business world. Under "Advantages," after writing that he would promote interest in aviation in both St. Louis and the nation as a whole, he let a bit of his personal passion seep in; in point 5, the lifelong machine lover noted how the flight would "demonstrate perfection of modern equipment." "Results" was the shortest list, with just two points: "1. Successful completion," which, as he jotted down, meant "winning $25,000 prize to cover expenses," and its polar opposite, "2. Complete failure," about which he chose not to elaborate.

"That...will do for a start," Lindbergh later wrote of his own reaction to this initial set of lists. "I'll add to it, improve it, and clarify it as time passes." Thus would his nervous tic propel him across the Atlantic the following May. Out of his lists of his equipment and flying procedures, which he would constantly check and recheck on this and every other flight he would ever take, would later also come the safety checklist. As Reeve Lindbergh has noted, this legacy of her "obsessively meticulous" father, which has saved the lives of countless pilots, may have been even more important than his historic flight.

A few weeks later, Lindbergh called his first potential backer, Earl A. Thompson, a wealthy St. Louis insurance executive, to whom he had given flying lessons. Offered the choice between a meeting at his office or at his home at 1 Hortense Place, Lindbergh opted for the latter. But after a maid escorted him into the living room, Lindbergh had second thoughts. As he later described the scene,

"I don't seem to fit into a city parlor. It would be easier to talk on the flying field."

Away from his workplace, which to him felt homier than the magnate's mansion, Lindbergh lost his self-confidence. Ticking off the items on his "Advantages" list, he mentioned to Thompson that a flight to Paris "would show people what airplanes can do." While the evening was not a disaster—Thompson remained interested—Lindbergh was unable to pry any cash from him.

But Lindbergh had better luck a few days later with Albert Lambert, the former Olympic golfer and aviation aficionado—Orville Wright had taught him to fly—whom he visited at his office rather than at his Hortense Place home (which was located next door to Thompson's). Lambert, whose day job was running his family's pharmaceutical company, promised one thousand dollars. *"I feel that my New York–to–Paris flight is emerging from the stage of dreams,* Lindbergh thought as he drove back to the field in his secondhand Ford. *"I have an organization under way.*

Like other obsessives, Lindbergh was clueless about how to handle intimate relationships, but he did develop a knack for networking with the powerful. This lover of propriety also learned how to dress for success. That fall, he shelled out $100 to buy a "traveling outfit," which consisted of seven sartorial items including a silk scarf and felt hat for which, Lindbergh conceded, he "didn't have the slightest use." But the right impression, he realized, "may be as essential for my Paris flight as a plane." He soon assembled a team of investors that also featured Bill Robertson, his boss; Harry Knight, a stockbroker and the president of the St. Louis Flying Club; and Harold Bixby, a bigwig at the State National Bank and the president of the St. Louis Chamber of Commerce. These men all believed in Lindbergh and his lofty aspirations for aviation. Promising that they would handle the finances, they told him to worry only about the technical details of the flight. The man who was used to going it alone was deeply moved. "I went to them hoping only for financial aid," he later wrote, "and...I...found real partners in the venture."

With the dollars secured, Lindbergh tried to acquire the Wright-Bellanca that he had long lusted after. Over the next few months, dressed in his elegant new togs, he made three trips to Manhattan to visit with the plane's Italian-born designer, Giuseppe Bellanca. While Lindbergh was quoted a reasonable price— $15,000—Bellanca's business partner insisted on "managing the flight to Paris" and selecting the two-man crew. These conditions were deal breakers. Since the Wright-Bellanca was the only off-the-shelf product that could do the trick, Lindbergh was forced to put his own engineering skills to the test. This setback, he soon realized, turned out to have a silver lining. "Every part of [the new plane]," he noted, "can be designed for a single purpose.... I can inspect each detail before it's covered with fabric." In the end, he would control everything to do with *The Spirit of St. Louis.* Lindbergh was not only its pilot, but also its father; the first of his many children would be a machine. And like Pygmalion, he would fall in love with his own creation.

On Tuesday, February 22, 1927, racing against the clock — several other pilots were also finalizing plans to make the first transoceanic flight — Lindbergh boarded a train to San Diego to meet the management team of Ryan Airlines. Soon after his arrival, Lindbergh and Donald Hall, Ryan's chief engineer, squirreled themselves away in the company's huge drafting room. As Lindbergh rattled off the requirements for his dream machine, Hall sketched. When asked where to put the cockpits for the pilot and his navigator, Lindbergh responded, "I've thought about it a great deal.... I'd rather have extra gasoline than an extra man." Though surprised, Hall immediately understood that this specification would mean a shorter fuselage. Ryan's CEO then also got on board, and a deal was consummated. For just $10,580, Lindbergh could expect his plane within two months.

Staying in San Diego, Lindbergh supervised Hall's every move. He devised a list of three principles to guide the plane's construction — "efficiency in flight," "protection in a crack-up," and "pilot comfort." He told Hall, "I don't see why cockpit in the rear doesn't cover all three." The conscientious Hall, who would put in eighty-hour weeks (and once worked thirty-six hours straight), would come to depend on Lindbergh's judgment. The pilot spent part of every day at the Ryan plant, looking over Hall's shoulder; Lindbergh was also busy compiling and checking the lists in his little black notebook in which he kept track of the maps, weather information — particularly wind currents — and landmarks that he would need to study. In the third week of April, with his plane nearly completed, he purchased the twelve items on his emergency equipment list, including his Armbrust cup, which could convert his breath into drinking water, an air raft, and five cans of Army emergency rations (chocolatelike bars).

Lindbergh then churned out a new series of to-do lists for each of the four cities his plane was to be in — San Diego, St. Louis, New York, and Paris. With his anxiety mounting, these lists had a robotic quality; they referred to items that he was unlikely to forget. Under "N.Y. Take-Off," he mentioned the need to notify the papers and cable St. Louis and San Diego. "Paris Arrival" also covered just the basics plus a reminder to cable his mother. He had no list for "Paris Take-Off." "I . . . concentrated so intensely on the preparation and execution of the flight," he later wrote, "that I had thought little about what I would do after landing."

On May 20, 1927, at 7:52 a.m., *The Spirit of St. Louis* took off from Roosevelt Field in Long Island. Exactly thirty-three hours, thirty minutes, and twenty-nine and eight-tenths seconds later, Lindbergh landed in Le Bourget Airport in Paris. The pilot was stunned when nearly 150,000 "cheering French," as the *New York Times* noted the next day in its banner headline, greeted him and began carrying him off the field. Amid the frenzy, Lindbergh kept worrying about the welfare of his beloved traveling companion. "Are there any mechanics here?" he shouted to no avail. "I was afraid," he later wrote, "that *The Spirit of St. Louis* might be seriously injured." French officials whisked Lindbergh away to a big hangar, where the American ambassador to France, Myron T. Herrick, congratulated him. Herrick, who would laud Lindbergh in the foreword to *We* as "an example of American idealism, character and conduct," offered the pilot shelter at his elegant residence at no. 2, Avenue d'Iena. Though Lindbergh was exhausted—he also had not slept his last night in New York—he insisted on seeing *The Spirit of St. Louis* before turning in. After a careful inspection, he discovered "that a few hours of work would make my plane air-worthy again." A relieved Lindbergh then stepped into the Renault, which took him to the ambassador's mansion by the Seine. After slipping into borrowed pajamas in the blue-and-gold guest bedroom, he provided laconic answers to the questions posed by reporters while sipping milk and munching on a roll. At last, at 4:15 a.m., he fell into the arms of Morpheus.

When Lindbergh awoke a little after noon on Sunday, May 22, 1927, he was already a luminary known throughout the world. The front page of newspapers in countless countries carried news of little else. That afternoon, he stepped out onto the balcony to wave to those who had been gathering below for hours, chanting, "Vive Lindbergh! Vive l'Amérique!" His privacy was a thing of the past. "If I had gone around the block," he later noted, "I would have been leading a parade." The hero was in constant demand. Decked out in a new tuxedo made by a Paris tailor, he shuttled from one ceremonial function to the next, collecting awards and gifts. On May 23, the French president, Gaston Doumergue, gave him the Cross of the Legion of Honor—the nation's highest civilian honor. But despite all the plaudits, separation anxiety continued to gnaw at him. "I did not have time," Lindbergh later lamented, "to be with my *Spirit of St. Louis.*" On Saturday, May 28, he could finally escape from the social whirl by going back to his favorite refuge—his plane's cockpit. Lindbergh circled over Paris before heading off to Belgium and England for visits with royalty. And then he stepped aboard the USS *Memphis*, which President Calvin Coolidge had assigned to haul the aviator and his plane back to Washington, D.C. While Lindbergh preferred to fly—he felt uncomfortable about "bind[ing] my silver wings into a box"—he chose not to disobey the president's directives.

The nonstop feting of the man and his machine would continue for nearly a year. Upon disembarking in the nation's capital on June 11, Lindbergh was reunited with his mother in the backseat of President Coolidge's touring car; with a quarter of a million people looking on, the president promoted him to colonel of the United States Reserve Corps. Two days later, on "Lindbergh Day," the financial markets were closed and four million New Yorkers lined the streets of downtown Manhattan for a ticker-tape parade. In July, Lindbergh took *The Spirit of St. Louis* on a victory tour to all forty-eight states. Over the next three months, he would ride in 1,300 miles of motorcades and be glimpsed by one-quarter of America's 120 million citizens. At the end of 1927, *Time*'s first "Man of the Year" flew his alter ego to a half dozen countries in Central and South America. On April 30, 1928, after completing a final four-and-a-half-hour flight from Lambert Airport, Lindbergh officially handed over *The Spirit of St. Louis* to the Smithsonian Institution, where it has safely remained ever since.

While Lindbergh smiled at the adoring crowds, inwardly he seethed. Like Kinsey, he hated engaging in small talk with his fans, or with just about anyone else. Fame did not make connecting any easier or more enjoyable. A quarter century later, when the author John P. Marquand—Lindbergh had gotten to know the bestselling novelist because Anne was a close friend of his wife, Adelaide—suggested that he go on a tour to promote his autobiography, Lindbergh responded that he could not do it. "I thoroughly dislike such things," he wrote, "and feel they are mostly a waste of time and life. I fulfilled a lifetime's obligations along these lines in the year or two following my flight to Paris. . . . I have the hope of never going to a big dinner party again." The Lone Eagle would always be a loner. Even Marquand, whose home Lindbergh visited on numerous occasions, found him "pretty tough to converse with as he does not understand the light approach to anything."

During their ten-minute chat at York House in late May 1927, the Prince of Wales—later King Edward VIII—asked Lindbergh about his plans for the future. "Keep on flying" was his response.

But not long after his marriage, aviation, as he later wrote, went from "a primary to a secondary interest." With the task of mapping out air routes for Trans World Airlines (TWA) not proving to be an adequate match for his grandiosity, he soon turned his attention to the mysteries of life and death. By the early 1930s, like Kinsey a half continent away, Lindbergh would switch obsessions; and his new all-consuming pursuit would be in the same field from which Kinsey was retreating—biology.

This was a return to an interest that he had abandoned when he took up flying. Ever since stumbling upon a dead horse in Little Falls, the farm boy had been fascinated by what "stopped life from living." Inspired by several Detroit relatives who had made significant contributions to medicine and science, he had once toyed with the idea of becoming a physician. But while the indifferent student did not feel capable of handling the academic grind, the world-famous aviator held no such reservations; now supremely self-confident, Lindbergh was convinced that he could do anything if he only put his mind to it. In 1928, he began devouring medical textbooks. The following year, he treated himself to a sleek, new gadget—a high-powered binocular microscope—and began fantasizing about building his own laboratory. After moving with his new wife into a farmhouse near Princeton, New Jersey, Lindbergh got permission from Princeton University's president to spend time at its labs. On one visit to campus, he observed the reactions of a decerebrate cat which, as he later noted, "seemed to…demonstrate the basically mechanistic qualities of life." For Lindbergh, the fact that a cat could still eat, see, and claw without most of its brain raised existential questions. The man who attached more readily to machines than to people wondered exactly what it was that differentiated the two. "Certainly," he speculated, "a decerebrate human would manifest similar reactions."

Biology might have remained a hobby for Lindbergh, had not a medical crisis struck the family. In 1930, Anne's elder sister, Elisabeth, whose mitral valve had been damaged during a bout of rheumatic fever, suffered a heart attack. She was just twenty-six, and the prognosis was grim. (She would die just four years later.) From the perspective of the onetime engineering student, his sister-in-law's "engine" was malfunctioning, and he did not understand why a surgeon could not take it out and fix it (while a temporary pump kept her going) or put in a new "artificial heart" to replace it. Not sure how to answer his questions, a New Jersey doctor directed him to an expert, Dr. Alexis Carrel, an experimental surgeon.

On November 28, 1930, Lindbergh drove in to Manhattan to meet the fifty-seven-year-old French émigré at the Rockefeller Institute for Medical Research. Still just twenty-eight and at the height of his fame, Lindbergh towered over the short, squat, and balding Carrel, then widely considered the world's top scientist. After listening sympathetically while Lindbergh detailed his mechanical solution to his sister-in-law's health woes, his host mentioned that he had long been interested in developing artificial organs. At present, Carrel explained, the risk of infection precluded the insertion of a pump to replace the heart. But taken by Lindbergh's curiosity, Carrel gave him a tour around his fifth-floor lab. Lindbergh got a chance to view up close the Frenchman's most famous experiment, begun in January 1912, in which he kept tissue from a chick's embryonic heart alive in a small flask. "These results showed that the permanent life [of tissues]," Carrel reported later that year in the *Journal of Experimental Medicine*, "was not impossible." After eighteen years, as an impressed Lindbergh observed while peering through a microscope, these chick heart cells were still alive.

After pointing to a sink, where Lindbergh scrubbed his face and hands with disinfectant soap, Carrel escorted his visitor up a spiral staircase to the black operating suite in the attic. *Black* was the operative word. It was the color of the paint covering the floor, the ceiling, the walls, the operating table, and the cabinets. And the surgeons and staff all wore black robes and hoods, and their specially sterilized instruments were covered in black rubber sheets and towels. According to Carrel, his favorite color cut down on glare, and the black outfits, by highlighting dust, were easier to keep spotless. For this biologist, Louis Pasteur, the father of germ theory, was not just a towering icon but also a patron saint.

Carrel proceeded to show Lindbergh his various attempts to keep the thyroids of cats, dogs, and chickens alive outside the body by means of a glass perfusion pump. As the Frenchman conceded, his gizmos invariably failed to prevent infections. "I was as impressed by the perfection of Carrel's biological techniques," Lindbergh later recalled, "as I was astounded by the crudeness of the apparatuses I inspected." The aviator then offered to help him design a better pump. It was a perfect match. Giving the new volunteer his own key to the black kingdom, Carrel would describe their relationship as "the marriage of [Lindbergh's] mechanical genius with my scientific research." Of Carrel, who soon became a mentor, Lindbergh later wrote, "there seemed to be no limit to the breadth and penetration of his thought."

By early 1931, Lindbergh was commuting four times a week from New Jersey to his "secret" Manhattan office—he refused to tell the inquisitive press what he was doing—sometimes staying until the wee hours. "The moment I entered the black-walled room," Lindbergh later observed, "I felt outside the world men ordinarily lived in." Like the sky (and later his European love nests), this escape hatch insulated Lindbergh from the angst of quotidian existence. For this product of two volatile parents, regular contact with others in the ordinary world—particularly, his own wife and children—would prove nearly unbearable. While unstructured domesticity could increase his anxiety, "the precision of trained efficiency" that permeated Carrel's aseptic workplace could mitigate it. The man who longed to get all the little things right enjoyed studying "every detail of his operating procedures in an attempt to make my designs conform to them." Lindbergh also burned some midnight oil looking through Carrel's microscopes. One night, he examined his own semen, which he described as "thousands of living beings, each one of them myself...capable of spreading my existence throughout the human race." (As Lindbergh aged, his interest in finding receptacles for his seeds would not let up.) As Anne recorded in her diary, she had "never seen him as happy as when he was working quietly there."

Within a few months, Lindbergh had designed a tilting-coil pump, which allowed a chick's carotid artery to survive for a few days before succumbing to infection. After this significant first step, Lindbergh worked on increasing the power of his instrument so that it could perfuse a whole mammal organ. Over the next few years—despite a hectic schedule, which kept him in the air for long periods of time—he would continue to sketch new versions. "[Lindbergh] is...very obstinate and tenacious," Carrel would later tell the New York Times, "so that he does not admit defeat." At Carrel's urging, Lindbergh returned to the lab just a couple of weeks after his firstborn's body was found. As a fellow obsessive, Carrel sensed that immersion in painstaking scientific research might boost the aviator's spirits, a hypothesis that turned out to be true. In April 1935, the engineering school dropout completed his high-tech three-chamber glass pump, which was able to keep alive a cat's thyroid for weeks at a time. Soon about one thousand different animal organs—hearts, lungs, livers, and spleens—had been kept alive for up to thirty days in "Lindbergh pumps." In June 1935, Lindbergh and his boss summarized their preliminary findings in an article for

Science, which they began expanding into a book entitled *The Culture of Organs*. Shortly after its publication in June 1938, when Lindbergh and Carrel were living on neighboring islands off the coast of France, *Time* put both men on its cover above a caption that read, "They are looking for the fountain of age." That same month, the *New York Times* heralded their development of "medical engineering," which the paper called as "of as much importance in the progress of medicine as Pasteur's discoveries."

But just as Carrel and Lindbergh were gaining worldwide attention for the fruits of their eight-year collaboration, politics intruded. From the beginning, their shared love of black hoods and efficiency had gone hand in hand with fantasies of racial betterment. And with Hitler now both committing unspeakable acts against Jews and readying his war machine, the public suddenly lost its appetite for the latest findings of "the men in black," as *Time* referred to the two celebrity scientists in its cover story. Antidemocratic to the core, Carrel wanted to replace "liberty, equality, and fraternity" with "science, authority, and order." In 1935, he had espoused eugenics in a pseudo-philosophical screed, *Man, the Unknown*. Translated into twenty languages, the blockbuster would sell more than two million copies. Going far beyond his standard praise for Pasteur and his longtime cause célèbre, "cleanliness," Carrel now promoted racial hygiene. He argued that "a genetic elite" should control human affairs and that the weak, the criminal, and the insane should be "disposed of in small euthanistic institutions supplied with the proper gases." His interest in artificial organs was inextricably linked with his goal of "remaking man." "The development of the human personality," he wrote, "is the ultimate purpose of civilization." Carrel's theories were in lockstep with the policies of the Nazi government, which in July 1933—just six months after Hitler's election as chancellor—passed a law requiring the sterilization of all Germans alleged to be suffering from genetic disorders. In fact, in 1936, Carrel added a few lines to the German translation of his bestseller in which he praised the Nazis for taking "energetic measures against the propagation of retarded individuals, mental patients, and criminals."

Due to his mechanistic view of human nature—which, given his obsessive temperament, he felt needed to be controlled—Lindbergh was easily seduced by the erudite Frenchman's twisted utopian vision. For years, he had nodded approvingly as Carrel expatiated on his crackpot sociology in their frequent conversations in the black halls of the Rockefeller Institute. And like his revered teacher, Lindbergh was receptive to vast chunks of Nazi ideology. These Teutonic sympathies only intensified after Lindbergh and his wife moved to Europe at the end of 1935 to elude the hounding by the American press corps.

From his farmhouse outside of London, which he rented from the renowned Bloomsbury writers Harold Nicolson and Vita Sackville-West, Lindbergh conducted diplomatic missions to Germany at the behest of the United States Army. In the summer of 1936, Major Truman Smith sent Lindbergh to Berlin to report on the state of German aviation. As usual, he would focus more on the machines than on the mammals in his midst. Blind to the cruelty of the recently passed "Nuremberg laws," which deprived Jews of their rights as citizens, Lindbergh praised the "organized vitality of Germany" that was busy creating "new factories, airfields and research laboratories." He attended the 1936 Berlin Olympics as the special guest of Hermann Goering, the commander-in-chief of the Luftwaffe and Adolf Hitler's right-hand man. To Carrel, he described Germany as "the most interesting place in the world today," adding, "Some of the things I see here encourage me greatly." While he didn't celebrate the virulent anti-Semitism, it didn't bother him, either.

In October 1938, at a stag dinner—wives were verboten—at the American embassy in Berlin, Goering presented Lindbergh with the Service Cross of the German Eagle, an award speckled with four miniature swastikas that had been commissioned by the Fuehrer himself. A horrified American press corps would vilify Lindbergh for not returning the medal, but a week later, the appreciative aviator wrote to Goering, asking him to "convey my thanks to the Reichschancellor." More entranced by Germany than ever, Lindbergh planned a move to its capital, Berlin. But after *Kristalnacht* —the pogrom of November 9, 1938, in which thousands of Jews were arrested and sent to concentration camps, hundreds of Jewish shops and synagogues destroyed, and dozens of Jews killed—the Lindberghs put that notion on hold. "I do not understand," a puzzled Lindbergh wrote in his diary a few days later, "these riots on the part of the Germans. It seems so contrary to their sense of order." Like other obsessives, Lindbergh was often hyperrational; disconnected from his own emotions (and those of everyone else), he had no idea that the Nazis' love of order masked their pathological aggression. The couple ended up choosing Paris instead. As Anne explained in her diary, they did not "want to make a move which would seem to support the German actions in regard to the Jews." Nevertheless, as *Time* reported in December 1938, what was "once the most heroic living name in the U.S." was now hated by a considerable swath of Americans. Paying deference to this wave of "anti-Lindberghism," TWA stopped calling itself "the Lindbergh line" in its advertisements.

As 1938 wound down, Lindbergh tossed in his black scientific hat, ending his experiments with Carrel. "Why spend time on biological experiments," he later wrote, "when our very civilization was at stake, when one of history's great cataclysms impended?" But while he no longer thought about how to prevent bacteria from infecting the organs in his pump, he kept worrying about abstract threats to racial purity. Moving back across the Atlantic to Long Island in the spring of 1939, Lindbergh began doing everything in his power to keep his country out of war with Germany. While nonintervention was popular among Americans of all political stripes, Lindbergh's rationale was curious at best and extremely naïve, if not downright delusional at worst. Not long after the Nazi invasion of Poland in September 1939, Lindbergh, recycling the racist doubletalk that he had honed with Carrel, explained his position in "Aviation, Geography and Race," an article for *Reader's Digest*. "We, the heirs of European culture," he declared, "are on the verge of a disastrous war, a war within our own family of nations, a war which will reduce the strength and destroy the treasures of the White race." Ignoring Germany's obvious bellicosity, Lindbergh insisted that England, France, and America should all cozy up to the Nazis. According to Lindbergh, who would keep on airing his Teutonic-friendly views in a series of high-profile addresses, this "peace among Western nations" would, in turn, provide protection against the real enemy—the Mongrels, Persians, and Moors.

After Germany attacked France and Britain, the aviator told a stunned congressional committee that he did not believe it was necessarily in the best interests of the United States for England to defeat the Germans. As the public face of the America First Committee, an antiwar coalition established in September 1940 by a group of Yale law students including future president Gerald Ford and future Supreme Court justice Potter Stewart, Lindbergh emerged as the most influential opponent of President Franklin D. Roosevelt's pro-British foreign policy. During an America First rally in Des Moines, Iowa, in September 1941, Lindbergh blasted American Jews, making sensational claims about "their large ownership and influence in our motion pictures, our press, our radio and our Government." Even more alarming, he declared that "leaders of both the British and Jewish races...for reasons which are not American, wish to involve us in this war." Lindbergh's speech was immediately denounced by dozens of prominent Americans, including Wendell Willkie, Roosevelt's Republican challenger in the

1940 presidential election, who called it "the most un-American talk made in my time." A week later, Luther Patrick, a Republican congressman from Alabama, waved a copy of *Mein Kampf* on the floor of the House, saying "it sounds just like Charles A. Lindbergh." The America First Committee did not dissociate itself from Lindbergh, but simply urged him to stop attacking the Jews. A few months later, after the Japanese attack on Pearl Harbor, the organization folded, ending Lindbergh's brief flirtation with politics. "Now that we are at war," he wrote in his diary on December 12, 1941, "I want to do my part."

In January 1942, the thirty-nine-year-old went to Washington to ask Secretary of War Henry Stimson if he could assist the Army Air Corps. With several cabinet members opposed—in a memo to President Roosevelt, Secretary of the Interior Harold Ickes described Lindbergh as "a ruthless and conscious fascist motivated by...a contempt for democracy"—the administration quickly rejected his offer. "What you say about Lindbergh," the president wrote to Ickes, "and the potential danger of the man, I agree with wholeheartedly."

Lindbergh turned to the private sector, testing planes first for the Ford Motor Company and then for United Aircraft; this second gig took him to the Pacific theater, where he flew on dozens of combat missions as a "technical advisor." Itching to get into the action, he eventually persuaded the Marines to ignore the limits of his official duties and let him dive-bomb enemy positions. "Lindbergh was indefatigable," recalled Colonel Charles MacDonald, the commander of "Satan's Angels," the acclaimed 475th Fighter Group. "He flew more missions than was normally expected of a regular combat pilot." He also taught the fighters of the 475th various ingenious ways to conserve fuel, which allowed them to extend their missions much deeper into enemy territory. Back up in the air, Lindbergh was doing what he did best.

Like Carrel, Lindbergh would have been much better off had he not strayed from his forte and ventured into social philosophy and politics. The aviator understood what made machines tick, but not human beings, much less nations. While it seemed as if he were taking directives from Berlin, his various Teutonic tributes never did amount to treason, as the Roosevelt administration contended. Lindbergh could not have been a good Nazi, even if he had so desired; he lacked the social skills. While he revered organization, he was too much the alienated loner to work within one. (He never would stick to a regular day job in corporate America.) The Lone Eagle's allegiance was not to National Socialism, but to Isolationism (both upper and lower case). "[My mother] said," his daughter

Reeve wrote in *Under a Wing*, her moving memoir of growing up Lindbergh, "that the very qualities that made him a success as an aviator doomed him as a politician. Isolationism…was a quintessentially personal characteristic…and a politically hopeless cause." While Lindbergh never renounced his racist rants, he did succeed in rehabilitating himself by his activities during the war; in fact, to commemorate his admirable service to his country, President Eisenhower would later make him a brigadier general.

In contrast to Lindbergh, Carrel kept pursuing his elitist utopia. In 1941, the surgeon set up a research foundation in Vichy France that was designed to "create a civilization that, like science, will be infinitely perfectible." After his mentor's death in 1944, Lindbergh continued to idealize him; decades later, he would call Carrel's mind "the most stimulating I have ever met." Their cocreation, the Lindbergh pump, while never leading to immortality per se, would have offspring such as the heart-lung machine, which can keep patients alive during open-heart surgery, and the artificial heart designed by Robert Jarvik in the 1980s. Likewise, contemporary efforts at biomedical engineering—particularly tissue engineering, where scientists create, for example, replacement urinary bladders out of a patient's own stem cells—can be traced back to "the men in black."

———

As he moved away from biology in the late 1930s, Lindbergh urgently sought a new focus for his compulsive energy. He was also on the lookout for new daily companions, which could replace his string of beloved machines—namely, his planes and pumps. The manuscripts that he began toting around in manila envelopes on his worldwide travels would meet both needs. The former engineering student who could not hack freshman English was now determined to become a writer. And his subject would be himself.

Lindbergh's perfectionism had first driven him into the writing business a decade earlier. A few days after his arrival in Paris, he began collaborating with a *New York Times* reporter on a book about his famous flight. When shown the galley proofs in late June 1927, he was outraged by the journalist's looseness with the facts. "It was highly inaccurate," he later noted, "and out of character. I decided immediately that I would not permit it to be published over my name." He decided to redo the entire book himself, even though that meant knocking out the forty-thousand-word manuscript in just three weeks in order to meet the deadline. He worked at a furious pace, delighting in the daily tally of his words. "My record for a single day," he noted proudly, "was thirty five hundred words." But while both his publisher and the public were more than satisfied with the workmanlike prose of the megaselling *We*, which eventually earned its novice author more than $250,000, not so Lindbergh. In October 1928, ten days after his first "air date" with Anne Morrow, he admitted to his future wife, the recipient of several writing awards during her days at Smith College, "I *wish* I could write." Living up to her literary promise, she would eventually pen thirteen bestsellers, starting with the Number 1 nonfiction book of 1935, *North to the Orient*, which described her flights with her husband in the early years of their marriage. She would also teach an eager Charles Lindbergh, who copyedited her literary debut, how to use the English language.

In November 1937, following in the footsteps of his wife, who would later publish several volumes of her diaries, Lindbergh began keeping a daily journal. At the time, as Lindbergh later recalled, he was thinking not so much about publication as about keeping "a private record" of his experiences, particularly his meetings with world leaders that his international celebrity had made possible. The following year, he also began a do-over of his do-over, vowing to complete a thorough hour-by-hour account of his trip across the Atlantic "without the pressure of time." Once again, he was concerned about creating "a record that was accurate." After discontinuing his diary at the end of the war, he moved full steam ahead on his revamped memoir, *The Spirit of St. Louis*. Over the next several years, this obsessive would write and write in an attempt to get everything just right. He would end up cranking out six complete drafts, rewriting some sections as many as ten times.

Lindbergh was as persnickety about his writing implements as about his prose. The former airmail pilot wrote his new book with Number 2 pencils, which he sharpened with a penknife, on pads of blue airmail paper. "He liked his erasers green and he chopped them up to specific lengths," his daughter Reeve told me. He would mark his location at the top of the page; these "geographical positions," as he later noted, included the Carrels' home off the coast of France, New Guinea jungles, and air bases in Arabia and Japan. After slaving over his words for a dozen years, he finally summoned the courage to show them to his wife. Anne would help him find his voice, encouraging him to adopt a conversational, yet precise prose style. "She functioned as his first editor, getting him to trim things, particularly the hyperbolic," added Reeve. And there were many more rounds of tweaks after he placed the book in the hands of his editor at Scribner's, who insisted that he cut another seventy pages. "He was the most fussy of authors, living or dead," observed publishing executive Charles Scribner. "He would measure the difference between a semicolon and a colon to make sure each was what it ought to be."

The result was what Orville Prescott of the *New York Times* called an "extraordinary experiment in autobiography." Lindbergh had turned his thirty-three hours in the air into a fast-paced and moving adventure story. Weaving in flashbacks from his past, including scenes from his childhood in Minnesota, Lindbergh conveyed both his thoughts as he headed to Paris as well as what it felt like to fly. While praising "this superb feat of writing," the *Times* reviewer did have one peeve: "excessive detail." And that was after years of slicing and dicing; his original stack of blue sheets was larded with minutiae about aviation mechanics and logistics.

With few critics expecting the middle-aged Lindbergh to pound out a literary masterpiece, rumors circulated that Anne had been his ghost writer. While his remarkable drive had powered his success—in addition to the ubiquitous raves, royalties amounted to $1.5 million—her influence was everywhere. Just as the writers of the 1930s who visited poet Ezra Pound in Italy were said to have attended the "Ezuversity," this University of Wisconsin dropout could be said to have finished up at the "Annuversity." "I don't think Anne will ever understand," Lindbergh wrote to John Marquand in early 1952, "how much part she has taken in the chapters of *The Spirit of St. Louis*. She taught me to see as I never did before, even to look back on past experiences." To Marquand, Lindbergh also mentioned how much he had absorbed by reading the books she left lying around the house as well as her manuscripts. "In the deepest sense," he added, "[it was] as if a lot of the pages had been done with her own pen."

Though proud to have completed the definitive account of his flight, Lindbergh was far from done setting the record straight. In the mid-1950s, he immersed himself in another massive autobiographical manuscript, at which he would plug away until his death. Over the next two decades, he produced a thousand typed pages of text as well as another two thousand pages of notes. He continued to go back over key events, eager to fill in new details and draw out new shades of meaning. To organize his mountain of words, he naturally came up with a list, "on writing autobiography," that outlined six steps, including one that required him to jog his memory to create another list—that of "scattered incidents." About a third of Lindbergh's pages would make it into the posthumously published *Autobiography of Values* (1978). His American mistress, the

Pan Am stewardess Adrienne Arnett, was the muse who inspired him to relate his "moral perceptions" in this memoir, which never did quite fly. In this case, his lists seemed to work to his disadvantage. The *New York Times* called this follow-up memoir "jerky [as it]...sometimes repeats the same episode or point with only variations in emphasis."

Lindbergh would also study the dozens of books written about him, compiling long lists of factual inaccuracies. His jottings on *The Hero: Charles A. Lindbergh and the American Dream* (1959) by historian Kenneth Davis, which his friend publisher William Jovanovich considered "a sympathetic biography," came to seventy-six typed pages. Like a dissatisfied moviegoer yelling back at the screen, Lindbergh talked back to the text. He did not like the author's emphasis on his shyness around women as a youth. "I was definitely interested in girls," he protested, "but never saw one I was sufficiently attracted to date until I saw the girl who became my wife." Paradoxically, the anti-introspective Lindbergh, who reacted scornfully when Anne or any other family member turned to psychotherapy, did not hesitate to put his biographers on the couch, based solely on what they said about him. "The author of this book," he wrote of Davis, "gives me the impression of being a confused and unhappy man. It seems to me he is dissatisfied with the world in general, and particularly with himself."

Enraged with what he perceived to be constant misrepresentations of his character, in 1969, Lindbergh decided to work up his decades-old diary for publication. In the introduction to *The Wartime Journals of Charles A. Lindbergh* (1970), William Jovanovich, now also his publisher, explained the "exceptional precaution" that "General Lindbergh took...to authenticate the fact that the journals were not rewritten at later times." Lindbergh passed on the leather-bound diary notebooks first to a transcriber, who, in turn, gave her handwritten pages to a typist. For each subsection—typically containing a week of entries—both secretaries would sign a statement, "It was copied from and carefully checked with the original," which Lindbergh would then initial. All this cross-checking was spelled out to prove to the world that he had not doctored anything in his text. But while Lindbergh did not add any new words, his emendations were not all cosmetic. Chopping down his manuscript by a third so that it could fit into a thousand-page book, as biographer A. Scott Berg reported, "he intuitively deleted many [of his anti-Semitic comments]. His admiration for Germany's accomplishments got soft-pedaled." Ultimately, this autobiographer was less concerned with accuracy than with control; what he sought was the ability to shape his own public image. But even with the effusive odes to the Third Reich removed, the diary did not strike a chord with readers; sales were anemic.

———

Lindbergh's concern about the lack of accuracy in reporters' accounts of his past is almost comic, given that his post–World War II private life was nothing but a string of secrets that he feared might leak out at any moment. Small wonder, then, that he disdained biographers. While he tried to pass himself off as an easygoing suburban family man, he was actually a high-strung sex addict who was spending a huge chunk of his time planning and engaging in his trysts. As with Kinsey, the family homestead—a four-acre plot of land in Darien, Connecticut, that he purchased in 1946—gave some clues to his little-known flip side. The stucco house was surrounded by disorder, except for "pockets of horticultural order here and there," Reeve Lindbergh has written. Right outside the door stood a young maple tree on the service line of an old tennis court. A wide variety of animals—deer, geese, snakes, and turtles—roamed the "unkempt wildness" of the land. And like Kinsey, Lindbergh also liked to shed garments in his backyard; he would skinny-dip in the nearby Long Island Sound and then lie naked on the beach.

When he was not tending to some project outdoors, Lindbergh squirreled himself away in his office, where he often went into a list-making frenzy. He began compiling lists of nearly everything, including events in his past such as all the planes he had ever flown and all the books he had ever read. And he was constantly updating his own to-do lists, which he divided into three categories, "Current," "Immediate," and "Near Future." In 1963, he downsized his Darien digs, moving from the cavernous Tudor house to a new spartan dwelling, which had no dining room. "As if we were on an airplane, we ate on trays by the fire," recalled his granddaughter Kristina, who often visited on school vacations.

He stayed with Anne and the children in Darien only a couple of months a year. And whenever he did return home, Lindbergh would invariably terrify them all. "This is a nonbenevolent dictatorship," he would repeatedly bark out. "He laughed after he said it, but I didn't," Reeve has written. "I wasn't in the mood."

Lindbergh ruled over his subjects not with an iron fist but with ironclad lists. He demanded that Anne compile and continually update a complex series of household inventories, which documented every article of clothing, book, and kitchen item owned by the family. As per his directive, she also kept track of all

her household expenditures, including every fifteen cents she doled out for rubber bands. When Anne did not comply, he got testy. An exasperated Anne was
just as likely to find herself retreating to her room to cry when her husband was
home as when he was away. And the paterfamilias who insisted on "Father"—
"Dad" was verboten—would keep extensive checklists on his children. On a
megachart, which had a column devoted to each of the five American Lindberghs, he would jot down—with his trusty Number 2 pencil—all their infrac-
tions such as "chewing gum," "reading comics," or "leaving shoes out in the
rain." As the no-nos added up, he would summon each child into his office for
some discussion and/or a couple of half-hour lectures on, say, "Freedom and Responsibility" or "Downfall of Civilization." And after the tête-à-tête, he would
place the appropriate check marks on his chart, indicating that domestic order
had been restored. The children felt otherwise. "I thought," Reeve has recalled,
"my father was, too often, both unfair and absurd."

By the late 1940s, Anne realized that her husband was incapable of maintaining anything resembling a conventional marriage, but she couldn't figure
out why. As Reeve Lindbergh told me, after his death her mother confessed that
she was constantly mulling over divorce in the decade between 1945 and 1955.
But this easygoing and thoughtful problem solver eventually decided to accept
Lindbergh for what he was. She made the most of her years of psychotherapy
with the controversial psychiatrist Dr. John N. Rosen. While this shrink could be
even more volatile than her husband—in 1983, Rosen would surrender his medical license when charged with dozens of ethical violations by a Pennsylvania
medical board, including, most notably, the verbal, physical, and sexual abuse
of hospitalized schizophrenic patients—he proved remarkably helpful with this
high-functioning and verbally gifted ambulatory neurotic. Rosen put his finger
on exactly what she was up against, explaining that her husband's "compulsive
outward orderliness" was compensating for his "*inward* disorderliness." And to
solve the existential problem that Lindbergh's bewildering behavior posed, this
introspective writer also turned to words. "My mother wrote her way back into
the marriage," Reeve stated.

Anne's writing for public consumption evolved into the protofeminist classic
Gift from the Sea. Begun in 1950 and released in 1955, this 127-page book of
philosophical reflections went on to sell nearly three million copies. "I began
these pages for myself," Anne wrote, "in order to think out my own particular pattern of living, my own individual balance of life, work and human relationships."

While her husband's eccentricity was extreme, the issues that Anne addressed were universal; she explored, for example, how couples inevitably grow apart after the "perfect unity" in the early years of marriage. To cope with such difficult periods in life and love, she advocated simple virtues such as patience and openness; she also stressed the joys to be found in solitude. In private, however, as revealed in *Against Wind and Tide* (2012), a collection of her letters and diaries from this period, Anne also decided to fight back. "As I read into the 1950s and 1960s and beyond," noted Reeve, the volume's editor, in the Introduction, "I recognized the person who had learned to stand up to a man whose good opinion she had once craved above all else." Avoiding direct confrontation with her husband, "she began to embrace his absences," Reeve told me. Relishing the chance to carve out her own life, Anne turned to other men to meet her needs for intimacy. Her lovers included Dana Atchley, the family doctor, and Alan Valentine, a prominent academic historian who served for fifteen years as the president of the University of Rochester. Anne stopped straying by the late 1950s, and Lindbergh never learned about these relationships. Though her husband was the sex addict, Anne was the partner who was saddled with the guilt. During her husband's lifetime, as she later told biographer Scott Berg, Anne suspected that he had been unfaithful, but only once, with a beautiful young Filipina, whose picture he had brought back from one of his trips to Manila in the 1960s. And a few years after his death, as Susan Hertog reported in *Anne Morrow Lindbergh: Her Life* (1999), Anne found love letters from Adrienne Arnett, the stewardess, with whom he carried on an affair between 1966 and 1972; however, she did not stumble upon any other evidence of his extracurricular activities.

It's not clear exactly when Lindbergh first became a serial adulterer. Hard evidence for any affairs before the mid-1950s is missing. But given his remarkable ability to control other people—with each German mistress, he insisted on a vow of "secrecy," threatening not to return if it was ever violated—this gap in the historical record doesn't necessarily mean that his hyperactive sexual self remained dormant until then. We know about his German escapades only because after the death in 2001 of Brigitte Hesshaimer, one of his three German "wives," her three children, who had discovered about 160 love letters on blue airmail paper sent to their mother by "C."—the same sign-off that the aviator tended to use in his letters to Anne, who also died in 2001—felt free to reveal the truth. In the summer of 2003, Dyrk Hesshaimer, born in 1958; Astrid Hesshaimer, born in 1960; and David Hesshaimer, born in 1967, announced at an international press conference held in Munich's Rathaus (town hall) that the famous aviator was their father. A DNA test conducted later that year confirmed their assertion. "At first, I was shocked," stated Reeve, who has since met and become friendly with all seven European half siblings and their families. "But after a while," she added, "I felt as if this news explained a great deal. Now I know why he was gone so much. I also understand why he was delighted when I was learning German and why he repeatedly advised me not to sleep with anyone you don't want to have a child with."

Lindbergh's three children with the dark-haired Brigitte Hesshaimer also spoke at length about their famous father to a German journalist, Rudolf Schroeck, with whom they shared the letters. Schroeck's ensuing book, *Das Doppelleben des Charles A. Lindbergh* (*The Double Life of Charles A. Lindbergh*), appeared in 2005 (it has yet to be translated into English). His four other European children have never spoken publicly. Since the release of this insightful biography, which was widely and positively reviewed in Germany, both Astrid and David Hesshaimer have shunned the media. "All you need to know [about my father's German families]," David wrote to me in a 2011 e-mail, "is already written in Rudolf Schroeck's book." In contrast, their elder brother, Dyrk, who appeared on European TV to promote the book, has occasionally fielded questions from reporters. In the fall of 2012, I became the first American writer to interview any of Lindbergh's seven German children when I met with Dyrk for four hours in a Munich hotel. He is tall and lanky, speaks fluent English, and has long worked as a software programmer in his native Germany. "Of course, the word *double life* in the title of the biography," he told me with a smile, "isn't quite accurate."

Schroeck's book also contains some basic information about Lindbergh's two other German families. With Marietta Hesshaimer, Brigitte's sister, who was also dark-haired, he would have two children, Vago, born in 1962, and Christoph, born in 1966. And with a Prussian blonde, whom Schroeck referred to as "Valeska," he would have two more children—a son born in 1959 and a daughter born in 1961. Seeking privacy, this mistress, who today resides in Baden-Baden, has not revealed her real name nor the first names of her two children. As children, Dyrk, Astrid, and David would often spend summer vacations with their aunt's two children, but they had no idea that they were actually half siblings rather than cousins.

Lots of people seek out lots of sex, but only a select few start four families, three of which are "secret"; and it is this aspect of Lindbergh's erotic life that is the most puzzling and puts him in a league of his own. His contemporary

Louis Kahn—the influential architect was born a year before Lindbergh and also died in 1974—came close, but he stopped at one wife, two mistresses, and three children—one with each partner. What Kahn, whose story was told in the 2003 documentary, *My Architect: A Son's Journey*, and Lindbergh shared was a preference for a nomadic existence, which may have had roots in their chaotic early lives. At three, Kahn also was victimized by a fire—it left permanent scars on his face—and emigrated with his impoverished parents from the Estonian island of Sarema to the United States.

Lindbergh, who had hardly felt connected to his family of origin, may have harbored a deep need for belonging that he did not know how to pursue in any other way. Fathering the children with his German mistresses may also have helped reduce his fears of abandonment by increasing their dependence on him. In contrast to his German lovers (particularly the Hesshaimer sisters, who rarely pushed back against his exacting demands), the American Adrienne Arnett, with whom he did not father a child, repeatedly threatened to throw him out whenever his teasing got out of hand, and she would not let him back into her life until he apologized.

While Valeska was the second of Lindbergh's German mistresses to bear him a child, he was already intimate with her before he met either of the Hesshaimer sisters. In the mid-1950s, he hired the attractive blonde, twenty-two years his junior, as his translator—he had found her by placing an ad in the *Süddeustche Zeitung*, Munich's leading newspaper. Blessed with a perfect command of English, Valeska had been working as a private secretary for Philip Rosenthal Jr., the flamboyant owner of a porcelain manufacturing business in Bavaria, with whom she had also been carrying on an affair. Lindbergh soon began sleeping with her both in Munich and in Rome, where he kept an apartment.

The tragicomic romantic complications, which would eventually require all of his obsessive skills to handle, didn't ensue until March 1957. That's when Lindbergh, accompanied by Valeska, paid a visit to a three-room, fifth-floor walk-up at 44 Agnesstrasse in Munich's Schwabing district, where he was introduced to both Brigitte and Marietta for the first time. The two sisters had been living together there since 1955 (though Marietta was soon to move out). This modest apartment, which its current tenants showed me in the fall of 2012, was where Dyrk was conceived toward the end of 1957 and where he lived until he was six. "My sister Astrid and I used to sleep with my mother in the bedroom," he stated, "except when my father came to visit; then we were exiled to the living room." Dyrk also told me of his fond memories of the pancakes that his father used to make in the small kitchen. "He was a good pancake flipper," Dyrk recalled. Lindbergh used to enjoy eating breakfast with Brigitte and the children on the small porch that jutted out from the living room and overlooked the building's interior courtyard.

At the time of Lindbergh's first visit to Agnesstrasse in March 1957, Brigitte— nicknamed "Bitusch"—was a thirty-one-year-old hatmaker and Marietta a thirty-three-year-old painter. Like Lindbergh, Valeska didn't know the Hesshaimer sisters; she had only recently heard of them through a mutual German friend, Elisabeth, who escorted the former aviator and his secretary to their Schwabing apartment that day. While Brigitte and Marietta were aware that Lindbergh was a married man and already had a mistress—Valeska—they were both instantly taken by the fifty-five-year-old celebrity, who looked much younger than his years. Their attraction to Lindbergh also had roots peculiar to their era. "For my mother's generation," Dyrk remarked, "there was a shortage of eligible men, and foreigners who had a second family in Germany were not all that unusual. After all, many German men died in World War II, and those who returned were often tormented."

A couple of days later, Lindbergh came back to 44 Agnestrasse by himself, and invited Brigitte out for a stroll. Like Marietta, Brigitte was partially disabled due to a bout with tuberculosis in childhood. Her right leg was lame. She took Lindbergh's arm, and they took the streetcar to Odeonsplatz in the heart of Munich. As with wife number one, the courtship was swift. As the pair walked past the lions near the Field Marshal's Hall, he told Brigitte the old saw about how when a man is in love, he can hear the stone lions roar. Putting his arms around her, Lindbergh added, "And I fell in love with you." A passionate kiss followed. Two days later, on March 21, 1957, on their second "ground date," Lindbergh was ready to declare his intentions. While he was not free to marry, he wanted to cement their union with some jewelry. Wearing a black beret over his comb-over— his thinning blond hair was now mostly gray—Lindbergh took Brigitte to the exclusive Andreas Huber jewelry store—Munich's Tiffany—where he bought her an elegant Swiss watch for 390 marks. She would proudly wear this gift on her wrist for the rest of her life. (She treasured the receipt, which Dyrk would later find among her papers.) Seeing the expensive watch on the arm of her sister,

Marietta soon put two and two together. For the time being, however, Valeska remained in the dark about her American lover's new lover.

In the early summer of 1957, Lindbergh returned to Munich, where he spent a few days alone with Brigitte in her apartment (Marietta was off in Baden-Baden, receiving medical treatment). A few weeks later, he set up a veritable ménage à quatre in his twelfth-floor pad on the Via Polvese in Rome. This was the rented love nest that he had heretofore used for trysts with Valeska. On this visit in July 1957, Lindbergh slept in one bedroom with Valeska. Marietta, who was in the Eternal City to take an art course, and Brigitte, who was on summer vacation, shared the other. Lindbergh's love life now resembled the plot of a romantic farce dreamed up by the master of the genre, French playwright Georges Feydeau. While all three German babes with whom he was cohabitating had fallen for him, his official mistress count stood at two—the seduction of Marietta was still to come. Though both Brigitte and Marietta knew about Valeska—and Marietta knew about Brigitte—Valeska still assumed that she was his sole mistress. And Brigitte, who would repeatedly bend over backward to accommodate Lindbergh, did not voice any objections to the status quo. For the next few weeks, accompanied by his harem, Lindbergh gleefully pranced around town and went on beach outings. "[The summer in Rome] was a wonderful time," he would write Brigitte later that year.

A few months later, after Lindbergh added Marietta to his list of conquests, he had to figure out how to smooth over the inevitable stickiness between the sisters. "We will work the various problems out," he wrote to Brigitte in early 1958. Reassuring her of a positive outcome, he added that "with the right approach everyone can end up with great happiness." For Lindbergh, *right* meant whatever would allow him to do whatever he wished. He was delighted that Brigitte continued to accept his double-dealing and triple-dipping without so much as a whimper; the same went for Marietta. In contrast, Valeska was initially irate when she found out that she was no longer his only European mistress. The passivity of both Hesshaimer sisters may have had something to do with their trying socioeconomic circumstances. In addition to their medical ailments, which had landed both in sanitariums for years at a time, they had endured a series of major traumas.

In 1936, before either was a teenager, their father, Adolf Hesshaimer, a wealthy chocolate manufacturer, died of a heart attack at the age of forty-five. At the end of the war, Marietta and Brigitte emigrated from Romania to Germany, where they fell on hard times, as the Communists ended up commandeering the entire family fortune. After they became pregnant, the Hesshaimer sisters both became financially dependent on Lindbergh, who proved to be generous, eventually helping them to buy houses. On most visits, he arrived armed with gifts, including toy fire trucks and foreign coins for the children (whom he presumably saw as obsessive collectors in the making). To Brigitte and Marietta, Lindbergh was a godsend who served as an insurance policy against a possible fall from bourgeois respectability. Not so to Valeska, who, as a descendant of Prussian aristos, was a woman of independent means.

Brigitte, who also had had an abortion a few years before meeting Lindbergh, seems to have been even more slavishly devoted to her American sugar daddy than Marietta. In late 1962, after explaining to Brigitte that he had fathered a child by Marietta "because it was really important for *her*" (italics mine), Lindbergh asked Brigitte to travel to Marietta's home in Switzerland to help her sister recover from the delivery. A month later, he wrote to thank Brigitte, noting that "[your assistance] touches me more deeply than I can explain to you." The sexagenarian sex addict was finally getting some of the unconditional mother love that Evangeline Land had never sent his way. But by then, it was much too late. For the rest of his life, the self-absorbed celebrity would continue to burden his concubines with his neurotic tics. As part of the deal, Lindbergh insisted that both Brigitte and Marietta—but not Valeska, as she had her own funds—compile household account books in which they tracked every pfennig of the allowance that he provided. "A few days before every one of my father's visits, my mother would take out all her receipts and start organizing them in order to update and balance the account books," Dyrk told me. "During this time, she was often very nervous and grumpy."

While Lindbergh was alive, Valeska's two children were informed of his real identity, but not the five children born to the two Hesshaimer sisters. Brigitte told Dyrk and his siblings that he was in fact a writer named Careu—"Charles" in Hungarian—Kent, as he alleged, though she did acknowledge that he had another family back in America. "When I was very little, I called him Father," stated Dyrk. "And afterwards, I called him Careu." To communicate with Lindbergh, who knew just a few words of German, Dyrk, whose English wasn't very good during his father's lifetime, relied on his mother as a translator. "As I got older," Dyrk noted, "I found it surprising that even though my father was an author no one seemed to know, he was so well connected. I was amazed that he had met with people such as Henry Ford, the Kennedys, Neil Armstrong, and Richard Nixon." Fearful that Dyrk and his younger siblings might make the connection in the weeks following Lindbergh's death in August 1974, Brigitte removed pictures of their father from the family's photo album. That summer, she also managed to prevent her three children, then aged between seven and sixteen, from seeing any of the obituaries that appeared in German newspapers and magazines and on German TV. However, about a decade later, a tearful Brigitte was forced to acknowledge the deception when confronted by a twenty-five-year-old Astrid, whose thorough library search on Careu Kent had come up empty.

———

It was Wednesday, April 5, 1961. Thirty-four springs after touching down in Le Bourget, the Pan Am consultant was a bit player in the aviation biz. The new air heroes were astronauts such as Russia's Yuri Gagarin who, a week later, would become the first human to journey into space. Comparing the two pioneers, the *New York Times* reminded readers that month, "Each won a race to which the entire world was an audience."

The master organizer's miraculous solo flights now took place not in the heavens, but on the ground, as he weaved across Central Europe, heading to and from each of his European families. His new vehicle of choice was a sky-blue Volkswagen Beetle—his "love bug"—that he had recently purchased in Switzerland. And for these arduous journeys, a key part of the challenge was to make sure that no one would be watching.

The former pilot was not quite the proverbial sailor with a lover in every port. His three main squeezes were located within driving distance of one airport—Frankfurt International.

Pulling into a VW dealership in Walldorf, not far from the airport, Lindbergh politely asked in English (he spoke not a word of German), "I've got a problem. Can you help me?"

"No problem," responded Gerald Schroeber, the English-speaking salesman who handled all the American customers. According to Schroeber, who recalled the conversation four decades later in an interview with Rudolf Schroeck, Lindbergh gave his true name and age. But when asked if he was the famous aviator, he said, "I'm often asked this question. No, the aviator is a distant cousin of mine."

Lindbergh explained that he was looking for a place where he could both park his Beetle and have it serviced, adding that he lived in America and flew in to Frankfurt four times a year, staying a few weeks each time.

By then, the fifty-nine-year-old Lindbergh had been romancing his trio of German lovers for several years, and three of his European children had already been born. His aim was to bring more order to his affairs.

For the next thirteen years, he would use the parking spot in Walldorf as his base, from which he would drive his love bug about 20,000 kilometers a year; his quarterly visits with each family would rarely last more than several days. A routine would be set in stone. First, he would drive 600 kilometers south to hook up with the Prussian Valeska and her two children, who were then living in the Swiss canton of Ticino located near the Italian border. Without telling Valeska his destination, he would next head west some 210 kilometers to Wallis, to the waiting arms of Marietta Hesshaimer and her two children. The last stop was 600 kilometers away in Bavaria where Brigitte lived with her three Lindberghs. And then it was another secret 400-kilometer trip in the Beetle back to Frankfurt.

After two hundred thousand kilometers, the Beetle's four-cylinder Boxer engine died. But the thrifty Lindbergh—with a history of deep attachments to machines—refused to consider tossing his car. Harking back to his days in the black laboratory, Lindbergh chose an organ transplant instead, plopping down 1,000 marks on a new engine. After his last ride in the spring of 1974, the speedometer of the VW with the Swiss license plate—GE-9473—recorded a figure just shy of three hundred thousand.

Like his planes of the 1920s, Lindbergh's love bug also served as a surrogate home. "My father," Dyrk told me, "had the seats redesigned so he could sleep in it in his sleeping bag. It was very well-organized and contained everything he needed, including a water tank as well as a steady supply of dried milk powder and Muesli."

Even though the young Dyrk didn't know his father was the famous aviator, his old man was still his hero. In a talk that he gave to his school class when he was about ten, Dyrk referred to his father—rather than any movie star or athlete—as his *Vorbild* (role model). "I was impressed that he knew a lot about a lot of different things," Dyrk stated. Careu Kent expressed particularly strong and informed opinions about the design of machines. He liked Volkswagens because they were simple. When the teenage Dyrk built a plastic model of the Concorde, his father couldn't help but jump in with his assessment, arguing that the jumbo jet used too much fuel and was not economical enough. "He was right, of course," noted Dyrk.

After reading Scott Berg's biography in the late 1990s, Dyrk was perplexed. "The portrait the author painted wasn't consistent with my experience. I never saw my father as a cold and unemotional tyrant," he recalled. "While he wasn't around much, he was always very engaged with us during his visits. In the United States, he had the burden of being a public person. But in Europe, where he could move around as he liked, he was relatively relaxed. My family was very fond of him. When I spoke to my mother about him in the 1990s, she still had a glimmer in her eyes. She never had an interest in finding another man. He was the love of her life."

————

On Friday, August 16, 1974, Lindbergh was trying to summon up the strength to organize a final flight.

The seventy-two-year-old was stuck in the Intensive Care Unit at Manhattan's Columbia Presbyterian Hospital. He was dying of cancer, and his team of eleven doctors said that even if they stepped up his chemotherapy, he was unlikely to live more than a few weeks.

"I want to go home," he told his startled wife, Anne.

Home was then some five thousand miles away in Maui. His doctors were reluctant to let him leave the ICU, much less fly across America. But as with his signature flight a half century earlier, he could not back down from the challenge. "No one," Anne later stated, "believed he could do either and survive."

Five years earlier, Lindbergh had built a modest two-story house with few modern conveniences—it had no phone—in the isolated Hawaiian town of Hana. Anne was not thrilled with the idea, but reluctantly agreed when he promised not to travel so much. But that was a ruse; he stayed in the house overlooking the Pacific Ocean at most two months a year. In the end, he had left Anne stranded on one side of the earth while he pursued his sexual adventures on the other. Knowing what we now do of his nefarious intentions, Anne's diary entries and letters penned from Hawaii, where she felt "dropped out of the world," can be painful to digest. "What a romantic C is! Imagine buying a vacation home without even trying out the climate and locale for one season!" a lonely Anne noted in her diary on February 1, 1969. Two years later, she complained to a friend, "This is the most isolated place on earth: 35–45 minutes from the nearest village."

That same day from his bed in the ICU, Lindbergh sent out a final love letter to all three German mistresses. The text was the same in each. "The situation is extraordinarily serious....All that I can send you," he wrote in blue pen on blue airmail paper, "is my love to you and the children." In a postscript, which he added to the missives to Brigitte and Marietta, he noted that he had set up a Swiss bank account to provide for the family after his death. To the self-sufficient Valeska, he would not leave any money. "My father made sure that we were well taken care of," stated Dyrk, who noted that neither he nor his siblings has ever sought any financial compensation from his father's American heirs. "We went public only because we wanted to be officially recognized as members of his family."

On the morning of Sunday the eighteenth, Lindbergh, lying on a stretcher, arrived at Kennedy Airport, where he was lifted aboard a regularly scheduled United Airlines DC-8 flight, which departed at ten thirty. Accompanying him in the first-class cabin were Anne and his sons, Jon and Scott, who gave him his medicine as they headed west.

As he awoke the next morning in Hana, Lindbergh began compiling a new series of checklists, as he turned his attention to his final journey—the one into the ground.

In the week of life left to him—he died after breakfast on Monday the twenty-sixth—though he would drift in and out of consciousness, Lindbergh kept planning the details of both his funeral services and burial. In the end, he arranged everything. Rejecting Anne's suggestion of Bach cantatas for his memorial service, which he requested be held a day or two after the burial service, he settled on Hawaiian hymns because, as he told the family, "no one will know what they mean." While he had hoped that his body would be wrapped in sheets made of pure cotton, he reluctantly agreed to a 50-50 cotton-polyester mix. He even instructed the pallbearers, local day laborers, what to wear, insisting on work clothes.

As if he were back looking over the shoulders of the engineers at Ryan Airlines, Lindbergh helped design both his coffin—one-inch planks of a special type of mahogany were to be used—and his gravesite. He specified the shape and size of the lava rocks that were to surround each side of the fourteen-by-fourteen-by-twelve-foot pit where he—and later Anne—were to be buried. He kept badgering his wife and children about every detail. "Father was obsessed about drainage," Jon Lindbergh noted.

Today the Lone Eagle still lies alone, as Anne later chose to be cremated rather than to be buried beside her husband.

Part Three

———

Celebrity Compulsives

6

Beauty: Estée Lauder

The Woman Who Couldn't Stop Touching Faces

> Good was not good enough....I know now that *obsession* is the
> word for my zeal. I was obsessed with clear glowing skin, shin-
> ing eyes, beautiful mouths.
> — Estée Lauder, *Estée: A Success Story* (1985)

Without a beauty business as an alibi, Estée (pronounced "Esty") Lauder might well have gone to jail for aggravated assault with deadly face powder or lipstick.

For this cosmetics tycoon, putting makeup on women's faces was not a chore; it was all that she ever cared about. It was not something that she did to build a company; she built a company so that she could keep on doing it. During her adolescence, as she later recalled, "I was forever experimenting on myself and on anyone else who came within range."

The adult Lauder would sidle up to perfect strangers whom she bumped into in elevators and on street corners in order to perform an instant makeover. In the early 1950s, a few years after starting her eponymous company, the forty-something entrepreneur was taking the train to Utah to open her counter at Auerbach's Department Store in Salt Lake City when she spotted a young woman decked out in a Salvation Army dress. *Just because you're in the service of the Lord,* she suddenly thought, as she later noted in her autobiography, *doesn't mean you can't be beautiful.* When asked if she wanted to be made up, her stunned interlocutor declined. But a persistent Lauder soon whisked her into a roomette, where she dabbed on some cream, a drop of Honey Glow face powder, and a hint of turquoise eye shadow.

A decade later, after overhearing the legendary designer Sister Parish, who was paying a visit to her Manhattan mansion, mutter to an assistant, "Oh, what I could do with this house," Lauder patted her guest's sagging cheeks and quipped, "Oh, what I could do with that face."

This habit would follow her to the grave—and beyond. "When I was attending grade school in the 1980s," her granddaughter Aerin Lauder, now the company's image and style director, told me, "she went to my parent-teacher conference. And she brought some product and did a makeover." Estée Lauder's idea of heaven, as she remarked toward the end of her life, took "the form of little angel girls on high, who could use just the teeniest dab of blusher, just the little drip of Super-Rich All Purpose Crème....I'll be there...to do the dabbing."

Today, nearly a decade after death, her compulsion remains the driving force behind the Estée Lauder Companies, a public megacorporation whose annual sales exceed $9 billion. As its marketing department stresses, this beauty colossus, which now hawks more than two dozen brands (including such stalwarts as Clinique, Origins, M-A-C, Bobbi Brown, and Jo Malone) in more than 150 countries, "touches" more than half a billion consumers around the globe. Every day, its army of beauty experts—a significant subset of its nearly thirty-five thousand employees worldwide—provide one-on-one skincare in the same obsessional manner as the founder to more than five million individuals.

While the company's raison d'être can be traced back to Estée Lauder's compulsion to touch faces, it first shot to prominence because of her extraordinary nose.

Nose is beauty-industry jargon for someone who mixes fragrance components into perfume. "In all America," stated the late Ernest Shiftan, long the chief perfumer of International Flavors and Fragrances, Inc., the world's leading creator of fragrances, a half century ago, "there is only one true nose and it belongs to Estée Lauder."

Lauder's nose, which forever changed the scent of the American woman, was as perfectionistic as the late Steve Jobs's eyes. Just as the Apple founder obsessed over the parts of computers that went unseen—he nixed the initial design of the circuit board inside the Apple II because the lines were not straight enough—she could not stop worrying about the parts of scents that went unsmelled. In 1973, when her company was launching Private Collection, she startled her colleagues by demanding that department stores send back early shipments, complaining that "it didn't have dunk-dunk in it." When told that "Nobody will *know* the difference," she responded, "But *I'll* know the difference."

This world-famous nose first made its mark back in 1953 when the beauty business that she ran with her husband, Joseph—an easygoing accountant, he kept the books and oversaw manufacturing—still sold just a handful of products, the most successful of which was its signature Estoderme skin cream. One evening while attending a dinner party, the workaholic and mother of two was seized by an idea. Examining a tray on her host's dresser—Lauder was the eternal snoop—she noticed three beautifully packaged but unopened bottles of perfume. "Perfume was the perfect gift," she later recalled. "*That* was killing it. . . . I'd convince the American woman to buy her own perfume, as she would buy her own lipstick." In America, as opposed to France, where Chanel No. 5 already ruled, women considered perfume a luxury and would use only a few dabs at a time.

The five-foot-four-and-a-half-inch blonde with the blue-green eyes and perfect skin, which she kept perfect looking as she aged—"You have only one face, so you better take care of it"—also had a nose for the bottom line. In the mid-twentieth century, perfume was just a tiny fraction of the $1 billion cosmetics and toiletries market—less than 1 percent—and gross margins (the difference between the cost of raw materials and the price) averaged a robust 80 percent, 10 percent higher than for most other beauty products. To induce middle America to change its ways, this always elegantly attired entrepreneur went into the fragrance biz "backwards." For years, she had been tinkering with a flowery scent, and now she finally decided to bring it to market, but as a bath oil rather than as a perfume per se. "It was feminine," Lauder later recalled, "all-American, very girl-next-door to take baths." And to make her new product, which she dubbed Youth Dew, more accessible to customers, Lauder did not seal the cap with cellophane or gold wire, as French manufacturers did. With the bottle easy to open, women who passed by the counters in the select department stores where she sold her wares—she was already in both Saks Fifth Avenue and Neiman Marcus—could easily take an experimental whiff.

"Youth Dew was an immediate success," her elder son, Leonard Lauder, recently told me. Leonard, who would succeed "Mrs. Lauder," as he used to refer to his boss, as CEO of the Estée Lauder Companies in 1982, was then a college student and his mother's part-time assistant. "We didn't even have proper distribution channels," he noted. "But it emerged as the engine behind the growth of the company." In 1953, the product brought in $50,000; three decades later, the figure came to $150 million.

Youth Dew, as Americans soon discovered, had magical properties. If Helen of Troy, as Renaissance poet Christopher Marlowe has put it, was "the face that launched a thousand ships," this was the irresistible fragrance that saved thousands of marriages. It could even revive the careers and romantic lives of Hollywood has-beens. The Mexican-born beauty Dolores del Rio, whose star had fizzled out in the early 1940s (at the same time as her highly publicized affair with wunderkind director Orson Welles), stated publicly that the secret to "driving men ga-ga" was putting some in her hair. Likewise, Joan Crawford, whose box-office clout was fast declining, revealed to an interviewer that Youth Dew helped her snag her fourth husband, Mr. Pepsi-Cola. "I can't stop dancing with you," Alfred Steele whispered in Crawford's ear, "you smell so exquisite." While contemporary companies have to pay big bucks—through the nose—for such endorsements, such kudos came unsolicited.

A superb networker, Lauder often contacted celebrities after she read about their use of her products in the press; and Joan Crawford became her lifelong friend who also stuck a free plug for Youth Dew in her bestselling 1971 memoir, *My Way of Life*. A decade later, when Crawford's tumultuous life made it on to the big screen in *Mommie Dearest*, Lauder rushed to the theater with her grand-daughter Aerin, the elder daughter of Estée's second son, Ronald, the prominent Manhattan philanthropist who has held numerous positions in the company over the years. Aerin was then a preteen, and one might think the campy biopic about a neurotic mother torturing her daughter might not have been on *her* list of must-see flicks. When asked to say more about this outing in a recent inter-view in her office, Aerin took a cue from her idol, the woman in the huge portrait taken by the photographer Victor Skrebneski that hangs behind her desk: "My grandmother was a private person, who didn't gossip with kids. All she said after the film was, 'That was someone I knew.'"

With Youth Dew stoking interest in her creams, lipsticks, and face powders, Lauder went back to touching and dabbing customers with her characteristic abandon. For this supersaleswoman, marketing depended upon personal con-tact. "Touch your customer, and you are halfway there," she would later instruct her staff. Like Heinz, Lauder also emblazoned her office with her favorite mot-toes, and she had "Bringing the best to everyone we touch" engraved on little squares of pale green glass next to the elevator banks at the company head-quarters in the General Motors Building on Fifth Avenue. Her specialty was the three-minute makeover, which, she insisted, "could change a life." The de-partment store mini-makeover, which has been the bedrock of the cosmetics business since the 1960s, has Lauder's stamp all over it. She was a hands-on businesswoman. Like Kinsey, who took the sex histories of science journalists in his attempt to bond with and control them, Lauder gave beauty editors makeovers. And whenever Lauder met with a male department store executive, she would pat a few drops of Youth Dew or one of her creams directly onto his hand—and she always sought out the right hand. "That was a brilliant insight, to seek out the dominant hand, which is the one people are likely to touch themselves with," explained Jane Lauder to me, while seated at her desk overlooking Central Park. Jane is Ronald Lauder's youngest daughter and a graduate of Stanford; *Fortune* has described her as "press-wary" and "serious." She has been a member of the firm's board of directors since 2009. Jane emphasized how market research backs up her grandmother's key teachings, adding, "Letting customers touch and put on the product has a tremendous impact on sales."

By the late 1950s, the Estée Lauder treatment line emerged as number three in the cosmetics industry behind Helena Rubinstein and Elizabeth Arden, companies that were then still run by the grande dames themselves. Lauder would pattern herself after these two pioneering businesswomen, each of whom would die at an advanced age in the mid-1960s. She even borrowed a few of their favorite sayings. Rubinstein's "There are no ugly women, only lazy ones" became Lauder's "There are no homely women, only careless women." In awe of her idols, Lauder showed some uncharacteristic restraint around them. When she first met Madame Rubinstein at a ball at the Waldorf-Astoria, she conceded that the octogenarian's face looked lovely. However, Lauder did insist that she could do wonders for her neck and sent her a Crème Pack a few days later.

Her son Leonard would be instrumental in helping her leapfrog over her rivals. In 1958, after completing a three-year stint in the Navy, he joined the company full-time, focusing on marketing and advertising. A Columbia business-school graduate, Leonard also created a research and development laboratory and brought in a new cadre of professional managers. In 1960, three quarters of a century after Henry Heinz, Estée Lauder made her first call on London's Fortnum and Mason. After gaining a foothold in England, she conquered France and then the rest of the world. In the 1960s, she began rolling out a string of new brands such as Aramis—upscale men's toiletries—and Clinique—a medically tested line of skin-care products. Like Heinz, she also believed in allocating previously unheard-of amounts of money to advertising and promotion—estimates have ranged from 30 to 60 percent of sales—a formula that also worked wonders for her. By 1995, when Lauder finally retired and the family-owned company went public, it controlled nearly half of the U.S. department store market, and annual sales were $3 billion, 40 percent of which came from outside the United States.

Despite the staggering success of the Estée Lauder Companies and all the accolades awarded to its founder—in 1998, she was the only woman who made it on to *Time*'s list of the top twenty business geniuses of the twentieth century—little reliable information is available about the dynamic entrepreneur who invented the beauty business as we know it. Lauder rarely spoke about herself, and when she did, she told tall tales that often contradicted one another. "I was not born in Germany, Czechoslovakia, Austria, or Hungary," Lauder wrote in her 1985 autobiography, *Estée: A Success Story*. "I have read that I was born in all of these romantic places." But she herself was the primary source for most of the misinformation disseminated in the various newspaper and magazine stories about her. "She was a terrible liar," Marylin Bender, who covered business for the *New York Times* for three decades and often lunched with Lauder, told me. "Estée constructed a lovely past for herself. But that made sense because her business required her to appeal to rich people." In the fall of 1985, just as two books on Lauder's life—her autobiography and Lee Israel's equally skimpy biography (which remain the only ones ever written)—were about to appear, the *New Yorker* noted that "Lauder keeps its corporate secrets and Estée Lauder keeps her private ones . . . she [has excelled] at garnering publicity . . . while maintaining a mystique. Many customers vaguely accepted her as some European aristocrat . . . or they confused her with the beautiful young women . . . in her advertisements." These false notions were, of course, just what Lauder wanted people to believe.

The nearly eighty-year-old Lauder was a most reluctant author. She started her autobiography only after she learned that Israel, whose previous biography was a *New York Times* bestseller on journalist Dorothy Kilgallen, was plugging away and that there was nothing she could do to stop her. Like Kinsey and Lindbergh, Lauder was horrified by the idea of a biographer rummaging around in her past. In her case, she feared not so much the dredging up of her countless sexual escapades—though she had had a few—but the puncturing of the myths about her origins. As the *Wall Street Journal* reported in its article, THE BOOK WORLD IS ABUZZ OVER LIVES OF ESTÉE LAUDER—AUTOBIOGRAPHY AND BIOGRAPHY RECOUNT DIFFERING TALES, published in September 1985, several writers before

Israel had attempted to write a biography, only to be "talked out of it" by some "good conversation" with the family, which may have been spiced with monetary inducements. Israel mentioned to the paper that she had received a message on her answering machine from someone representing the family, which offered her six figures to break her contract with Macmillan. When asked recently about that message, Israel told me in a phone interview that the financial offer was preceded by the words, "The old lady is very upset." While Leonard Lauder acknowledged to the *Journal* that he had heard about the taped message, he denied that the family had anything to do with it. After Lauder's death, Cindy Adams of the *New York Post* also revealed that she had once tried to tell her story, only to be deterred by the family's lawyer, the late Roy Cohn. "I was parrying," the columnist wrote in 2004, "with the smartest and the toughest."

Rushed into print in an attempt to beat its competitor to press, each Lauder life turned out to be unsatisfying and incomplete. In her book, which came out in mid-October 1985, just two weeks before Israel's, Lauder, assisted by an uncredited ghost writer, covered just the basic facts—she finally acknowledged, for example, that she had Jewish roots. Like the other obsessives profiled in this book (with the notable exception of Ted Williams, who, with the help of a co-author, produced a moving bestseller about his personal struggles dating back to his boyhood), Lauder had little capacity for self-reflection; she provided just a two-dimensional picture of her emotional life. Like Jefferson, whose autobiography abruptly stopped in 1790 when he was in his late forties, she got bored with talking about herself halfway into her book; from that point on, the narrative turned to business tips. In contrast, while Israel did some valuable digging into her subject's family background and key relationships, *Estée Lauder: Beyond the Magic, An Unauthorized Biography* suffered from its prosecutorial tone. Attacking Lauder as a heartless social climber, Israel failed to capture her subject's spark and ingenuity. Israel admitted as much to me when she called her effort "a bad book." In both the marketplace and the book pages, neither did well. Writing in the *New York Times Book Review*, Marylin Bender characterized Lauder's prose as "gush cranked out by her publicity department" and Israel's style as "incoherent."

And in a curious twist, subsequent events in Israel's own life have cast a shadow on her factual findings, which by and large come across as plausible. "I guess there is a certain irony," Israel admitted to me, "in my questioning Estée's veracity." After her Lauder biography tanked, Israel descended into alcoholism and poverty; and in the early 1990s, in a desperate attempt to stay afloat, she turned to forging letters of such literary notables as Dorothy Parker and Noël Coward. This descent into criminality, for which she was convicted but not sent to prison—the penalty was five years of probation and six months' house arrest—became the subject of Israel's controversial 2008 memoir, *Can You Ever Forgive Me?*

Besides dispelling a few common falsehoods such as the foreign birth—this Queen of Beauty was actually born to middle-class European immigrants in Queens, New York—the two biographies added little to the public's understanding of Lauder. Israel's publisher, Macmillan, promised several "bombshells," nearly all of which the cosmetics tycoon acknowledged in one form or another so as to take away Israel's thunder. (In the months preceding the launch, the rival publishers, Macmillan and Random House, kept close tabs on one another.) But by the mid-1980s, the two juiciest bits of new info—Lauder's Jewishness and her divorce from Joseph in 1939, which was followed by remarriage in 1942—were hardly tantalizing enough to set many tongues wagging.

In retrospect, what is most revealing about Lauder's book is what she left out. On the subject of her Jewishness, despite her promise "to be candid," she noted only that her mother was half-Jewish; she said nothing about her father's religion. Noting that her maternal grandmother was a French Catholic, she alluded to her "ecumenical approach to religion." But her family was actually Jewish on both sides. And she was raised as an observant Jew, as were both of her sons. While Leonard and Ronald have long been open about *their* religious heritage—1987 saw the birth of the Ronald S. Lauder Foundation, which assists European communities ravaged by the Holocaust—only after their mother's death in 2004 did they begin to embrace *her* Jewish identity. As Ann Friedman, director of the New York Landmarks Conservancy's Sacred Sites Program, informed me, Leonard Lauder's generous donations have been instrumental in restoring the Congregation Tifereth Israel—the synagogue is the oldest building in Queens—where Estée Lauder worshipped as a child a century ago. Inside are bronze plaques with the names of both her parents. (This Queens landmark also has ties to another prominent self-made woman. In 1979 and 1980, Madonna lived in the building across the street that once served as the temple's Yeshiva.)

The careful fudging about her religious background in the autobiography underlines how much Lauder was a creature of control. Like Kinsey and Lindbergh, she sought to shape her public image, down to the smallest details. As she saw it, the story of her life was essentially the story of her brand; hence, the stakes were far from trivial. "She sold herself as a brand," Leonard Lauder told me. "The ads say, 'Estée Lauder says.' Everything depended on her authority." Her company peddled not just beauty products but a lavish lifestyle; and in post–World War II America, Lauder concluded, not entirely unreasonably, that coming out as a Jewish girl from Queens would reduce her cachet. By the mid-1980s, Lauder also had another compelling reason for describing herself as ecumenical rather than Jewish—the marketplace in the tense Middle East. At the time, the Arab League boycotted many companies that traded with Israel, and Lauder was forced to do business with one side or the other. And in contrast to her Jewish-owned competitors such as Revlon, she chose the Arabs, who were big fans of her pungent fragrances, over the Jews. Like Jefferson, she enjoyed sweating the small stuff. "God is in the details," she would often say (though the nonreader had no idea that she was recycling a phrase often attributed to novelist Gustave Flaubert or architect Ludwig Mies van der Rohe). In the end, she produced a book that was as carefully packaged as any of the lipsticks in her company's vaunted Christmas lines.

In Lauder, this desire for control was combined with a fiercely competitive nature. "She taught me to be the best at whatever you do, even if that's selling peanuts. Second best wasn't good enough for her," stated her son Ronald in a phone interview. Agnes Ash, the now nearly ninety-year-old former editor of the *Palm Beach Daily News*, who was a good friend for half a century, recalled going to a polo match with her in the 1980s to watch Prince Charles: "The conversation came around to the possibility of her sponsoring a polo team. Estée then suddenly stated out, 'But what if they didn't win! My products have to be associated with a winner.'"

As with other obsessives, Lauder often sought to impose her will on others. "My grandmother was a very determined woman," William Lauder, Leonard's son, now in his early fifties, who became the company's CEO in 2004, noted in an interview in his office. "There were two ways to do things with her—you could do it her way, or you could compromise and do it her way," added her grandson, who has served as executive chairman since stepping down from the top job in 2009. "My grandfather [Joseph Lauder] used to say, 'Here we go again' before giving in." However, in the one-on-one of the sales arena, she knew just how far to push; and her gentle but firm persistence was precisely what made her a supersaleswoman. "Customers flocked to her because of the force of her personality. She loved people," Leonard Lauder told me. While the first statement is undoubtedly true, the second is debatable. Her charm with customers, like Kinsey's compassion with interviewees, did not come naturally. It was something that she turned on to achieve her objective. Away from the department store counter, she often came across as both intimidating and detached. In a recent phone interview, a retired executive who provided consulting services to her company from the 1960s to the 1980s and who did not wish to be identified, stated, "I learned never to argue with Mrs. Lauder. I had no choice but to acquiesce." In the autobiography, she stuck in an analogous throwaway comment: "I must admit that I'm not terribly democratic in my business, and neither is my son, Leonard."

In contrast to his mother, who never went beyond high school, the Ivy League–educated Leonard is a careful and systematic thinker. However, he shares her quirky and demanding temperament. Now eighty and one of America's fifty wealthiest men—he's worth more than $7 billion, according to *Forbes*—Leonard has always been fidgety. As a middle-aged man, when stuck in traffic on the highway, he used to head for the nearest exit and drive in the other direction so that he could keep moving. As Allan Mottus, a beauty industry consultant, told the *New York Times* in 1987, just as Leonard was coming out from under his mother's shadow, "he's secretive, confidential to the point of obsession. Leonard's a very studied person. . . . He is acting a role." Leonard has also sought tight control over media coverage. "He used to ask to review my stories before publication, but I had to tell him that we didn't do that at the *New York Times*," Marylin Bender told me.

In contacting family members and former business associates for this chapter, I repeatedly came up against a kind of omertà. Many would refuse to talk, and those who did sometimes insisted on anonymity; even then, on a couple of occasions, I heard, "Leonard is going to kill me for saying this." Given the family penchant for privacy and control, the recent sex scandal involving his son William struck Bender as "highly un-Lauder-like." (During his five-year stint as CEO, as the *New York Post* revealed in 2007, William carried on an extra-marital affair with Manhattan socialite Taylor Stein, which resulted in "a love child.") While Leonard built the company up by creating a well-oiled organization and focusing on the numbers—say, achieving sales goals—he was careful to preserve, as he told Harvard Business School professor Nancy Koehn in the late 1990s, "the intuitive, gutsy feel of Mrs. Estée Lauder." So too have Leonard's successors, including the Italian-born Fabrizio Freda, who took over as CEO in 2009.

And Estée Lauder's sensibility, which continues to guide the company, was shaped in her Jewish childhood in Queens, which she spent her whole adult life running away from.

———

In her early days, America's preeminent nose was forced to breathe in some horrific scents. Corona, Queens, where Josephine Esther Mentzer was born on July 1, 1908, was literally a dump. The Brooklyn Ash Company used the mostly working-class Italian neighborhood—the total number of Jewish residents, who had first begun settling in the still-sylvan community around 1900, then came to only 150—as the site to spill the waste collected on its railroad cars. In addition to the thick clouds of foul-smelling smoke that emanated from the smoldering refuse, the future beauty tycoon also had to inhale the stench from the manure-filled barges left at the nearby docks. "In her youth, because of all the garbage," Queens historian Vincent Tomeo said in a recent phone interview, "Corona was known as 'the dumps.' It also had a serious rodent problem." WAR DECLARED UPON RATS, ran the headline of a *New York Times* story, published on November 4, 1920, which discussed the plan of New York health commissioner R. S. Copeland to exterminate the rats that infested both Corona's meadow dumps and its residential neighborhood. "Commissioner Copeland," the paper reported, "in a communication to the Corona Civic Aid Society said inspectors of his department had found conditions to be as bad as described." Corona would not get a serious makeover until the late 1930s, when it was selected as the venue for the World's Fair.

"Terrible place" was the assessment rendered by Tom Buchanan, the old-monied, Yale-educated villain of F. Scott Fitzgerald's 1925 novel, *The Great Gatsby*. Buchanan's depressed proletarian mistress hails from Corona, which the novelist described as a "valley of ashes... bounded on one side by a small foul river." One of the early titles of the Fitzgerald classic was "Among the Ash Heaps and the Millionaires." To cross over to the ranks of the millionaires, Esther (or Estelle, as she was then also called—no one ever referred to her as Josephine) would completely erase her past, just like the self-made financier Jay Gatsby, who, as Fitzgerald wrote, "sprang from his Platonic conception of himself."

Her mother, Rose Schotz, was a Hungarian Jew who had immigrated to America, accompanied by her five children, in 1898. In New York City, the twenty-nine-year-old Rose was reunited with her Hungarian husband, Abraham Rosenthal. But a few years later, Rosenthal was gone.

A struggling single mother with little education—as census records reveal, she could neither read nor write—and in a strange land, Rose Schotz was beside herself with grief. As Rose later said little about what happened other than to label this blow a "burden," Lauder was never sure whether her mother's first husband died or simply abandoned the family; the latter scenario was more likely, as she would acknowledge in her memoir.

This loss compounded the other major events that Rose had endured back in Hungary. When she was a little girl, her mother dropped dead after eating a spider hidden in a cup of water drawn from a well. Rose was then reared by a nasty stepmother. To escape her unhappy family predicament, she had run off with Rosenthal, an older cousin, at the age of fifteen.

But before Rose could give in to despair, she was rescued by a knight in shining armor—though he did not joust, he was quite the able equestrian—another Jewish immigrant from Hungary, Max Mentzer (the family name was derived from the German city of Mainz). With her second husband, Rose had two more children, Grace (called Renée) and Esther. Mentzer first worked as a tailor and did other odd jobs. The 1920 census identified him as a driver for a bakery. In the early 1920s, he opened up a hardware store at 107th Street and Corona Avenue, above which the family lived. His new business venture did well, and by 1930, as census records show, the family's real estate was worth a hefty $50,000 ($650,000 today). As his fortunes improved, Mentzer also built a stable next to the house. In the late 1930s—after Lauder had gotten married—Mentzer would move into the largely Jewish Washington Heights section of Manhattan and become the director of the Beth El Cemetery in Paramus, New Jersey; at his new place of employment, he could show off his equestrian skills by taking mourners (and family members) on horseback rides. The entire family, including Lauder, is buried there.

Though Lauder finally did cough up the key facts about her childhood in her autobiography, she still spun several hard-to-believe yarns; a few revolved around the supposedly aristocratic backgrounds of her parents. She claimed that the Austrian emperor Franz Joseph had personally selected Mentzer as the man whom one of his nieces should marry—an offer he allegedly declined because the bride-to-be weighed three hundred pounds. Lauder also insisted that her mother went to spas in Carlsbad and Baden-Baden for beauty treatment—though the family had some means by the early 1930s, it's highly unlikely that she or her husband ever traveled back to Europe. (For Jews of that generation, Germany was not exactly a favorite tourist destination.) And while Lauder stated that her mother spoke "a very broken English, with a predominantly German accent," that phrase is misleading. Yiddish was the mother tongue of both her parents, as noted on the 1920 census, and was the language spoken at home. Years later, Lauder could still hold her own in Yiddish, though she never let the press know.

While the tall, handsome, and affable Mentzer was the answer to Rose's prayers, one gnawing problem remained: her traumatic anxiety. She was terrified of being abandoned by Max just as she had been by her first husband (and by her mother, who had suddenly died on her). And her fear that her dashing husband might run off with another woman was magnified by the difference in their ages—he was a full decade younger.

In an effort to hold on to her man, Rose engaged in an elaborate beauty ritual as soon as he left the house in the morning. "My mother began brushing her hair," Lauder later wrote, "even before she opened her eyes." Rose was obsessed with staying attractive and young looking.

And just as the young Henry Heinz became "his mother's little helper," Esther became her mother's little personal beauty assistant. "My very first memory," Lauder later wrote, "is of my mother's scent, her aura of freshness, the perfume of her presence....Her hair didn't escape my attention, either. As soon as I was old enough to hold a brush, I'd give her no peace." A script was thus implanted into little Esther's brain, one which Estée Lauder would replay time and time again. She would always equate her own well-being with her ability to help the women in her midst look their best.

The lifelong addiction to making up women was already under way in early childhood. "Esty, you've already brushed my hair three times today," her mother would complain. Likewise, her irked father would oft repeat, "Stop fiddling with other people's faces." Once she started going to school, the first thing Esther would do when she got home was pat the face of her older sister, Renée, with her mother's skin cream.

"But this is what I liked to do—touch other people's faces, no matter who they were," Lauder wrote in her autobiography, "touch them and make them pretty. Before I'm finished, I'll set, I'm certain, the world's record for face touching."

This feat she would accomplish, just as Kinsey would set records for collecting both galls and sex histories.

For Lauder, the obsession with glowing skin and shining eyes was forever tied to her own deepest needs for love and connection. If she could only keep her mother beautiful, little Esty must have thought, she could keep her family together and thus guarantee herself the love of both her parents. "My mother was so beautiful that a man fifteen years younger married her," she told the *New York Times* in 1967, stretching the truth by five years. "Now my purpose is to keep women looking younger and younger." This pursuit was not just what Lauder ended up doing for a living; it became her reason for living. And her obsession could translate into a phenomenal living because her mother's predicament was universal; while Rose Mentzer's fear of abandonment was extreme, many women share her dread of aging and losing their looks. Like Heinz, who targeted his products to stressed-out mothers eager to put fresh food on the table, Lauder could also tap into a huge market.

While the adult Lauder would describe herself as the "coddled baby of the family," the evidence suggests otherwise. Like Lindbergh, she came from a topsy-turvy family where the traditional child and parent roles were reversed. As a child, she kept herself busy tending to the needs of her anxious parents, particularly her mother. And like other obsessives who received little nurturing, she took on various adult responsibilities at an early age. Just like Melvil Dewey, who compiled an inventory of the items in his father's general store, as a teenager Esther organized the wares in her father's hardware store. Mothering her own parents would be a lifelong assignment. In the 1950s, when the forty-something executive was zipping across the country on sales trips, she would feel compelled to call Max and Rose nearly every night to allay *their* anxiety about her stressful existence.

And the little girl eager to please her parents would evolve into a merchant eager to please patrons. "Let's listen to our customer," she would state in a lecture to fashion students toward the end of her life. "She's trying to tell us something—and the word she is trying to tell us is *service.*"

In her autobiography, Lauder summed up her childhood as nearly idyllic. In her cheery rendering, the only blot was "the specter of an infantile paralysis epidemic [that] loomed over New York." Due to this public health catastrophe, the anxious Rose fled with her two preteens to the home of Sarah Gottlieb—her younger sister—in Milwaukee for several months. Lauder did not mention the date of the move, but it was probably in or around 1916; from June to November that year, the death toll in New York City from polio amounted to a staggering 2,407 persons, 98 percent of whom were children under sixteen. Of the five boroughs, Queens was hardest hit; its death rate was .90 per 1,000 residents, more than twice the average for the city as a whole and three times more than that of Manhattan. New York's Department of Health attributed the epidemic to "insects migrating by themselves or on the body of some animal host like a rat"— a widely circulated conclusion that must have left Esther feeling even more ashamed about her borough of origin. Like Kinsey, so too was this neatnik and order freak created at least in part from early exposure to too much dirt and to too many rats.

But Lauder would never acknowledge any of this angst. All she mentioned about the epidemic was that after the family's return from Milwaukee, Renée contracted polio and had to wear a brace until she turned fifteen. "When trouble struck," she wrote, "my sister, not I, absorbed the blow." In her autobiography, she also said nothing else about Milwaukee except for that quick allusion to her stay there when she was around ten. But she would actually go back to live with her relatives a decade later and work as "a little clean-up girl" in beauty shops. In interviews in the 1960s and 1970s, Lauder would occasionally reference Milwaukee sojourns, but she would embellish her rather modest living conditions with her aunt Sarah. "In Milwaukee," she told the New York Times in 1967, "a woman used to come to our house every day just to brush my mother's hair."

As a girl, her role models were not her parents, but the Leppel sisters— Fanny and Frieda. Eleven years older than Esther, Fanny was married to her half brother Isidor; Frieda was Fanny's older sister and was married to another Isidore. Together with their husbands, the two sisters transformed their father's dry-goods store—originally called Leppel's, it was renamed Pflaker and Rosenthal—into a department store that became known as "the Macy's of Corona." "Pflaker and Rosenthal," Lauder later wrote, "was my gateway to fancy. It was Dress-up Land for me. I loved to play with the beautiful clothes." Schmoozing with the Jewish customers in Yiddish and the Italians in Neapolitan, Fanny and Frieda were skilled saleswomen who knew how to move product. "I whetted my appetite for the merry ring of a cash register," Lauder later observed. "I learned early that being a perfectionist and providing quality was the only way to do business."

In the Leppel, Rosenthal, and Mentzer families, traditional gender roles were turned inside out. The women often took the initiative; the men, in contrast, tended to be less ambitious and to patrol the kitchen. One of Lauder's relatives, who did not wish to be identified, told me: "Ours was a matriarchal family. Fanny and Frieda ran the store." Now in his late sixties, this family member recalled attending a Passover Seder with Estée Lauder and her parents in the 1950s: "Her father, Max, made the best matzah balls. They were tight and firm like cannonballs. They sank right to the bottom. Fantastic."

In contrast to her father, Esther did not like to cook. "One day, in the mid-1960s, while I was walking along Worth Avenue in Palm Beach, Lauder drove up to me in her pale blue Cadillac and invited me over to her English-style mansion for 'some tea and Sara Lee.' I was stunned," Marylin Bender told me. Lauder's lack of a food sense has been confirmed by numerous other sources. As her granddaughter Aerin recalled, "When we used to visit her in Florida, she would insist on hot lunches. She would prepare for us her favorite foods—spaghetti and meatballs and hot dogs, which she called frankfurters." In her house in southern France, her American maid would serve caviar on Ritz crackers.

As an adolescent, Esther ventured into the kitchen not to work on matzah balls with her father but to assist her uncle John—her mother's younger brother—as he produced his skin cream over the gas stove. During World War I, John Schotz, a chemist who may have had a Ph.D., was visiting from Hungary, and he decided to stay in America. "I loved his creams, loved his potions," Lauder later wrote. She now had a new excuse to go on face-touching binges. In high school, Esther didn't have "a single friend who wasn't slathered in our creams," as the beauty tycoon later put it. "If someone had a slight redness just under her nose…she'd come to visit."

In the mid-1920s, at about the same time Esther was finishing Newtown High School in Corona, Schotz set up a laboratory on West Forty-Second Street in Manhattan, where he manufactured several beauty products such as a Six-in-One Cold Cream. While Schotz was a clever inventor, he had no idea how to sell anything. But Esther would figure that one out. Renamed "Super-Rich All Purpose Crème," Schotz's signature concoction would later emerge as the bedrock of Lauder's own burgeoning beauty business. "All [her products,]" the *New York Times* would report in 1959, "are based on formulas that Mrs. Lauder's uncle, a dermatologist, turned over to her." (A decade later, she would invent a few more analogous relatives, telling the *Boston Globe* that her beauty empire

was launched with a face pack devised by her "four Viennese doctor uncles.")
According to Schotz's nephew, Alan Carlan, the chemist did recall giving her
the formulas. However, Carlan was not sure if Schotz, who died penniless, ever
received a share of the profits.

———

In the late 1920s, while vacationing in the family's tiny bungalow in Mohegan
Lake in New York's Westchester County, Esther, then nearly twenty, met her first
beau, Joseph Lauter, a man six years older, whose parents were also Jews from
Eastern Europe. After studying accounting and shorthand at New York's High
School of Commerce, Joe launched a series of small businesses that sold everything from buttons to textiles; none would do particularly well. (She would later
also remove the blemishes from his résumé, telling the *Boston Globe* that Joe was
"a Wall Street financial consultant" when she first met him.) But he was cordial
and kind, and that was what won her heart. "All at once I felt noticed, cherished,
grown-up, amused, amusing, happy," she later wrote. Everyone seemed to feel
comfortable around Joe. "He was very approachable and easy to talk to," a relative told me. As the years went on, his unflappable demeanor may have been
aided by alcohol, as Lauder herself appeared to acknowledge. In her autobiography, she noted that Joe had "a royal constitution for holding down four or five
Scotches without visible effect."

After a three-year courtship, they were married on January 15, 1930, at the
Royal Palms Ballroom on 135th Street and Broadway in West Harlem, then a
Jewish neighborhood. While Lauder would later claim that her wedding picture
appeared in the rotogravure section of the *New York Times*, the couple was not
yet that socially prominent. That month, the *Times* did mention a "Mr. and Mrs.
J. H. Lauter," among the recent arrivals at the Bermudiana Hotel, in Bermuda,
where they spent their honeymoon. But the couple initially lacked the funds to
move into an abode of their own. The 1930 census, taken a few months later,
listed them as living in Corona along with her parents as well as with her sister
and her husband, Herman Shapiro.

In March 1933, a couple of years after the couple had made the move to their
own modest apartment on the West Side of Manhattan, Leonard Allan Lauter
was born. The woman who had not been the beneficiary of much mother love
dreaded the prospect of being cooped up alone at home with her son. Like the

male icons profiled in this book, her identity would come primarily from pursuing her obsessions and compulsions rather than from nurturing others. "It was not enough," she later wrote, "for me to stay home and play Mommy." She preferred "mothering my zeal for experimenting with my uncle's creams," which she continued to cook up in her kitchen. Lauder also began performing in small parts at the Cherry Lane Theatre in Greenwich Village. "She was not much of a success as an actress," her grandson William Lauder stated. "But she took something from that experience. She learned how to tell stories in the retail environment." For Lauder, teaching women about how to take care of their skin would always have a dramatic element. "Pure theater—in the end, that's what it was, this rendering of beauty," she would later write.

She got her first chance a few years later. As a young mother, she enjoyed getting her hair done once a month at the House of Ash Blondes, a beauty salon on the Upper West Side run by Florence Morris. One day, in response to a question from Mrs. Morris about how she kept her skin so lovely, Lauder promised to bring in her beauty products. A few weeks later, the excited customer could not wait until her next scheduled visit. She returned to the House of Ash Blondes with four of her uncle's concoctions—the cream, a cleansing oil, skin lotion, and face powder—and applied a few dabs from each one directly onto Mrs. Morris's face. An impressed Mrs. Morris offered her a small counter at the new salon that she was opening on East Sixtieth Street. "This was my first chance at a real business," Lauder later wrote. "I would pay her rent; whatever I sold would be mine to keep. No partners (I never did have partners)." Like the Lone Eagle, Lauder would be characterologically incapable of flying with a copilot and would make her mark without one. When her company was formed a decade later, she and her husband agreed to "be equal partners in every sense of the word." But her true feelings are more likely contained in that parenthetical aside. As a good obsessive, equality was anathema to her, and she would wield considerable control over her future partners—Joe and Leonard.

And she would put her new name, Estée Lauder, on her jars, which were at first black and white. (Several years later, after doing some snooping around in the homes of her rich friends and clients to determine "what color would look wonderful in any bathroom," she would switch to pale turquoise, aka "Estée Lauder blue.") This perfectionist who would later put considerable energy into coming up with le mot juste to describe her products—think of Youth Dew, which held the promise of rolling back the clock by natural means—first had to name herself. She wanted to sound old-Europey, if not French, and "Esther" had to go. However, she would never acknowledge that her new name was her own creation. In a 1969 interview with the *Boston Globe*, she stated that a nurse at the hospital where she was born was responsible for "the very chic" mistake. In her autobiography, she came up with another story, claiming that an "enterprising" Corona schoolteacher gave her the accent when her father tried to register her in grade school. But there is no indication that this budding entrepreneur was ever known as Estée until "Estée Lauder" first popped up in the Manhattan phone book in 1937. Of her new last name, she asserted that "Joe and I decided that we would return his name to the integrity of the original." But the decision may not have been mutual, as Joe still went by Lauter for a few more years. And her claim that Lauder was a return to the original spelling "in Austria where Joe's father was born" is contradicted by the 1930 census, which listed Joe's father's place of birth as Russia. Even if the Lauter family name was originally spelled as she said it was, given her tendency to run away from—rather than embrace—her family's origins, her desire to come across as less Jewish must also be considered a possible reason for this tweak.

As sales of her products took off and Lauder received offers to run concessions at other salons, she needed to clone herself; as she discovered, standing behind a counter, she could touch only about fifty faces a day. "Girl to assist beauty specialist," ran one of her early ads in the *New York Times*. "Interesting work with high-class clientele." The face-touching army, the same one that circulates in department stores around the world today, was born. Just as Kinsey trained his staff when to push forward and when to pull back in interviews, Lauder taught the proper degree of assertiveness with customers. She instructed her assistants not to ask, "May I help you?" but to say, "I have something that would look perfect on you, madam. May I show you how to apply it?" Lauder, who liked to coin phrases as well as names, came up with "Telephone, Telegraph, Tell-A-Woman" to describe her word-of-mouth campaign that was instrumental in stoking sales of her products in those early years.

Her husband suddenly had a new rival—her work. "Business," Lauder later wrote, "marries you. You sleep with it, eat with it, think about it much of your time. It is…an act of love." She would often leave Leonard at home with Joe and a maid to go on "working vacations" to swanky hotels, where she could dab faces poolside. Her jaunts in those days were limited mostly to Gatsby country on Long Island. In an effort to fit in, she would dress to the nines. "I knew," she later mused, "I had to look my best to sell my best." Dressing for success was to become an article of faith. (Decades later, as Cathie Black, the former head of the Hearst Magazines, noted in her memoir, Lauder would approach employees at her annual Christmas party and yank the back collar of their dresses to examine the label.) She also rarely went out hatless, explaining, "Try to walk in a hat, it makes you look like someone." Like other obsessives, Lauder had a one-track mind. Business was everything. She never developed any hobbies or other interests. By the late 1930s, she began questioning whether she could stay married to Joe, who lacked her ambition. "When he wanted to talk," she later wrote, "I'd usually be off in another world, thinking, projecting, planning...my mind awhirl." In April 1939, she got a divorce.

Still only thirty, Lauder moved with the six-year-old Leonard to Miami Beach. Over the next few years, the attractive, flirtatious, and impeccably dressed divorcée would date a series of older, high-powered men, a couple of whom were still married. One beau was the bachelor Charles Moskowitz—a top executive at Metro-Goldwyn-Mayer, dubbed by some gossip columnists as "Mr. MGM"—who, as she wrote in her autobiography, "showed me a world I'd never even imagined...Hollywood, stardom." Another was Dr. John Myers of Palm Beach, a British oral surgeon who made a fortune manufacturing flanges. A man with multiple talents—he was a noted actor and painter—Myers also headed a nonprofit that supported the arts. His then twenty-something daughter, the late Jeannette Vitkin, who later went on to head the Myers Foundation, was startled when her father's new girlfriend gave her face the once-over. "You shouldn't wear that lipstick," Lauder could not help but mention. "It's not right for you." Lauder was also seen arm-in-arm with Arnold van Ameringen, a Dutch-born head of a big perfume company, who later became the head of International Flavors and Fragrances. Lauder and Ameringen stayed friendly after their break-up, which was caused by his unwillingness to leave his wife. In the early 1950s, Ameringen provided considerable financial support to her growing business; this perfume tycoon may well also have passed on some of the ingredients of Youth Dew.

After a three-year separation from Joe, Lauder no longer wished to play the field. To her credit, she realized that success meant little without stable human connections, and they got remarried. "Look for a sweet person. Forget rich," as she later advised others, was the principle that guided her. Ronald, born in 1944, was the product of her return to Joe for a second lap around the track.

Lauder thus steered clear of the excesses exhibited by other beauty tycoons such as her chief rival in the 1960s and early 1970s, Charles Revson. Known as "the Nail Man," the founder of Revlon was a fellow obsessive, who also lived for his business, which doubled as his religion. As Andrew Tobias revealed in his juicy biography, *Fire and Ice* (1976), Revson ran roughshod over everyone, including three ex-wives, one whose name he couldn't remember, countless short-term lovers, and "hundreds of shell-shocked, verbally assaulted, overworked... executives," many of whom he wiretapped. That was the road not taken by Lauder. Nobody could stand Revson. In contrast, Lauder could maintain a genial demeanor and was capable of cordial relationships. "She was a family person, and I could relate to her. That was certainly not the case with Revson," Marylin Bender told me.

Agnes Ash had a similar take. "Estée was no phony. I was fond of her," stated Ash, who enjoyed their leisurely lunches during her long tenure as editor of the *Palm Beach Daily News*. "You could just sit and talk about your family and career; she would give wonderful tips about who you should get to know." Given Ash's influence in the community, Lauder's kindness was not unconnected to the promotion of her brand. Lauder also turned into a tipmeister for Mary Randolph Carter, beauty editor of *Mademoiselle*. "The first time I met Estée Lauder," Carter wrote in 1976, "I was eight months pregnant, so we talked a lot about babies and mothering. It was a happy meeting and she left me with all kinds of advice and good wishes." When asked about her relationship with Lauder in a recent phone interview, Carter, now the creative director for Ralph Lauren, said, "She could be a bear, but not with me. You felt taken care of when you went to her office for a new product launch. As soon as she saw my baby bulge, she made sure that I had a glass of water or juice."

However, while Lauder, unlike Revson, could come across as genuine and concerned, connecting was always something that she had to work at. Easygoing and relaxed with others she was not. In contrast to her two sons, who both idealize her as an all-loving mother, her grandchildren are well aware that her solicitousness could be awkward, if not downright irksome. "I was staying at her cottage in the south of France when I was about twenty," Leonard's son William recalled. "There wasn't much to do and I wanted to go to the beach with my friends. She started asking all kinds of questions about where we were going. Fortunately, my grandfather was there to calm her down."

Just as Clara Kinsey mothered Alfred, Joe Lauder would mother Estée. But in contrast to the sex researcher, the beauty-tycoon-in-the-making would not take her spouse for granted. Instead she became deeply appreciative. "I knew I needed him," she would later write, "not only for emotional support but to keep me in line financially." After the remarriage, the number-savvy Joe officially abandoned his own career and began managing the practical aspects of her business. But while Joe encouraged her to fulfill her dreams, he had his limits. Thirty years later, when President Nixon offered her the ambassadorship to Luxembourg, Joe told her, "If you go, you go alone. I won't go along to carry your bags." She got the message and declined.

In 1946, Lauder launched her company with Joe's savings and a loan from her father. With the war now over, she no longer had to worry about the shortages of such critical supplies as plastic and glass as well as fats and oils. She and Joe set up a small factory in a former restaurant on West Sixty-Fourth Street. She initially sold her wares only at beauty salons and through the mail, but she soon set her sights on the department store where customers shopped using a new tool—the store credit card, which allowed for impulse buying (bank-issued cards such as Visa and MasterCard were not yet available). But discount outfits such as Macy's or Gimbel's would not do. She aimed only for the high-end stores, and Saks Fifth Avenue was the top of the line.

Her characteristic persistence would come in handy; the store's cosmetics buyer, Robert Fiske, was, as she later wrote, inundated by "experimental merchandisers who would sell their souls to sell from Saks." Lauder kept bugging Fiske every which way. Every Wednesday and Friday afternoon for weeks on end during buying hours, she sat outside his office along with fifty other merchants. She put pressure on him by repeatedly asking her clients to call the store. She also touched the faces of as many women with ties to Saks as she could find; her prey included an assistant buyer whose skin had been scarred in an auto accident, and the daughter of a prominent executive, whose acne crisis had forced her to wear a little veil over her skin. And when that full-court press did not achieve any results, Lauder tried an end run. In 1948, after a speech at a benefit luncheon at the nearby Waldorf-Astoria, she handed out to the audience free $3 lipstick in metal cases—a fancy touch at the time, as the war had led to the widespread use of plastic tubes. "As the luncheon broke up," Fiske later noted, "there formed a line across Park Avenue and across Fiftieth Street into Saks asking for these lipsticks, one after another. It convinced us that there was a demand for the Lauder product." Sold, he placed his first order for $800 worth of merchandise. "Breaking that first, mammoth barrier," Lauder later recalled, "was perhaps the single most exciting moment I have ever known." Her first order sold out in two days. By 1950, she was also in Manhattan's Bonwit Teller and Lord and Taylor.

Lauder still faced enormous challenges. In the late 1940s, as the *New York Times* reported, the roughly $1 billion beauty business was America's eighty-fifth largest industry in size, but the second largest in advertising expenditures. And she had a limited budget; in the company's first year, total sales were just $50,000. Over the next few years, its only print ads were those subsidized by department stores. The name Estée Lauder first appeared in the *New York Times* in April 1948, when Saks hailed "Estée Lauder beauty props" as "the pretty cosmetics of the . . . perfectionist making." By the end of the decade, with about $50,000 in the bank, Lauder tried to hire a major New York City advertising agency to spread the word about her brand. But when her paltry savings did not allow her to get a foot in the door, she was forced to improvise. Confident that customers would snap up her products if only they tried them, Lauder gave away samples and more samples. The businesswoman who as a girl had been desperate to earn and keep her parents' love had developed a remarkable knack for forging connections with the consumer. Her competitors thought she was nuts. An executive at the perfume manufacturer Charles of the Ritz muttered, "She'll never get ahead. She's giving away the whole business." But she was on to something. "People trooped in to get the free sample," Leonard Lauder has stated, "liked it and bought it again." She also recruited new customers by devising the clever innovations Gift with Purchase (G with P) and Purchase with Purchase (P with P), which have since emerged as standard operating procedure in countless industries. Even after the company began investing heavily in print advertising in the early 1960s, it kept passing out all the freebies.

Premium department stores would always remain her focus. "We're prestige," Lauder told the *New York Times* in 1967, "and we refuse to go into stores that are not prestige." She nixed the idea of following her competitors such as Revlon that sold products at drugstores and supermarkets. According to Lauder, while wide distribution might increase sales in the short-term, it inevitably backfired over time. In the 1980s, as a guest lecturer at a Fashion Institute of Technology class on the cosmetics industry, she stated: "What I'd really like to do, if I could get away with it, is cut my distribution by a third." Such a shift, she was convinced, could increase her profitability by 50 percent. "Less is more," she emphasized. Today, the company is still using the same playbook.

"The founders, who were my parents, had two very simple ideas," Leonard Lauder recently noted, "product quality and narrow distribution to high-end retailers. We never went mass."

After first conquering Manhattan, Lauder faced the challenge of placing her brand not in more types of stores, but in more of the same kind of stores. To take the rest of the country, throughout the early 1950s she took to the rails. Like Jefferson, Lauder had her share of phobias, and one was a fear of heights, which then prevented her from flying. (But this she would eventually conquer, and by the late 1960s, she was working without any apparent discomfort in her new office on the thirty-seventh floor of the new General Motors Building.) Her compulsion to sell turned her family inside out. She left her two sons in the care of a maid and her husband, who was now also working seven days a week from 8 a.m. to 7 p.m. Leonard, then attending the Bronx High School of Science, would make afternoon runs on his bicycle to deliver goods to Saks from the firm's two small plants in Upper Manhattan. (Since her elder son was already versed in every aspect of the business, Lauder considered letting him run the company while she took a vacation with her husband; but the adolescent came down with the chicken pox, forcing her to abandon the idea.) Though Lauder would not admit it, due to her restless temperament, like Kinsey and Lindbergh, she may well have preferred being on the road to staying at home. One year, she was away twenty-five weeks. While neither of her boys would ever complain, her frequent absences presumably led to considerable confusion and anxiety.

She began the 1950s by opening her two-foot-long counter at the Neiman Marcus flagship store in Dallas. "Estée Lauder came in without an introduction," the late Stanley Marcus, who took over as company president that same year, told the New Yorker a couple of decades ago. "Barged her way in. She was a cyclone on the selling front. She'd outsell me any day." After countless phone calls and considerable cajoling, the store finally let her open for business on January 2, 1950. On New Year's Day, Lauder appeared on a Dallas radio show at 8:15 a.m., the only time she could get. Remarkably, in her autobiography, she boasted of the tall tale that she told that morning: "I'm Estée Lauder just in from Europe with the newest ideas for beauty.... Do let me personally show you how to accomplish the newest beauty tricks from Paris and London." (At the time, the only connection between her and France was the accent aigu in her faux first name.) "Start the New Year with a new face," was her sign-off. It worked. Wearing her signature hat with a pink rose, she was inundated by customers early the next day. Her lipstick sold out so fast that she instructed her salesgirl: "Go ahead and sell the tester!"

During the week that she spent in each town opening up a new store, she followed a carefully honed protocol that relied heavily on her obsessions and compulsions. Before attaining vast wealth, she owned just one or two expensive outfits, which she wore over and over again, and everything about her appearance was perfect, including, of course, her personal hygiene. "I'd always be immaculate," she later wrote. "If you looked shabby or tired or messy, no one in the world would be interested in your opinion on what sells in the beauty field." She would meet with and touch the face of every beauty editor in town. Behind her perfectly decked-out counters—making the most of every inch, the detail-oriented designer turned each one into "a tiny, shining spa"—Lauder would also touch the face of every customer in sight. And she was goaded on by her relatively mild number fetish. While she wasn't a rabid counter like Jefferson, Heinz, Dewey, or Kinsey, this hard-nosed businesswoman still enjoyed doing a certain amount of tallying. "Measure your success in dollars, not degrees" would emerge as a favorite maxim. For each day, she set monetary goals—typically a nice round number such as $1,000. Toward the end of business one afternoon in Houston when she was making her first foray into the Sakowitz store, she took off her shoes and counted her receipts. Her take stood at $998, which threw her into a temporary tizzy. "Oh no," she said to herself, as she rushed to meet a woman who had just made it through a closing door. Quickly slipping her shoes back on, she started hawking some eye cream that sold for $2.95. In an effort to clinch the sale, she startled the customer by announcing that the cream would smooth out the wrinkles on the side of her mouth. "That did it," Lauder later wrote. "Letting my shoes drop off, I sank into my chair and grinned my most victorious grin."

But like other obsessives, Lauder would rarely stay put for long. "She rests," a colleague once told *Mademoiselle*, "by doing something else hard."

———

To use a beauty metaphor, Youth Dew, first introduced at Bonwit Teller in 1953, would lay the foundation for Lauder's worldwide cosmetics empire. By the mid-1950s, the perfume, which she would compulsively spritz wherever she went—including elevators and restaurants—would generate about 80 percent of her sales at department stores. "It was impossible to get rid of the smell. It lasted forever," recalled Marylin Bender. And Lauder would mine this core characteristic to bring Youth Dew (and thus her entire treatment line) to the land of Chanel. When the buyer at the Galeries Lafayette in Paris would not see her, Lauder spilled a considerable amount on the floor. Over the next couple of days, as the fragrance lingered, customers kept asking about the source, and the department store soon had no choice but to carry it. Spritzing became a permanent part of her playbook. "Whenever I have a fragrance promotion," she wrote in 1985, "I ask my salespeople to spray some scent on the counters, and in the air to attract the customer.... My little Parisian 'accident' set the stage."

With Youth Dew putting her on the map, Lauder felt emboldened to make an experiment. In 1957, she brought out a moisturizing cream called Re-Nutriv—the moniker highlighted its supposedly medicinal properties—for which she charged a staggering $115 ($950 today) for a sixteen-ounce (one-pound) jar. While critics insisted that the sticker price would scare away customers, she sensed that the opposite might be true. Her gamble was a radical move. Until then, all her products had been moderately priced; Youth Dew Bath Oil, for example, cost from $3.75 to $22.50, depending on the size of the container. Likewise, the upscale creams manufactured by competitors such as Helena Rubinstein typically retailed for under $30 for an eight-ounce jar.

As Lauder predicted, her "Crème of Creams" elicited lots of free media coverage precisely because of its sky-high price. She also took out full-page ads in *Harper's Bazaar* and *Vogue* featuring a Hitchcockesque model under the headline, "What Makes a Cream Worth $115?" (Lauder had not yet begun hiring her string of famous blonde and blue-eyed models, such as Karen Graham, the company's official representative in the 1970s and 1980s, whom the public often assumed was her.) By way of explanation, the accompanying text alluded to "the rare perception of a woman like Estée Lauder who knows almost better than anyone how to keep you looking younger, fresher, lovelier than you ever dreamed possible." It would be hard to contest this assertion, as Rose Mentzer's youngest daughter had indeed been thinking of little else for decades. The ad also referenced some rare ingredients, such as turtle oil and royal jelly, and twenty secret ingredients, to which only members of the family were privy. The claim of high production costs noted by her copywriters, however, was less well grounded, as Lauder herself would acknowledge.

Quoting from the sales spiel that she delivered in department stores across the country, she wrote in her autobiography: "'Why do you spend so much for a Picasso? The linen under his painting costs two dollars and seventy-five cents, each jar of paint he used was perhaps a dollar seventy-five—perhaps the material cost a total of eleven dollars. Why, then, do you pay a small fortune for a small picture? You're paying for creativity, that's why.'" Remarkably, few customers, journalists, or industry analysts were troubled by her grandiose comparisons, and the cream flew off the shelves. This campaign, wrote British author Mark Tungate in his book, *Branded Beauty: How Marketing Changed the Way We Look* (2011), "combined all the best (or worst) attributes of beauty marketing: snobbery, emotional blackmail, the cult of celebrity, faux continental sophistication, and pseudo-science." She had devised a magic formula, which would transform her industry. While Lauder was still a relatively small player—sales did not hit $1 million until 1960—rival firms were already beginning to copy her when developing and marketing new products.

By 1965, sales were up to $15 million, as Re-Nutriv led to huge new income streams. In its new manufacturing plant on Long Island, the company also churned out large jars, which looked like Fabergé eggs, priced at a few hundred bucks a pop. Lauder also stuck tiny dabs in other products, such as face powder and lipsticks, which helped her justify the high prices for her "prestige brand." In 1962, for example, she charged $3.50 for her new "French Peach" lipstick, which, as the *New York Times* ad noted, featured "the creamy richness of her Re-Nutriv formula." That year, few other lipsticks ran anywhere near $3; Arden's Regal Red Lipstick cost $2 and Revlon's Lustrous Lipstick cost only $1.10. As a rule, retail prices for lipstick have always been based on higher markups than any other beauty product. As Andrew Tobias has reported, the Nail Man's costs for Lustrous Lipstick came to only 9.6 cents per tube; her gross margins for those Re-Nutriv–laced lipsticks were, in all likelihood, also over 90 percent.

Lauder plowed a sizable chunk of her excess cash into trophy real estate. As with other obsessives, her homes emerged as a vehicle through which she could express her love of organizing and collecting. In 1955, after reaping the first wave of Youth Dew profits, she moved out of her West End Avenue apartment and into her first Upper East Side town house, which, despite its gold-plated bathroom fixtures, she would later dismiss as "informal." A few years later, she bought her first place in Palm Beach, a small Spanish-style dwelling located on Route Trail, then the least fashionable part of the tony town.

Over the next decade, she upgraded. In 1964, she switched to a villa on the ocean in Palm Beach—"an English home, not a beach home," as she was fond of saying. Three years later, she dropped $500,000 (about $10 million today) on a twenty-five-room, eight-bathroom, nine-fireplace town house on East Seventy-Fifth Street in Manhattan, which most visitors referred to as "a castle." As the *New York Times* reported shortly after her move-in day, the living room, whose walls were draped with Flemish tapestries, was so massive that the grand piano in the corner "looked like an abandoned toy." The powder room on the main floor was lined with shelves overflowing with her cosmetics—lipsticks, face powders, and rouges, as well as her Re-Nutriv Cream (fittingly enough, as it was "the cream that bought the house"). As she proudly reminded the *Times*, her crème of creams, whose price was then $20 an ounce, "is the most expensive in the world and is our greatest seller." Of her rationale for leaving out all that product, she explained: "I want my guests to be able to do their faces over completely." (That explanation may have been only half true; she probably also relished the chance to get in a little extra face touching.)

By 1967, Lauder also owned a villa in Cannes, which she described in her autobiography as "immaculately clean." According to the *Boston Globe*, the neatnik "liked lots of shine" in her homes; maids were constantly waxing her *already waxed* drawing room floors with furniture polish. Not one to deny herself any material comforts, Lauder would later acquire an apartment in London— the blue-and-white wallpaper in her bedroom was modeled on that used by Jefferson in Monticello—as well as a massive home with Corinthian columns on Long Island. But like Lindbergh, she felt more comfortable on the go than at any of her palatial homes stuffed with Chippendale furniture and Meissen china. As the late fashion maven Eleanor Lambert has stated, "Estée let her houses live her...she didn't live in them."

By the early 1960s, Lauder had finally attained the vast wealth of which her public persona ("Estée Lauder") had long been boasting and her private persona ("Esther Mentzer") had long been dreaming. She now set her sights on developing the prominent social connections that she might have already had, had she actually descended from Viennese aristos. This step was all about business. "Her Palm Beach social life," William Lauder told me, "embodied what the brand stood for." The society pages constituted another theater in her ongoing war with her rivals such as Revlon—which, in the late 1960s, was still more than ten times the size of her company—and the fierce competitor dug in her heels. "The icons of fashion, those were the sophisticated people whom we were trying to reach," said Michael Gibbons, a retired marketing executive who began his long career with the company in 1967.

Of Lauder's attempts to ingratiate herself with her rich and famous "targets," Erica Titus Friedman, a frequent luncheon companion, has stated, "She tried too hard, but she was *very* determined." Just as Lauder used gifts to win customers, she distributed baskets of her products to gain entry into the balls and benefits held at Palm Beach's exclusive venues such as the controversial Everglades Club (which to this day has few, if any, Jewish members). In the mid-1960s, she reeled in the biggest fish of all—the Duchess of Windsor, whom she called "the most attractive woman in the world." In Lauder's version, they first met aboard an ocean liner and it was the Duchess who was eager to meet *her*: the Duchess had long been such a fan of hers that the Elizabeth Arden rep who made her up before parties used Estée Lauder products. But a more likely explanation, now widely accepted, is that their relationship began through a carefully orchestrated surgical strike; one day, just as the Duchess and her husband, the former King Edward VIII, were about to board a train bound for New York at the West Palm Beach station, Lauder "accidentally" bumped into her in front of a photographer, whose snapshot soon was transmitted around the world. However the bond was forged, it solidified quickly.

Within a couple of years, Lauder was hosting the couple's anniversary dinner and papers were reporting that her personal friend the Duchess does not "hesitate to test the newest Lauder products and tell [her] buddy if it's good or bad." Her social circle would also include Princess Grace of Monaco and her Palm Beach neighbor Rose Kennedy, a frequent visitor to her home for afternoons of tennis and a makeover.

As a CEO, Lauder could appear flighty—in business meetings, she often rambled—but she was totally focused when she had to be. "She sees and absorbs everything," a company executive once told *Vogue*. "You may think she has forgotten or not noticed, but when there is a scrap of information to fit in with a lot of others, it's there—been there all along." Michael Gibbons recalled a trip to Chicago with her in 1969 to open up a counter at Bonwit Teller, which had just completed its move across Michigan Avenue. "At a party at the store the evening before the opening, a Revlon executive was upset with its company's location on the floor. Afterwards, at dinner, she told me and my colleagues, 'They are going to move us.' We did not think it possible. But she insisted that we go back after dinner. At 11:30 that night, we moved our booth back where it was originally supposed to go."

By the late 1960s, Lauder had handed off the day-to-day operations of the company to Leonard, then in his thirties. The working alliance between the self-described "stern taskmaster...[who] expected perfection...and then a little more perfection when perfection is offered" and her elder son was not always smooth. A decade earlier, on Leonard's first day on the job, Lauder announced that she and Joe were going on a two-month vacation to Florida; while Leonard was often jolted by her mercurial and demanding ways, after several years, they ironed out the kinks. She remained the company's public face who had final say over all products—she hated false eyelashes, so they were nixed.

In 1973, when the thirty-nine-year-old Leonard officially replaced her as president, he described himself to Marylin Bender as a cross between his parents. A perfectionist like his mother, he was driven by a fierce ambition that could "keep everyone on their toes." To motivate his staff, Leonard would blurt out, "I *want* you nervous. I want you to be nervous. Are you nervous?" And like his father, he could "direct and organize vast logistical movements." In contrast to Leonard, who said nothing publicly about the tension, Lauder alluded to "many heated discussions" in her autobiography. "My father," William Lauder explained to me, "was her son as well as her business partner and rival. But the relationship was symbiotic. They both recognized that they needed each other. He could not do what he wanted without her, and she could not do what she wanted without him."

Both sons are chips off the old block. Ronald and Leonard also have obsessive traits, though Ronald has never been as excited about business as his elder brother. Ronald's heart has always been in collecting. "I first became interested in art at thirteen," he told me. "I guided my parents, who never had time to learn about it. I grew up around great style, and I knew what they liked." The man who founded Manhattan's Neue Galerie Museum for German and Austrian Art in 2001 bought his first canvas of the Austrian great Egon Schiele with his bar mitzvah money. As the *New Yorker* noted in its 2007 profile, "An Acquiring Eye," this megacollector—Glenn Lowry, the director of the Museum of Modern Art, has called his private holdings "the finest collection of modern art assembled by an individual in the world today"—has "given himself the grand, cultured Viennese heritage to which Estée Lauder pretended." While most of Leonard's obsession-ality has been plowed into the company, he, too, has dabbled as an art collector. He has made several donations of prominent American artworks to Manhattan's Whitney Museum. Ever since the age of six—back when he was coping with the interregnum in his parents' marriage—Leonard has also been accumulat-ing postcards; he started by spending his five-cent allowance on five cards of the Empire State Building. At present, his collection, which he plans to donate to Boston's Museum of Fine Arts, features 125,000 items encompassing numerous subgenres, such as artists' postcards, sports postcards, advertising postcards, and fashion postcards. His late wife Evelyn, Leonard told the *New Yorker* in 2012, "often said my postcard collection was my mistress."

Estée Lauder wanted both her boys to work in the family biz, and in the mid-1960s, not long after finishing business school at Wharton, Ronald also came on board. In 1968, when she rolled out Clinique, a new line of medically sanctioned skin-care products, she named Ronald its executive vice president. Under his leadership, a decade later, Clinique's sales came to $80 million, nearly 30 percent of the company's total. After dabbling in politics in the 1980s—in 1983, he worked in the Reagan Defense Department as deputy assistant sec-retary, and in 1986 he was appointed U.S. ambassador to Austria—he spent a decade as chairman of Estée Lauder International. In 1995, Ronald also became chairman of Clinique—now the bestselling prestige makeup line in the United States and most of the 130 other countries in which it is sold—a position that he still holds. As peripatetic as his mother ever was, Ronald now also runs several businesses of his own, including a leading TV station in Central Europe.

———

On October 16, 1979, the seventy-one-year-old Lauder, having already enjoyed a couple of decades of spectacular wealth and fame, was forced to endure fifteen minutes of terror. At five thirty that afternoon, three gun-toting intruders stormed past her maid and into her Manhattan mansion. Lauder immediately locked her-self in her third-floor bedroom, but two of the robbers rushed up the stairs and kicked in the door, threatening to kill her if she did not cooperate. After one man smacked her across the face, she opened the two wall safes containing her jew-elry. Though tied to a chair, a relatively unscathed Lauder made a rather gutsy move that could have been life-threatening. Wiggling around on the floor, she activated the silent alarm button that was hooked up to police headquarters. After noticing what she had done, the thieves collected their heist and immediately dashed out of the house. Two minutes later, the police arrived. As with other obsessives, Lauder's nervous system worked backward. While too little to do could raise her anxiety level, too much to do—or even danger—could reduce it. The police sergeant who spoke to her that afternoon told the *New York Post* that she was "quite calm, unusually calm" about the robbery, in which she lost about a million dollars in jewelry as well as $6,000 in cash. "I'm not a bit disturbed," she told the paper. This perfectionist would always pride herself on her emotional control. "They took a few things that were lying around," she added, "but nothing important." In her autobiography, however, she would finally acknowledge the truth, stating, "I gave them everything." For the rest of her life, she would be protected by bodyguards.

Three years later, Lauder was felled by another blow, one from which she would never fully recover. On January 15, 1983, the fifty-third anniversary of her first wedding, Joe collapsed and died during a dinner at Ronald's Manhattan home. Lauder's remarkable control over her public image (and the news media) came through loud and clear in the vague *New York Times* obituary. The paper of record was reduced to guesstimating her husband's age, reporting that he was "in his 70s." He was actually eighty.

While many women of her generation were reluctant to reveal their age, Lauder's desire to keep her birthdate hidden was extreme. As her grandson William told me, when he was carrying her passport on a trip to Austria in the mid-1980s, she insisted that he not take a peek. So determined was she to keep her secret that she also kept a tight lid on the age of other family members— namely, her husband and elder son. Leonard was under strict orders not to be open about his age, unless otherwise directed. As Lauder acknowledged in her autobiography, when asked, Leonard would reply, "I'll have to ask my mother.…I'll check on what I am this week and let you know." In 1988, in an effort to keep *her* secret, she would ask her fifty-five-year-old son to paint *his* graying hair. The 1983 *Times* obituary also failed to mention where her husband's burial took place. The venue, the Beth El Cemetery in Paramus, New Jersey, where her father, Max, had once roamed with his horses, may well have struck the family as too Jewish.

The loss of her husband was overwhelming. Joe had been not just her spouse, but also her surrogate mother, who had given her the attention that she had never received from the anxious and overburdened Rose back in Corona. For the next several weeks, Lauder retreated to the upstairs bedroom of Ronald's nearby Manhattan town house. Her nose, she figured, could help bring her out of her despair, and over the next couple of years, she put her energy into developing a new fragrance, Beautiful. As she was racing around the country during the launch in 1986, she told the *New Yorker*, "Hard work never killed anyone.... Smile and the world smiles with you, cry and you cry alone.... I found that out after Joe died." But for the first time in her life, burying her emotions in her work was no longer working. "After 1986, she was meaningfully less active. At the time, we did not appreciate how much of an effect my grandfather's death was still having on her," William Lauder told me.

From then on, her public appearances would be limited. In December 1988, Raisa Gorbachev, who was in Manhattan to attend an event at the United Nations, headed up to the thirty-seventh floor of the General Motors Building, where she sampled Beautiful and a few other perfumes. After their forty-five-minute meeting, Lauder, apparently frustrated because she did not get to dab her visitor, told the *New York Times*: "I want her to come back and talk about skin." Two years later, when Leonard Lauder introduced Origins, a frail Lauder would head down to its retail outlet in Soho with William, then the vice president of this line of natural skin-care products. "She loved standing behind the counter," her grandson stated, "and waiting on customers." By 1993, when she went to Florida for the last time, Alzheimer's was starting to set in. "Both her mother and her sister, Renée, suffered from the disease. Her sister's came quite early when I was still in my teens," added William. Lauder would die, attended by nurses, in her Manhattan town house in 2004. She was ninety-five.

By the end of this Queen of Beauty's long reign, her family knew exactly how to defuse the rough edges of her obsessionality. In 1989, as the company was reshuffling its offices in the GM Building as part of an expansion—Lauder's office was moved up from the thirty-seventh floor to the fortieth—Leonard was nervous about showing his mother the renovation. Relaying the story to me, a smiling William Lauder explained: "My father told one of his assistants, 'Break something. Something that isn't important.' The next day, as my eighty-year-old grandmother was entering her new quarters, she stopped and snapped, 'The door handle isn't working. They didn't do it right. That needs to be fixed right away.' She then let out a big sigh of relief and was quiet for the rest of the day. Order was restored."

7

Sports: Ted Williams

"Show Me Your Swing"

I...insist that regardless of physical assets, I would never have gained a headline for hitting if I [had not] kept everlastingly at it and thought of nothing else the year round.... Then [in childhood] as now, I only lived for my next time at bat.

—Ted Williams, July 1941 interview with the *Boston Evening American*

TED WILLIAMS SMACKS SMACKER.

Thus ran the caption on the front page of the *Boston Globe* on September 29, 1941, below the AP photo of "the Kid" kissing his bat after the season-ending doubleheader against the Philadelphia Athletics. Entering the day's action hitting .39955, which rounds off to .400, the twenty-three-year-old Red Sox left fielder could have sat out and still etched his name into the record books. While players often quit while they are ahead rather than risk losing a milestone, for Williams, that was not an option. Choosing to "play it all the way," the six-foot-four, 175-pound John Wayne look-alike collected six hits in eight times at bat, raising his average to .406, the highest in the major leagues since 1924 (and 47 points higher than the second-place finisher). Baseball is a game of numbers, and during his annus mirabilis he racked up some of the best ever. In addition to his ninth-inning walk-off homer in the All-Star Game, Williams hit 37 home runs and drove in 120 runs; he also finished with 145 walks, while striking out a paltry 27 times. His on-base percentage—bases on balls plus hits divided by at bats—came to a staggering .551, a mark that went unmatched for more than sixty years (when it was broken by Barry Bonds who, as critics charge, may well have had some biochemical assistance). No batter has hit .400 since. Analyzing and contextualizing these stats, the late Harvard biologist and baseball aficionado Stephen Jay Gould has called Williams's accomplishment on the diamond that year "a beacon in the history of excellence, a lesson to all who value the best in human possibility."

On that early autumn day, a jubilant Williams was clearly mugging for the cameraman stationed in the visitors' locker room in Philadelphia, but his lust for lumber was no passing fancy. That year, his Play Ball baseball card described him as "an enthusiastic ball player who would rather wield a bat than eat." The bat was to him what the machine was to Lindbergh—his emotional anchor, his most profound connection. "It was," he wrote in his bestselling 1969 memoir, *My Turn at Bat*, "the center of my heart, hitting a baseball." Like the security blanket tethered to the fingers of Charles Schulz's Linus, his bat was a transitional object, to which he repeatedly turned for comfort. Speculating about the thoughts that shaped the perennial All-Star's inner world, sportswriter Roger Kahn wrote in 1959, a year before Williams's retirement from the Red Sox, "I never needed anybody. I always had my bat."

His love affair with the bat began in boyhood, when home plate substituted for a real home. "[Hitting] was my whole life," he told *Harper's* in 1969. "It was the only thing I wanted to do." Like Lindbergh, Williams grew up in a tense and severely dysfunctional family. His parents, too, could not stand each other and were mired in a perpetual cold war. During Ted's grammar school days in San Diego, rarely was any adult present in the family's small frame house at 4121 Utah Street until 10 p.m. His father, a sometime photographer, was typically out carousing; and his mother, a Salvation Army zealot, was busy trying to save the town's drunks and prostitutes. After school, Ted would go straight to the nearby diamond at North Park to practice his hitting until 9 p.m., when the lights went out. He would continue swinging his bat in his backyard until one of his parents finally showed up. He would imagine himself at the plate in various situations, something he would continue to do as a Red Sox star. ("We're in Detroit. [Hal] Newhouser is on the mound. The count is two and one. Here he comes," Williams would bark out to a Sox teammate during batting practice a couple of decades later.) The next day at dawn, he would be in his backyard, going at it again. "When I wasn't sleeping or eating," Williams later noted, "I was practicing swinging." He got to school just as the janitor opened the building so that he could squeeze in some hitting before class. And if the janitor happened to be late, he climbed through a window to grab the bat himself. "By the time the other kids showed," he recalled for *Time* in 1950, "I'd have the bat in my hand, to be the first up." When he couldn't get hold of a bona fide bat, he would make one out of paper and swing at anything in his midst, including berries and stones. At Hoover High, he would bring his beloved bat to class. "I always took subjects [like shop] that wouldn't have much homework," he later stated, "because I wanted more time for hitting." The only course, besides phys ed, in which he excelled was typing, for which the perfectionist won an award by cranking out thirty-two words a minute without error.

And the bat for Williams, like the machine for Lindbergh, was also the primary means by which he drew other people into his life. His baseball coaches would become his surrogate parents. As an adult, his standard conversation starter was "Show me your swing." It's a request that Williams would ask not just of fellow ballplayers, but also of kids, sportswriters, old men in wheelchairs, and even nubile women, for whom it sometimes did double duty as a pickup line. He could not imagine that anyone might not share *his* pressing preoccupation. And once he got a response, Williams relished the chance to help his interlocutor tweak his or her stroke to get in a little more hip action—a necessity for hitting the ball with power. At the Fenway Park memorial celebration held after his death in July 2002, former senator John Glenn, who served in the Marines with Williams during the Korean War, recalled how a half century earlier in Kyoto, the Sox outfielder had befriended a Japanese boy whom he spotted taking phantom swings with an imaginary bat. "The boy hitter swung again," stated Glenn, "but this time Ted scowled at him. He went over to where the boy was standing, put him in a batting position and proceeded to correct his form!" Stepping away, Williams then threw an imaginary baseball toward the boy who demonstrated his newly tailored swing. Williams immediately ducked, as if a searing line drive were coming straight for his head—a gesture that led the batter and his young companions standing next to him to jump for joy. After his retirement from baseball, the bat would still cement connections, though it would not be quite as central to his social life as its successor, the fishing rod. Casting both spinning and fly rods with the same precision as he swung a bat, in 1999, Williams would be inducted into the International Game Fish Association Hall of Fame.

For Williams, bats were not just the tools of his trade, but holy relics. During his Red Sox career, he would make a pilgrimage every winter to Kentucky to speak with those responsible for creating his favorite companions. "He was one of our best clients; he loved us and was loyal to us," said Nathan Stalvey in a phone interview. Stalvey is the curator of the Louisville Slugger Museum and Factory, the bat company that still supplies about 70 percent of major leaguers with their lumber. When Bud Hillerich, the CEO of batmaker Hillerich and Bradsby, died in 1946, Williams was the only player in all of baseball to wire condolences to the exec's loved ones. "As far as our family is concerned," an appreciative John Hillerich, who was Bud's son and successor, told the *Boston Globe* the following year, "Ted can have the best in bats." Williams would not settle for anything less. He would often slip the Louisville Slugger lathe operator, Fritz Bickel, a twenty spot, in order to ensure that his bats had more grain lines per inch—the closer the grain lines, the higher quality the wood—than those sent to other players. Whenever he got a shipment of bats, he would dash over to the post office to weigh them; he wanted to make sure that they were exactly as advertised. Toward the end of summer, he would do a retest, as his bats often gained a half ounce due to the humidity. In the mid-1950s, Williams sent back to Louisville a box of twenty bats, complaining that they did not feel right. Upon examination, the company realized that he was correct; the bat handles were five-thousandths of an inch off. And he was constantly providing lots of tender loving care. "I always worked with my bats," he later wrote, "boning them down, putting a shine on them, forcing the fibers together.... I treated them like babies." In the Red Sox clubhouse, his bats were assigned their own locker, adjacent to his.

Williams was not just an expert practitioner; he was also a hitting savant. He was one of the first players to switch to a lighter bat to increase bat speed. In contrast to Babe Ruth, who used a forty-ounce bat to slug sixty homers in 1927, Williams used a thirty-two-ounce bat in 1941. Today most players still heed his wisdom. "Lord knows I wasn't much of a student," the intellectually curious autodidact, who once described *why* as "a wonderful word," later recalled. "But baseballically, I was a cum laude." More than a generation before stats geeks such as Bill James launched the field of sabermetrics, Williams was already compiling data. Soon after arriving in Florida for his first spring training with the Red Sox—for moral support, he toted his own bat to camp—he began gathering info on opposing pitchers, which he kept in a little black book. Like a dogged investigative journalist, he would dig and dig and dig. To get the full scoop on a given pitcher's habits, he would quiz not only any veteran who would listen to his flood of questions but also umpires. Blessed with a phenomenal memory, he could remember the sequences of pitches in a given at bat for decades after the fact. "Ted didn't need a computer to track pitchers. He was his own computer," Frank Malzone, the Sox All-Star third baseman in the late 1950s, told me. Williams also did a systematic study of every big-league park, learning about the slope of the batter's box—in Fenway, it was a tad higher in the back, enabling him to plant his back foot more firmly—and the prevailing wind currents. His fieldwork also included a visit to the physics lab at Cambridge's Massachusetts Institute of Technology, where he learned about the trajectory of baseballs upon impact. "Some people called it monomania," Richard Ben Cramer observed in his landmark 1986 *Esquire* article, "What Do You Think of Ted Williams Now?" of the thoroughness with which Williams studied hitting, "but with Ted it was serial (multimania?) in eager furtherance of everything he loved."

A master of his craft, Williams continued to excel even as injuries and advancing age slowed him down. In 1957, at thirty-nine, the left-handed slugger stunned the baseball world by making another go at .400, finishing at a robust .388. The following year, he won his seventh batting title; he remains the oldest man ever to win a batting crown. In his last at bat, in September of 1960, he slammed his 521st home run. (If he had not lost nearly five full seasons in his prime due to military service, most experts agree that he might have challenged Babe Ruth's longstanding record of 714.) For his career, Williams hit .344, higher than any other power hitter, including Ruth, and his lifetime slugging percentage (total bases divided by at bats) is second only to Ruth's. Moreover, his lifetime on-base percentage (OBP) of .483 is tops. While an OBP anywhere north of .400 is indicative of a stand-out season, only three times in nineteen seasons did Williams's OBP dip below .450. At the plate, this perfectionist came closer to perfection than any other hitter in history, reaching base nearly one out of every two times he ever came to bat. The adolescent who vowed to become "the greatest hitter who ever lived" remained true to his word.

At the center of Williams's methodology was a simple concept: "Get a good pitch to hit." This was the advice that he received from Hall of Famer Rogers Hornsby (the only man besides Williams ever to win the Triple Crown—to lead the league in batting, home runs, and RBIs—twice), his batting instructor during his stint with the Minneapolis Millers of the American Association in 1938. In *The Science of Hitting*, the influential manual Williams wrote after his playing days were over, he divided home plate into seventy-seven baseballs. As he explained, he strove to hit at pitches in "his happy zone"—the fifteen baseballs in the middle—where he could expect to hit .400. In contrast, he could hope to hit only .230 when he swung at pitches in the low-outside corner. Approximately

95 percent of the time, he took the first pitch so that he could study how the pitcher was throwing. He would do his best to avoid anything outside the strike zone. And in the late innings, with the game on the line, he might try to hit the bottom half of the ball in order to increase his chances of hitting a home run. He ended up with a higher percentage of game-winning home runs than any other player, including Ruth.

While Williams was convinced that he knew best, he made some allowances for individual differences. As he told numerous players, including his successor in left field at Fenway Park, Carl Yastrzemski, "Don't let anyone change your swing." Though he was horrified by the approach of the Yankee Hall of Famer Yogi Berra ("The son of a bitch got his bat on the ball" was how Williams described his rival's style), he conceded that the Berra Method might work, but only for a select few. In direct contrast to the Splinter, Berra was a "bad-ball hitter," meaning that he wouldn't hesitate to swing at high or inside pitches off the plate. "As I always said," Berra explained to me, "if I could see it, I could hit it. Ted wouldn't swing at too many pitches I would. But we had one thing in common. Neither of us struck out much." But Berra's OBP was never above .400 in any season—it was just .348 over the course of his career—and his lifetime average was a not-quite-majestic .285.

In the batter's box during a game, Williams, unlike Berra, was a paragon of rationality, precision, and patience. "No other player," John Updike mused in the famous *New Yorker* profile published after Williams's final game, "so constantly brought to the plate that intensity of competence that crowds the throat with joy." The same was true in those two other places to which he later transferred his exceptional hitting prowess—the airplane where he became a decorated fighter pilot and the boat where he evolved into one of the world's best fly-fisherman. However, just about everywhere else, even on other parts of the baseball field, he was more a disorganized jumble of raw nerve endings than an apotheosis of anything.

Rarely could he sit still, as his attention easily wandered. Early in his career, he would infuriate managers by turning his back to the action in right field—he did not move to left field until his second season with the Sox—in order to practice his swing with an imaginary bat. He remained a lackadaisical fielder who looked, as *Time* reported in 1950, "like a tired and slightly bored businessman" while standing in front of Fenway Park's Green Monster. Impulsive by nature, he often let his emotions hijack his brain. A notorious F-bomb hurler, "he was," wrote Leigh Montville, author of the definitive *Ted Williams: The Biography of an American Hero* (2004), "the best curser in the history of the human race." Before the fans got to the park, to get himself psyched for that day's game, he was prone to yell at the batting practice pitcher, "I'm Ted fucking Williams, the greatest hitter in baseball." His actions could be as crude as his adjectives. Too thin-skinned to tolerate any booing, he would vent his rage with the Fenway Park faithful by performing obscene gestures and spitting in their direction. For one of his legendary "great expectorations," in 1956, an exasperated Sox general manager Joe Cronin fined him $5,000, which was 5 percent of his annual salary (the equivalent of about a million bucks today, since stars of his magnitude now make upward of $20 million).

Like other obsessives, Williams did not do intimacy. He rarely hung out with teammates, preferring the company of sycophants such as clubhouse attendants who were in awe of him and would agree to do as he pleased such as consume the evening meal in the late afternoon. "Bing, bang boom, get it the hell over with" was how the slugger approached the dinner plate. He could not handle the give-and-take of real relationships. "With women, he had a reputation for being a pig," veteran *Boston Globe* sports columnist Dan Shaughnessy told me.

Scouting out for company for the night (or the afternoon), the playboy, who would quickly alienate all three wives with his constant barrage of vicious epithets, would blurt out to unsuspecting strangers, "Do you fuck?" (Given that he was Ted Williams, his boorishness didn't doom him to a microscopic batting average.) Wife number two, Lee Howard, a statuesque blonde whom he married in 1961, threw him out after just a couple of years. "If we went fishing," the former model recalled, "he would scream at me, call me dumb, and kick the tackle box." When asked by the judge at her divorce hearing whether there was any chance of reconciling with her husband, a startled Howard responded, "Are you kidding?"

And like his parents before him, Williams neglected his three children—his daughter Bobby-Jo, from his first marriage to Doris Soule; and his son, John Henry, and daughter Claudia from his third marriage to Dolores Wettach. He was not present for any of their births, and for long stretches of time he pretended as if they did not exist. Late in life, as he found love in the arms of an older woman, Louise Kaufman, he recognized and tried to make amends for his wayward ways. "I was," he would confess to anyone who would listen, "horseshit as a father."

But though "Terrible Ted," a nickname that emerged shortly after his major-league debut, often mistreated his nearest and dearest, he could be a charmer and a lively conversationalist. With his booming voice—his hearing soured after his service in Korea—he entranced interlocutors on many subjects besides hit-tingology. "He was a student of everything," stated John Underwood in a phone interview. Underwood, his coauthor on *My Turn at Bat*, added that Williams would spend hours burying his head in his *World Book Encyclopedia*. After devouring William Manchester's critical volume on his hero, Gen. Douglas MacArthur, the lifelong conservative with the photographic memory got into a friendly argument with Doris Kearns Goodwin. "I didn't agree," the armchair historian told the bestselling author, whom he liked to needle by calling her Pinko, "with [the biographer] in certain things." Williams was also capable of nearly otherworldly empathy and generosity.

For decades, he was the face of the Jimmy Fund Clinic, the pediatric cancer center in Boston, for which he worked tirelessly to help raise tens of millions of dollars. "Ted was a teddy bear," recalled Suzanne Fountain, the charity's direc-tor of community relations. While Williams never raked in anything near what today's All-Stars make, as a retiree in Florida, he would not hesitate to write $10,000 checks for fellow ballplayers down on their luck. And he had an abid-ing sense of justice. At his Hall of Fame induction ceremony in 1966, he urged baseball to honor "the great Negro players." "His speech had an impact," former New York Giants outfielder Monte Irvin has noted. "The powers-that-be at the Hall of Fame had to kind of perk up and take notice." Five years later, Satchel Paige became the first black player to be enshrined in Cooperstown.

———

Williams's sensitivity to racial discrimination—in 1959, he also took under his wing the first black player on the Sox, Pumpsie Green—had roots in his deepest fears. While most baseball fans, even die-hard members of Red Sox Nation, as-sume that Manny Ramirez was the first great Hispanic player to patrol the Green Monster, that distinction actually belongs to Williams. (Ramirez's quirky temper-ament was also foreshadowed by Williams; two generations before the Fenway Faithful resigned themselves to "Manny being Manny," Ted set the gold standard for eccentricity.) Ted's maternal grandparents, Pablo and Natalia Venzor, both hailed from Mexico, and his mother spoke Spanish at home during her childhood in Santa Barbara. His younger brother, Danny, who had dark skin and a round face, looked Mexican. Ted, in contrast, resembled his father, Samuel, who was of English-Welsh extraction. "If I had had my mother's name," Theodore Samuel Williams later wrote, "there is no doubt I would have run into problems in those days, the prejudices people had in Southern California." Like Lauder, the young phenom wound up creating the personal identity that best suited him (and his obsession). To the press, the Sox star stated that his mother was French (the family had ties to the Basque region). And he officially changed his date of birth from August 30 to October 30 during his rookie year because, as he later told the *Boston Globe*, "I didn't want to celebrate my birthday during the playing season."

Samuel Williams was a nonentity in Ted's life. "My dad and I," the retired ballplayer would note in his memoir, downplaying the truth, "were never close." Ted hardly got to know his nomadic father. Born in Mount Vernon, New York, at sixteen, Samuel Williams ran away from home to join the United States Cavalry. After serving for a few years in the Philippines, Corporal Williams was stationed in the Hawaiian Islands, where he met his future wife, Micaela ("May") Venzor. The couple was married in Santa Barbara in 1913 before settling in San Diego, where Ted was born in 1918. The stern and moody Samuel Williams, who has been described as a "semiderelict," cared more about getting his next drink than about spending time with his growing family, which by 1920 included Ted's brother, Danny. In the mid-1930s, with his photography business floundering, Samuel Williams moved up to Sacramento to take up a position as a state jail inspector. He also took up with his secretary, whom he later made his second wife. Ted felt that his father had shortchanged him, as the now ninety-something Bobby Doerr, the Red Sox Hall of Fame second baseman who also played minor-league ball with Williams in California, noted in a phone interview. In late 1936, Doerr invited his teammate to dinner at his family's Los Angeles home. In contrast to Williams, Doerr had a warm relationship with his father, who gave him whatever he needed to begin his baseball career. "As we left," Doerr recalled, "Ted told me, 'You're lucky to have a dad like that.'" As Ted metamorphosed into a celebrity, Samuel Williams kept trying to wangle money from his son. When his father died in a Bay Area nursing home in 1952, Ted chose not to attend the funeral.

Like her husband, May Williams, known up and down the Southern California coast as "Salvation May," frequented taverns; the teetotaler went not to

imbibe, but to collect money for the Salvation Army. After her son became famous, the avid proselytizer's pitch to patrons ran, "I'm Ted Williams's mother.
Empty your pockets." May first took up the cause as a teenager in 1907, and
she kept at it for the next half century. Not so Ted, who hated marching in pa-
rades with his mother and dropped out of Sunday school as soon as he could.
"I'd stand behind the bass drum," Williams later wrote, "trying to hide so none of
my friends would see me." While his mother's religious fervor made Ted squirm,
her single-minded determination proved to be a model. A fearless and tireless advocate for the needy, she thought of little else. "Mrs. Williams," the *San Diego
Sun* noted in 1936, "*is* the Salvation Army." Tambourine in hand, she would ride
hour after hour on the city's two streetcar lines, shouting in her booming voice,
"Praise the Lord!" A slick networker who befriended many of the state's leading
politicos, including Governor Frank Merriam, she once held the world's record
for selling the most copies of the Salvation Army paper, *War Cry*, in a calendar
year. But she ignored the needs of her family. "Always gone," Williams wrote in
1969. "The house dirty all the time. Even now I can't stand a dirty house." Thus
was made the germaphobe, whose bachelor pads would be remarkable for their
cleanliness and order, and who, before sitting down to a meal, would insist that
everyone at the table scrub their hands.

In contrast to Ted, who filled the nurture deficit with baseball, the unathletic
five-foot-four-inch Danny turned to petty crime. Dubbed "the city's most incorrigible youth," by the San Diego Police Department, the teenage Danny did not
hesitate to filch from the family; he once pawned his mother's coronet. But by
the 1950s, the former juvenile delinquent turned to the straight and narrow, became a contractor, got married, and started a family. He died of leukemia in 1960
at the age of thirty-nine.

In the late 1950s, the cancer-stricken Danny moved back into his boyhood
home with his wife, Jean, and sons Sam and Ted, then in grade school. Today
Ted Williams, the nephew of the baseball slugger, runs his own graphic design
firm in the Bay Area. "Living with my grandmother wasn't easy," the Hall of
Famer's nephew told me. May Williams once swatted him with a broom, complaining that he was getting in her way. "My mother had to tell her not to hit
kids," he added. Noting that his father, Danny, also beat him, Ted Williams sus-
pects that May also hit both her sons when they were boys. "My uncle Ted, like
my father, had a temper, and they must have learned that behavior at home," he
added. While the future Sox star presumably did not take to his bat solely to de-

fend himself against his mother's broom, he could connect with it much more easily than with her. Bill Swank, now a retired San Diego probation officer, ran into May Williams in 1957 when he was working as a shipping clerk. "Mrs. Williams," Swank stated in a recent phone interview, "was kinda nuts. She was in her own little world. She would jabber nonstop about God. It was impossible to figure out what she was saying."

By then, May Williams was in her midsixties, and a bad back, stemming from a bus accident, prevented her from marching around town on behalf of the Salvation Army. No longer able to pursue her all-consuming obsession, her mental state began to deteriorate. "She was depressed, but if she started talking about the Lord, her face would light up," recalled her grandson Ted Williams. While she once collected objects that held meaning for her, such as tambourines and all the published materials about her son, she turned to junk. She became both a compulsive hoarder, filling every room from floor to ceiling with old newspapers, as well as a serial shoplifter. In addition, May developed hypergraphia; she could not stop jotting down gibberish on the newspapers and on the backs of old photos. "My uncle Ted used to scold her," the graphic designer said. "He would give her a photo of his daughter Bobby-Jo, and tell her, 'Don't write on this.'" In late 1958, Ted Williams sent Danny a letter in which he urged him to place their mother in a nursing home so that she could get "the proper care which she obviously needs so badly." Suffering from the early stages of dementia, May Williams eventually moved in with a sister in Santa Barbara, where she died in 1961.

Growing up with a domineering mother whom he feared, Ted Williams was too shy to go out on any dates in high school. "[If] a girl looked at me twice," he later wrote, "I'd run the other way." And the little that the girls saw, they did not like. High school classmate Ruth Browning has recalled thinking he was "very arrogant, conceited." The adolescent with the thinnest of ties to his own mama had not yet figured out that girls were separate human beings (a fact that he never quite could get his arms around). According to the late *Boston Globe* sportswriter Will McDonough, in his minor-league career Williams was "like a Neanderthal." In 1938, a few minutes into one of his first dates, as a clubhouse attendant was driving him around town, Williams jumped a woman in the backseat of a car. "He didn't know," said McDonough, "that maybe you were supposed to talk to each other, maybe eat dinner, whatever." Journalist John Underwood, who was a friend of Williams from the 1960s until his death in 2002, noted, "He never paid attention to the normal rules of male-female relationships."

Left to his own devices by his neglectful parents, the San Diego boy managed to find a series of surrogate fathers who helped him develop his athletic prowess. At the age of five, Ted dragged his bat across the street to the house of his neighbor John Lutz, a twenty-four-year-old chicken salesman, whom he got to pitch to him. Lutz also taught him how to hunt and fish, sometimes taking him on day trips to Mexico. At nine, the budding ballplayer told his mother that he'd "ruther [*sic*] be a Babe Ruth than a captain in the Salvation Army," and turned to Rod Luscomb, the director at the North Park playground and a former minor-league ballplayer, for guidance. Six days a week for the next seven years, he and Luscomb would pitch to one another for hours at a time. "He was a baseball nut, too," Williams noted.

At Luscomb's urging, the gawky boy began to beef himself up. His daily exercise regimen included squeezing tennis balls to strengthen his wrists and doing dozens of daily fingertip push-ups, a practice he continued for decades. Convinced that he would not have made it to Cooperstown without Luscomb, whom he later called "my first hero," Williams mentioned this mentor in his Hall of Fame induction speech along with Wofford Caldwell, his baseball coach at Hoover High. Caldwell used the stick more than the carrot. To get Williams to run faster, he would chase him around the bases with a switch.

In 1934, Williams chose to attend Hoover High over the larger and more established San Diego High, the school located in his district, for reasons baseballic. "I didn't think," he later told the *Boston Traveler*, "that I had a chance of winning a letter on the San Diego High team." As a teenager, the gangly Williams, who was a born right-handed hitter, could not drive the ball with power consistently. At Horace Mann Junior High, he struggled to make the baseball team and was far from a standout performer. For Williams, as for NBA legend Michael Jordan, who was cut from his varsity basketball team as a high school sophomore, this brush with failure would just add fuel to his competitive fire.

To fulfill his dream of getting to the major leagues, Williams was willing (and eager) to hit and hit and then hit some more. "From the time I was eleven years old," Williams later stated, "I've taken every possible opportunity to swing at a ball." At the beginning of each season, before his hands developed calluses, he would bat until he bled. While the hero of *The Natural*, the Robert Redford baseball film, was partly based on Williams (Roy Hobbs wore the Sox outfielder's uniform number, 9, and hit a homer in his last time at bat), the man himself had to work at everything. "Hundreds of kids have the natural ability to become great ballplayers," Williams later told *Time*, "but nothing except practice, practice, practice will bring out that ability."

Like San Diego High, Hoover High was also a big school—it had a student body of about 1,500—and the competition to make the starting lineup was keen. In his first season, the *San Diego Union* reported, Williams was used primarily as "a reserve outfielder." He went to the plate just eighteen times, swatting six hits. The following spring, Williams initially worked his way onto the field as a pitcher. "He was a skinny bastard," his coach recalled. "But he could rear back and really throw the ball in there." In an April game, he struck out sixteen batters. And then when he finally got a few chances to start at first base and in the outfield, Williams began tearing up the league. As the season wore on, the sixteen-year-old, who swigged milk shakes to bulk up, emerged as a hitting sensation, batting .588. With Williams also winning four games on the mound, the Hockers from Hockerville, as the upstart Hoover High team was referred to (and denigrated) by the locals, pulled off a surprising victory in the league championship. After another stellar season, in which he hit .403, scouts from the New York Yankees and the St. Louis Cardinals came calling. Unwilling to let her boy leave home, May Williams insisted that he turn down all contract offers from big-league teams. In June of 1936, three days after his last high school game, he signed on with his hometown team, the San Diego Padres of the Pacific Coast League. Though Williams was not yet a high school graduate—he would not finish up until the following February—he would be earning $150 a month as a professional ballplayer.

While the Splendid Splinter's Red Sox career, as John Updike has observed, fell into three phases—Jason (Youth), Achilles (Maturity; like the Greek warrior, he pouted), and Nestor (Old Age)—his run-up to the major leagues was another matter. Before becoming anybody's idea of a Greek hero, the obsessive with no social skills often floundered. In the spring of 1939, as Williams was about to begin his rookie season in "the Show," the *Boston Globe* noted, "He was notorious throughout his minor league career for his screwball tactics." In his first year with the Padres, Williams startled his roommate Cedric Durst, a veteran assigned to watch over him, by jumping up on his bed one morning at six o'clock, shouting, "Christ, Ced, it's great to be young and full of vinegar." In the second appearance of his pro career, the still just 147-pound athlete was forced to abandon his pitching aspirations. "I got hit," Williams later noted, "like I was throwing batting practice." For the Padres in 1936, as a part-time, mostly eighth-place hitter, he batted a modest .271 with no homers. The following year, as a regular outfielder, he upped his average to .291 and banged out 23 homers. Part of the reason for the relative dearth of power was that the fences in Lane Field were far away— 350 feet down the right-field line and 500 feet to dead center. Remarkably, those would be the last two seasons Williams would dip below .300 until his injury-plagued 1959 campaign with the Red Sox, who obtained him from the Padres in December 1937.

Two months later, Sox general manager Eddie Collins, who was aware of Williams's reputation for eccentric behavior, asked Bobby Doerr, then about to start his second season in Boston, to escort his fellow Californian to spring training in Florida. Williams met up with Doerr and two other players: Babe Herman, a veteran who had hit .393 for Brooklyn in 1930, and Max West, a young first baseman with the Boston Bees (Beantown's National League team), in El Paso, Texas. Soon after their train left the station, the four ballplayers found themselves at one end of a long, mostly empty car; at the other end were four oldish women. The excitable, fingernail-chomping motormouth, who hardly slept at all on the three-day trip east, immediately began quizzing the former Dodger star about hitting. "And Ted," Doerr later recalled, "he's pumping Babe, and being loud like he is, using pillows for swinging the bat. These women finally told the porter, 'Can you shut that guy up a little bit? He's too loud.'" Each morning when the train stopped, Max West would open the window and do a double take. "There's Ted," stated West years later, "walking up and down and balancing himself on the rails. And he's got a newspaper or a magazine in his hands, making like he's hitting a ball."

Once in Florida, his batting stroke quickly convinced reporters that he was likely to be the next incarnation of Babe Herman, if not Babe Ruth. But though Williams was ready for the major leagues, he was still an emotional basket case. He called everyone in the Red Sox camp in Sarasota "Sport," including his manager, Joe Cronin. To the San Diego boy whose central relationship was with something made out of wood, the concept of a social hierarchy was alien. Assuming that all institutions were as rudderless as the Williams family, he was not trying to challenge authority figures; he just had no idea that they existed, even when staring them in the face. When introduced to California's then governor Frank Merriam, the adolescent stuck out his hand and said matter-of-factly, "Hi, Guv." Likewise, when entering the office of Hoover High principal Floyd Johnson for a chat about baseball or hunting, he did not hesitate to put his feet up on Johnson's desk. "I'd be enjoying the conversation so much," Johnson later mused, "that I'd be oblivious...to his unconventional way of talking to the principal." Not so forgiving was the dumbfounded Cronin, who banished "the Kid," as the nineteen-year-old was nicknamed on day one, to Daytona Beach, the spring home of the Sox top minor-league team, the Minneapolis Millers, after just a week.

Williams would spend the entire 1938 season with Minneapolis. The nonstop nonsensical chatter continued, as did the other quirky manifestations of his internal disorganization. At a dinner party with new neighbors, Williams went up to a top-level executive at Woolworth's and patted him on the stomach, saying, "Good evening, Whale Baby." When chasing after a fly ball, the right fielder would slap his butt and shout, "Hi-yo, Silver." He would also ride his bicycle to the refrain of "Yippy-Yi-Yo" on the outfield grass before games. "He was just a cuckoo guy," Millers pitcher Lefty Lefebvre, whom Williams once took for a hundred-mile-an-hour spin in his Buick, later recalled. "A loner." Referring to him as "Peter Pan," his Millers teammates would keep their distance in an effort to stay safe and sane. Williams's temper tantrums were what most exasperated his manager, Donie Bush, a former major-league shortshop. After a rare off day at the plate, he might tear up towels or punch the water cooler. When Bush threatened to quit, Sox GM Collins responded, "The day Williams doesn't put on his uniform, don't bother to put on your uniform, either." The moody star was also hitting like crazy, and Collins knew that the future of the Sox was inextricably tied to Williams.

Over the course of the season, he put up staggering numbers: 43 homers, 142 runs batted in, and a .366 average. Though those totals were good enough for the Triple Crown, Williams wasn't voted the American Association's Most Valuable Player. The only award the sportswriters agreed that he should get was the league's "screwball king." A pattern was set. Though Williams would later win the AL MVP trophy twice, he was denied the honor in his two Triple Crown years—1942 and 1947. With the exception of Yankee great Lou Gehrig in 1934, no other Triple Crown winner has ever failed to win the MVP, and few other players would succeed in alienating "the knights of the keyboard" as much as Williams.

Williams would eventually lament his lack of "a businesslike attitude" in his pre-Boston years in pro ball. "I mean hitting was so important to me," he later wrote, "consumed so much of my desire, was so much more exciting to me that

I tended to let other things go." And over the course of his nineteen seasons in the majors, his single-mindedness at home plate would make an indelible mark on the "National Pastime."

————

"Cronin's Big Problem of 1939," as the *Boston Globe* referred to the socially mal-adjusted Williams in the spring of his rookie year, got off to a shaky start. In an April preseason game in Atlanta, after striking out with two runners on base in the top of the eighth, the twenty-year-old can't-miss prospect dropped a foul pop-up in the bottom half of the inning. With his frustration mounting, the right fielder picked up the ball, turned around, and hurled it out of the stadium.

Fortunately for Williams, Cronin decided not to apply the measure recommended by the *Globe*, which was to use a screwdriver to force him "not to cut loose with his eccentricities." Instead, after immediately removing his temperamental rookie from the game, the player-manager—the All-Star shortstop would hit fourth or fifth in the lineup, right after Williams—sat down with him for what would be the first of several "fatherly chats." "I just can't understand what goes on in your mind," said Cronin, who, in the course of his storied career, had never witnessed a similar outburst. "See if you can't explain it to me." Though the Kid could not figure himself out either, he apologized. To express his gratitude for Cronin's patience and understanding, he would use his bat. He started hitting. A couple of weeks later, in his first Sunday game at Fenway, Williams thrilled the hometown faithful by going four for five, including a towering homer into the center-field bleachers, an area previously reached only by the game's most feared sluggers. In early May, in Detroit, after he belted the longest homer ever in Briggs Stadium, the *Globe* predicted that he would "become the biggest hitting sensation since Babe Ruth."

Despite a slump in June, which prevented him from being selected to the All-Star team—from then on, he would be a fixture in the midsummer classic—Williams led the league in RBIs with 145, the first rookie ever to do so. He ended up hitting a robust .327 along with 31 homers. Though his discipline at the plate was impressive—he had 107 walks compared with only 64 strikeouts—his first-year jitters precluded the eye-popping totals that would soon become his trademark. Then, as now, seasons with 100 or more strikeouts were common for power hitters, but he would exceed 50 strikeouts only two more times;

his next highest total was 54. Likewise, his OBP for 1939 was .436, lower than any other year except 1959, as his walk totals would typically be much higher (thrice surpassing 150). As Williams would later acknowledge, in his rookie season he was still swinging at pitches an inch above his shoulders. Even so, all the hours of practice at North Park had already paid big dividends. "I can't imagine," Williams later wrote, "anyone having a better, happier first year in the big leagues....Every day was Christmas." Babe Ruth agreed. At the time, baseball did not yet have its Rookie of the Year award, but the recently retired Sultan of Swat designated Williams "the best rookie."

The Babe would soon go further and anoint the Kid as his successor, an honor that Williams tried his best to live up to. In their first face-to-face meeting, before an exhibition game in Boston in 1943, Ruth, as the papers widely reported, told Williams, "You remind me a lot of myself. I love to hit. You're one of the most natural ballplayers I've ever seen." In a recent interview, Mike Epstein, who played under Williams in the late 1960s and early 1970s as a member of the Washington Senators, told me that his manager liked to tell a different version of this story. Attempting to channel Williams, Epstein said, "And the Babe comes up to me and tells me, 'I used to study Shoeless Joe Jackson [the great left-handed hitter for the Chicago White Sox accused of betting on the 1919 World Series] before games to copy him because I thought he had the prettiest fucking swing I have ever seen. But no, Williams, you've got a prettier fucking swing.'" Hearing such praise from the mouth of the Babe just a few years into his career moved the Red Sox outfielder deeply. "I was flabbergasted," Williams recalled years later. "After all, he was Babe Ruth." In the early 1990s, when compiling *Ted Williams' Hit List* with sportswriter Jim Prime, a book in which he would rank the twenty-five best hitters of all time, the Splendid Splinter would put Ruth at the top, followed by Lou Gehrig. While his findings reflected more than just a "dry statistical analysis," Williams put a premium on slugging percentage and on-base percentage. And he ended up not ranking himself, sticking a section on his career in an appendix. "But it was clear from our conversations," stated coauthor Jim Prime in a recent phone interview, "that Ted thought he was second only to Ruth." Though Williams was in awe of Ruth, the perfectionist could not help but point out his flaws. "Ruth struck out too many times," wrote Williams, proud that his 709 lifetime total of Ks paled in comparison to Ruth's 1,330.

With expectations sky-high, his second season in the majors turned out to be a bust. But only Williams could hit .344 — just eight points behind the league leader, Joe DiMaggio—and be accused of having an off year. Critics pounced on his inability to hit the long ball; he ended up with just 23 homers, the lowest total of his career for a full season. What highlighted his power outage was that in an effort to help Williams, the Red Sox had shortened the right-field fence in Fenway Park by twenty feet. Frustrated by his performance, Williams popped off, as only he could. Midway through the 1940 campaign, in response to an innocent question from a reporter at the *Boston American* ("What's the matter with you, Ted?"), he let loose, saying he hated everything about Boston, its fans, and its writers. After his tirade—minus the F-bombs—hit the newsstands, the war between Williams and his adopted hometown was officially on; Jason was fast becoming Achilles, whose rage knew no bounds. Psychoanalyzing "the problem child," the *Boston Globe* argued that Williams had a "repressed desire to dominate the Red Sox and afterward, perhaps, the American League." But the severity of his case of arrested development didn't allow for much repression. "Terrible Ted" would be forever mired in the "terrible twos." "TELL THEM TO ALL GO FUCK THEMSELVES" was the message that Williams asked the rookie reporter at the *Boston Record* to pass on to his colleagues.[3] What the toddler wanted above all was to spend endless hours of quality time with his bat. For Williams, both the writers as well as the fans were intruders; to tip his cap to the fans after a homer, which he stopped doing after his rookie year, would be to acknowledge that he and his bat did not have the right to be left alone. Like Jefferson and other obsessives, to combat his considerable social anxiety, he was prone to pretending that other people didn't exist.

Rebounding from his "sophomore slump" in 1941, Williams put together his season for the ages. But .406 wasn't the number that had Americans buzzing about baseball that year; it was 56. From May 15 until July 16, Joltin' Joe DiMaggio did the unthinkable; he got a hit in every game. And after being held hitless in Cleveland on July 17—and thus missing out on the $10,000 that the H. J. Heinz Company was prepared to pay had his record-setting feat reached the magic 57—the Yankee centerfielder started another streak of 17 games. With Joe D. hitting .357 and knocking in 130 runs, five more than Williams, and the Yankees winning the pennant by 17 games, the Kid came in second in the MVP

---

[3] To capture Williams's booming voice and larger-than-life personality, journalists have often used caps when quoting the words he used in his tirades.

voting. "Hell," Williams would later declare, "I'd'a voted for DiMaggio myself." But Williams was himself guilty of getting caught up in the DiMaggio hype. During his streak, DiMaggio hit *only* .408; during the same stretch, Williams hit .412; Williams essentially did for an entire season what DiMaggio could manage for only a third. Even more surprising, Williams failed to nab the MVP in 1942, when he won his first Triple Crown with an otherworldly 36 homers and 137 RBIs to go along with a .356 average. That year, the award went to another pennant-winning Yankee, second baseman Joe Gordon, who hit a modest .322 with just 18 homers and 103 RBIs.

Williams did not win the first of his two MVPs until 1946, when the Red Sox led the American League in batting and were in first place most of the season. That September, *Life* could not help but attribute the team's stunning success solely to Williams's hitting, lauding "his monomaniacal attempt to perfect himself in the one thing he really cares about." For the first time since 1918 and for the only time in his career, Boston won the pennant, finishing twelve games ahead of the second-place Detroit Tigers. But the World Series against the St. Louis Cardinals turned out to be a disaster. The highly favored Red Sox lost four games to three, and Williams hit .200, eking out just five puny singles. "I was so disgusted, so unhappy," Williams later recalled. "Shell-shocked. And so disappointed in myself." In this instance, his rigidity, rather than being an asset, seemed to work against him. During the Series, the Cardinals employed a "right-shift" against Williams, a strategy devised earlier that season by the Indians manager Lou Boudreau, which featured four infielders on the right side of second base. The day before the decisive seventh game, Williams told the *Boston Globe* that he would not change his batting style, "now, next year or ever." Obsessives are addicted to their routines, and the thought of changing his approach on the fly was anathema to Williams. According to his calculations, the shift still left thirty feet of open space between first and second base, and he had little interest in slapping the ball to left field. "Don't let anyone fill you up with the baloney," he emphasized, "that the Cards' defense has me worried and has caused me to press." But his actions suggested otherwise. Right after finishing that locker-room interview with the *Globe*, Williams got undressed and picked up a bat, which he toted all the way to the shower. With nothing—not even bat bonding—able to quell his jitters, the third-place hitter in the Sox lineup went hitless in the Series finale. On the train out of St. Louis, he broke down and cried. "I was looking out the window," he later recalled, "so I had to shut the shade."

April 30, 1952, was "Ted Williams Day" at Fenway Park. Boston was paying homage to its thirty-three-year-old star because on May 2, he was due to report to a U.S. Navy base in Willow Grove, Pennsylvania, to begin a seventeen-month tour of duty. In pregame ceremonies, the left fielder was showered with numerous gifts, including a memory book signed by four hundred thousand fans from across the country, a movie camera, and a light blue Cadillac. "This is the greatest day of my life," an emotional Williams told the crowd of 24,764. "I'll always remember it." In the seventh inning, in what both Williams and the fans assumed would be his last time at bat—he was not counting on a comeback at thirty-five—he parked a curveball eight rows deep into the right-field stands. Despite the wild cheering, the "Hub Kid" failed to tip his cap (as would also be the case on September 28, 1960, when he bid adieu for the final-final time with another long ball).

This would be Williams's second stint in the armed forces. He had signed up in May 1942 and first got called up that November, a couple of months after completing his Triple Crown–winning season. Of all the branches of the military, Williams enlisted in the most demanding, Naval Aviation—the Air Force was not established until 1947. When asked why he did not seek out something less perilous, he quipped, "Because I like to hit!" For Williams, the bat and the machine gun were first cousins.

His decision to take to the air, as he later acknowledged, was inspired by the exploits of his boyhood idol, Charles Lindbergh. At the age of nine, Williams had seen Lindbergh fêted in a packed San Diego Stadium not long after his return from Paris. "Lindbergh," he said in the 1960s, "had this great obsession to want to be alone and to want his own life." (The Splinter was of course no different.) "He [Lindbergh] is still doing great things," Williams added. "I'd put him among the five men that I admire the most that I've ever known in my lifetime."

Like Lindbergh, the lackadaisical C student turned into an academic whiz once his studies were geared toward a goal that excited him. In November 1942, the high school graduate, who had little idea what a college was—on a visit to Harvard University that June, he had commented, "It's old, right?"—began a civilian pilot training program at Amherst College. "I'm not batting .400 in this flying course yet," he told the *New York Times* after a couple of weeks, "but

I'm going to do it." Williams handled all subjects, including advanced math and physics, with aplomb. "He mastered intricate problems in fifteen minutes, which took the average cadet an hour," stated his Sox teammate and fellow cadet, Johnny Pesky, who struggled academically at Amherst that winter. And surprisingly, like Lindbergh, the fiercely independent Williams also took to military discipline. As opposed to the outfielder, the cadet was capable of controlling his moods. Squadron commanders considered Williams a model soldier, with one calling him "enthusiastic, industrious and cooperative."

The following year, Williams began intermediate flight training in Pensacola, Florida. Due to his preternatural hand-eye coordination, he excelled. In aerial drills, he repeatedly tore the sleeve target to smithereens, setting all kinds of records for hits. On May 2, 1944, he earned his wings, becoming a second lieutenant in the United States Marine Corps. That same day, he married Doris Soule, whom he had known since his days with the Minneapolis Millers (she was the daughter of his Minnesota fishing guide). While his bride met his specifications—(1) hourglass figure, and (2) likes to hunt and fish—their relationship would be stormy. Soon after their arrival in the Everglades for the honeymoon, Doris spotted a snake, and she shut herself in the cabin while Williams fished by himself.

Having demonstrated remarkable ability and composure in his new line of work, Williams stayed on in Pensacola as a flight instructor. In mid-1945, he headed to San Francisco, where he began preparing for combat duty in the Far East. After the surrender of the Japanese in August, he was transferred to Hawaii, where he spent the rest of the year playing baseball in a Navy league. Williams was discharged from the Marines in January 1946.

As he left the armed forces, Williams signed up for the inactive Marine Reserves. Like most exiting soldiers, he figured that his military days were over. But six years later, with pilots in short supply and a new war to fight, the Marines came calling. In private, the Red Sox star fumed, but in public, for the sake of his country, he bit his tongue. (Aware of his tendency to pop off, he also repeatedly gave reporters the slip.) The war in Korea he supported; his recall he hated. "I didn't think it was right," he later said, "to be called up again." And this time around, he would go directly to the front.

During his eight-week refresher course in Willow Grove, Captain Williams, as he was now called, chose to work with the new kids on the block: jets. "Easy to fly," later observed the technology geek, who also liked souped-up cars and cameras, "easier than props because they had no torque, less noise, tricycle landing gear. Wonderful flight characteristics." Early on, he got a huge scare when a pilot crashed his F-9 near the Pennsylvania base. Rushing to the scene, a horrified Williams saw the only remains of the crumpled soldier, a shoe and a leg. "So I was never a totally relaxed flyer," he later recalled, "because I knew it was my ass if I didn't pay attention."

After completing several months of jet training in Cherry Point, North Carolina, Williams headed for Korea, arriving in early February 1953. The hut in Pohang that he shared with two roommates looked like "a real dog box," as he later put it. Due to the cold and damp conditions, he would do frequent battle with viral infections as well as with Communists on the other side of the Thirty-Eighth Parallel. On a busy day, his elite squadron, whose roughly three dozen members included John Glenn, the future astronaut and senator, flew about thirty sorties into enemy territory. "There was certainly nothing 'bush' about him [Williams] as a Marine combat pilot," wrote Glenn in his autobiography. "He gave flying the same perfectionist's attention he gave to his hitting." And if Williams had not displayed his characteristic conscientiousness in the cockpit, he might never have made it home alive.

On February 14, after a couple of test flights and some target practice on an old bridge, he flew his first combat mission. Two days later, Williams took part in a massive air attack, in which a couple of hundred planes from several bases pounded a troop-and-supply area twenty miles south of Pyongyang, the capital of North Korea.

February 16, 1953, turned out to be the most harrowing day of Williams's life.

That morning, soon after dropping a few 250-pound bombs on buildings in enemy territory, Williams noticed that he had been hit. He did not feel a thud, but suddenly nothing worked. The light indicators were out of whack. The stick in his hand was gyrating wildly. The radio was dead.

Figuring he could not complete the return flight, Williams took his Panther jet out over the Yellow Sea, which was half-frozen. He thought about ejecting, but worried that he wouldn't be able to get out. "Not for this boy," he said to himself. Just then, a squadron mate, Lieutenant Larry Hawkins, spotted Williams's plane going in the wrong direction. Flying up alongside, Hawkins used hand signals to guide him back to the base.

Fifteen minutes later, as Williams was above a field near the base, smoke was coming out of his tail and fuel was leaking. His plane was on fire. But Williams could not tell exactly what was happening and decided to crash-land. He was going 225 miles an hour—twice the speed of a normal approach—and he could not do anything to slow down. Only one wheel popped down, and neither his dive brakes nor his air flaps were functioning. Once he hit the ground, he kept skidding and skidding, causing him to yell, "When is this dirty S.O.B. going to stop?" (The neatnik was trying to tar his malfunctioning machine with the ultimate insult.) The landing strip was 11,000 feet long, and about 2,000 feet from the end, his plane finally came to a halt. Just a few minutes after he stepped out, it burst into flames.

The next morning, without missing a beat, Williams was back in the cockpit. He would fly a total of thirty-nine combat missions before being sent to Japan for medical treatment in mid-June. Besides numerous bouts with the flu, which more than once progressed to pneumonia, he was suffering from inner ear problems.

Ted Williams was now more than just a great hitter. Proud of his military record, which earned him a handful of medals and gold stars, Williams would call the Marines "the best team I ever played for."

"Ted served his country in two wars," President George H. W. Bush has stated. "As a Marine pilot, he set a tremendous example for other celebrities in America. He believed in service to country, and indeed he served with honor."

———

Williams returned to the United States on July 9, 1953. He received a thunderous ovation when he threw out the first pitch at the All-Star Game on July 14. He had missed his favorite companion. As he told reporters, he had touched a bat just once during his entire time in Korea, when he and Lloyd Merriman—a pilot who, before he started shooting at Communists, patrolled center field for the Cincinnati Reds—gave their fellow Marines a brief demonstration of how the game was played.

On July 28, Williams was released from the military. That same day, he returned to Fenway Park, where he took batting practice several hours before a scheduled game. He wowed the couple of hundred onlookers by knocking nine straight balls out of the park. Afterward, when he ran into Sox GM Joe Cronin, he yelled, "What'd you do to the fucking plate while I was gone?" Something was wrong, Williams insisted. A few days later, the surveyor who checked out the batter's box determined that the dish was off by an inch.

Williams got into his first game at the end of August. "He don't look like he used to," Yogi Berra said after Williams feasted on Yankee pitching in a Labor Day doubleheader. "He looks better." In his 91 at bats, the revered elder statesman— Achilles had morphed into Nestor—would hit .407 with an astonishing 13 long balls. (Except for Barry Bonds in 2001, no player has ever hit that many homers per at bat over the course of a full season.) Despite his abbreviated season, Williams came in a close second in the voting for Comeback Player of the Year.

While Williams and lumber reconnected quickly—once again, he was always toting a bat around, swinging it and measuring it—he and Doris were done. In January 1954, she petitioned for a separation. According to a widely circulated UPI story, Doris charged him with beating her, making her life "an impossible burden," and using "language that was profane, abusive and obscene." Another stress on the marriage, which ended in divorce the following year, as biographer Leigh Montville has reported, was that the sexually hyperactive Williams had come down with "a social disease" while in Korea. The shame associated with this secret may well account for why the foul-mouthed Williams later turned to *syphilitic* as his epithet of choice.

For the man who had grown up without any intimate attachments, nothing was more horrifying than monogamy. As Doris told the press at the time of her divorce, "I don't think he ever wanted to be married." Even when living with Doris in Boston during the season, Williams would arrange for some getaway time in local hotels. After they split up, he became the incarnation of the "swinging bachelor" made popular by the recently launched *Playboy* magazine. He was infinitely more discriminating about the pitches he swung at than about the women he slept with. Just about anyone would do—at least for the very short term. At autograph shows, he wouldn't hesitate to print his Boston address— "Room 231, Hotel Somerset"—next to his signature before passing back the baseball to any woman he found appealing.

For companionship, as opposed to sex, he turned elsewhere. One might be tempted to argue that just as the adolescent Kinsey bonded with bugs, the adult Williams took to fish; but ever since his days in North Park, he much preferred the inanimate over the animate. By the late 1950s, he was a devoted and talented fisherman; yet catching (and releasing), as opposed to collecting, was what he was after. His goal was a thousand each of "the Big Three"—tarpon, bonefish, and salmon—and he dutifully recorded his progress in his log books. His closest bonds were with his flies—Mr. Meticulous was constantly inventing and tying his own, an activity that he dubbed "the pièce de résistance"—and with his fishing rods. Like bats, these tools, which he kept in neatly organized collections, could also provide comfort. Late in his career, after taking a called third strike, a disgusted Williams flung his bat into the stands in Fenway Park, accidentally hitting his manager's housekeeper in the head. Before going out to dinner that night, he calmed down by sequestering himself in his room at the Somerset Hotel for an hour, tying flies. Yet even with his fishing paraphernalia, sudden breakups were not rare. If a big fish managed to swim away with his lure, Williams might smash his rod in two, yelling, "Here, you lousy son of a bitch," before tossing the alleged offender into the water, adding, "Take that, too."

The Red Sox teams during his last years were terrible, but Williams continued to excel at the plate. In his first full season after Korea, Williams won the batting title with a .345 average. In 1957, the ageless wonder not only hit .388; he also banged out 38 homers. The hittingologist attributed his surprising .388, which, as the years went on, he was even more proud of than the .406, to a series of experiments. After the previous season, he had Hillerich's send him a couple of extra-heavy bats weighing about 60 ounces, which he kept swinging all winter. And that spring, he officially switched to a 34½-ounce bat, two ounces heavier than the one he had been using. As the weather got warm, he went back to hitting with a slightly lighter bat. "I never hit the ball harder," he later recalled, "than that year."

Everything clicked in 1957. On two occasions, he hit three homers in the same game, the first American League player ever to do so. In mid-September, after missing a couple of weeks with pneumonia, the perfectionist hit four homers in his first four official times at bat, en route to a remarkable streak in which he reached base safely (on a walk or hit) in sixteen consecutive plate appearances. Later that month, Red Sox clubhouse attendant Johnny Orlando told the *Globe* that "practice is everything to Williams....When Ted was sick recently...he takes it [an extra-heavy bat] back into his room and he's practicing swinging it while he's sick."

The following year, Williams again won the batting title; he got five hits on the last weekend of the season to pass teammate Pete Runnels and finish at .328. In 1959, bothered by a pinched nerve in his neck, Williams hit a fully mortal .254 (the only time he fell below .300). In 1960, the forty-two-year-old rebounded by hitting .316 with 29 homers and 72 RBIs as a part-time player; that final year, his home-run percentage was 9.4, the highest of his career.

In February of 1969, baseball, as the *New York Times* sports columnist Arthur Daley observed, got "a shot of Adrenalin." The Kid—with Williams incapable of growing up, the old moniker still applied—was back in the game.

To keep pace with the Washington Redskins, who had excited the capital's sports fans by hiring the legendary Vince Lombardi as their head coach, Bob Short, the new owner of the Washington Senators, snagged the retired Sox star, the biggest name he could get, as his manager. The price was steep; the Hall of Famer landed the biggest contract ever given to a field general, a five-year deal, which, with stock options, was worth more than $1 million.

Since his final at bat, the monomaniacal loner had not done much but fish. Back in 1960, he had signed a contract with Sears Roebuck to test and market hunting and fishing gear; as a sales rep, he no longer needed to put in too many hours to pick up his one hundred grand (roughly the same salary as he earned from the Sox in his final years). Also appointed a Red Sox VP after his retirement, he did little for the team but tutor hitters at spring training, an assignment that he gave up in 1967 when he abruptly left its spring-training camp in Winter Haven after just a couple of days. "Ted was a helluva hitter, but a pain in the ass. He disrupted my camp," recalled the late Dick Williams, the Sox manager that year, in a phone interview in early 2011. A disciplinarian who ran a tight ship, the skipper of the pennant-winning "Impossible Dream" Team complained that the retired star "kept corralling my pitchers to pick their brains about hitting."

While Ted Williams had nothing but contempt for the other segment of the baseball fraternity—"The only thing dumber than a fucking pitcher," he would bark out, "is two fucking pitchers"—he rarely could resist the temptation to discuss his favorite subject. The new Sox manager may have actually felt less annoyed by his jabbering than threatened by his very presence. Ted Williams had twice turned down the Sox job, and when Dick Williams was signed, several Boston scribes protested, "It's the wrong Williams."

As Ted Williams headed to the Senators' spring-training facility in Pompano Beach, the *Boston Globe* described his hiring as the "most exciting off-field event" since the signing of Jackie Robinson by the Dodgers in 1946. His charisma generated buzz, but so, too, did his unpredictability. "Manage twenty-five men," mused the paper, "heck, he can't even manage himself."

Facing a barrage of reporters for the first time in nearly a decade, Williams declared that he was up for the challenge. "I still love fishing," insisted the fifty-year-old, who no longer qualified as a Splinter, as his weight was up to 230 pounds. "But I found that I had fished most places already. Peru, Alaska, Costa Rica, Nova Scotia. It was time for something new."

He also had a new family to support. About a year earlier, the still handsome and imposing Williams had married Dolores Wettach, a former Miss Vermont, nearly two decades his junior. In March 1964, just as he was divorcing wife number two, Lee Howard, after only two and a half years of marriage, he and the *Vogue* model both happened to be flying back to America from Down Under in the same first-class cabin. He began the conversation by popping spitballs that folded out into notes in her direction—a first move that reflected both his crudeness and his charm—and several hours later, after a dinner in San Francisco, they were in the sack.

In the aspiring actress, who had just missed landing the part of Bond girl Pussy Galore in *Goldfinger*, Williams was looking for an occasional squeeze; only after she accidentally became pregnant did he start thinking about tying the knot. His first son, John Henry, was born in August 1968; a daughter, Claudia, would follow in 1971. "Dolores was a beauty," said Senators slugger Mike Epstein, who recalled a lunch when Williams hurled Dolores's plate against the wall. "He had picked at her salad, and she had told him, 'Just take it.' You never knew what was going to set him off." As Dolores once put it, "Ted can be a Dr. Jekyll and a Mr. Hyde." The inevitable divorce came in 1973.

The Washington Senators team inherited by Williams was pathetic. The players, with a few notable exceptions, such as All-Star outfielder Frank Howard, were a bunch of rejects. In its previous eight seasons, the expansion club had never won more than 76 games. In 1968, the Senators had finished in tenth place, 37½ games out of first, and had drawn just 547,000 fans, less than half the league average. With expectations low, Williams would feel free to manage the team exactly as he saw fit. What did he have to lose?

"I may turn out to be a horseshit manager," he told the press, "but I'm going to try." To fix all that ailed the Senators, Williams devised a simple cure: he would steep his players in his own obsessions.

On day one in Florida, the man who had practiced his swing more than just about anyone else who had ever lived (with the possible exception of Hall of Famer Ty Cobb) set up extralong batting practice sessions. Hitting was first and foremost on the agenda. "Early in camp, the infielders were practicing a pickle play [a drill in which infielders throw to each other to catch a would-be runner trapped between the bases]," Mike Epstein told me. "The coaches were arguing about how to conduct it properly. Williams comes out of the dugout and says, 'What's this all about? Fuck it, let's hit.'" The paragon of patience at the plate also emphasized concentration in the chess game between batter and pitcher. "What the hell are you thinking about up there, bush?" he would ask his players.

Williams identified as candidates for special tutelage the power hitters Frank "Hondo" Howard and Mike Epstein. The six-foot-seven, 290-pound Howard, then thirty-two, had been a solid hitter for nearly a decade, but Williams sensed that he was capable of being great. Cutting to the chase, the new manager asked the All-Star outfielder about his previous year's stats: "How can a guy hit 44 home runs but get only 48 bases on balls?" He accused Howard of going after "that first little swifty," the first fastball that he saw. Eagerly taking the medicine, "Hondo" told reporters that spring, "Repetition is the most important part of learning to hit." The effects would be dramatic. That season, Howard's average jumped from .274 to .296, his walk total nearly doubled, and his on-base percentage jumped from .340 to .402. Howard also had career highs in both homers, 48, and slugging percentage, .574. Epstein, who turned twenty-six that April, had been a minor-league MVP but had yet to do anything in the majors. In 1969, the six-foot-three, 230-pound, left-handed hitter, who reminded Williams of himself, would have his best year, hitting .278 with 30 homers. His on-base percentage was .416, up nearly 100 points from 1968. "Learning the mental side of the game from Williams," stated Epstein, who today passes down his former manager's lessons at his hitting school in Colorado, "was a phenomenal experience."

Williams also worked wonders for several other Senator hitters, even Eddie "Wimpy" Brinkman, his six-foot, 170-pound, great-field, no-hit shortstop. In his previous eight seasons, all with the Senators, the once promising twenty-eight-year-old, who had hit .460 while playing high school ball with Pete Rose in Cincinnati—most scouts considered him the better prospect—had been a nonentity at the plate. In 1968, Brinkman, whose career high was stuck at .229, hit an embarrassing .187. In camp, the manager who carried a bat on the bench at all times ("something to hold on to") insisted that Brinkman also take his bat with him wherever he went. And that spring, Williams taught his shortstop to choke up and slap the ball to all parts of the field. "Williams," Brinkman later recalled, "beat it into my head what I had to do." By the All-Star game, Brinkman was batting .287 with a team-leading 102 hits; he would finish at a respectable .266, his career high.

As a rule, Williams encouraged his players by telling them that with hard work and concentration, anyone could be successful; however, he could also be brutally honest. When the light-hitting second-baseman Tim Cullen once asked for reassurance, Williams fired back, "Timmy, you're one of the dumbest fucking hitters I've ever seen in my life." With the exception of Cullen, who hit .209 in 1969 and was soon out of baseball, Williams's batters thrived. In 1969, the team hit .251, up from .224 in 1968; while the Senators' walks went up from 9 to 11 per 100 at bats, their strikeouts dipped down from 18 to just 6 per 100 at bats.

Even more remarkable, Williams revived the Senators' pitching staff with the same one-dimensional approach. Adopting the mind-set of hitters, his pitchers discovered that they were better equipped to do their job. "I just listened to everything he said to the hitters," reliever Casey Cox later recalled, "and turned it around. If this was the situation they wanted to create, the 2-0, 3-1 count, then it was the situation I wanted to avoid. The most important thing was to throw strikes." The inverse of Williams's hitting mantra—"Don't get into a situation where you have to throw a good pitch to hit"—also proved useful. Cox had his best year in the majors, going 12-7 with a 2.78 ERA. Starter Dick Bosman went from 2-9 to 16-12 with a league-leading 2.19 ERA. "He [Williams] taught me to pitch from the neck up," stated Bosman. The team's ERA was fifth in the league in 1969, up from tenth in 1968.

The superior hitting, combined with the dependable pitching, translated into wins. "Williams has refused to act like a rookie manager," wrote the *Washington Post*'s Shirley Povich on July 4, 1969, alluding to the "sorcery he has used to bring forth feats from athletes who are surpassing themselves." The 1969 Senators were the first Washington ball club since 1952 to be five games over .500 by the All-Star break. By July 14, home attendance was already 11,000 more than for all of 1968. For the year, the team went 86-76, its best record in twenty-four years. Proud of how hard his players worked, on the last day of the season, Williams rewarded each one with an object dear to his heart—not a bat, but the next best thing, a fishing rod, which he placed in their lockers. Though the Senators finished in fourth place in the American League East, more than twenty games behind the first-place Orioles, the turnaround was so remarkable that the Associated Press named Williams the AL Manager of the Year. The whole city exulted in his triumph. Richard Nixon, who also moved to the nation's capital in early 1969, personally wired his congratulations. (Years later, Williams would call Nixon "the greatest fucking President since Abraham Lincoln.")

Williams had once again shown that he could control his behavior to meet a given objective. As a player, he had infuriated the writers and charmed the umpires (so that he could keep pumping them for info on hitters), but as a manager, he did just the opposite. "He gave us fantastic copy," stated Russ White, who covered the Senators for the *Washington Daily News*, in a recent interview. "He was colorful, and he didn't lie." After a game early in the 1969 season in which Morganna, the blonde bombshell known as the "Kissing Bandit," ran onto the field, reached up and pecked Frank Howard, the manager told White, "Hell of a butt on her." In Washington, in sharp contrast to Boston, Williams was beloved for his wit, intelligence, and strength of character. When the Senators manager met Vince Lombardi for the first time in the summer of 1969, he said, "I understand that you can walk on water," to which the Redskins coach responded, "I understand that you can, too."

But Williams couldn't keep up the magic. In 1970, the Senators reverted to form, winning only seventy games. And the team's fortunes went downhill from there. Much of the blame can be heaped on team owner Bob Short, who made a series of ill-conceived decisions, such as trading several key players for a controversial has-been, pitcher Denny McLain. Williams got embroiled in a bitter feud with the former All-Star, who suffered a league-leading twenty-two losses in his only year with the team. Early in the 1971 season, to balance his books, Short sold a couple of his best players, including Mike Epstein; that fall, the mercurial executive abandoned Washington in favor of Arlington, Texas. A frustrated and bitter Williams stayed on and became the first manager of the new Texas Rangers. One of the few highlights of his disastrous 1972 season—the Rangers lost more games than any other team in baseball—was a pregame hitting exhibition at Fenway Park on August 25, when the paunchy fifty-three-year-old-thrilled the Boston fans by picking up a bat and promptly knocking one into the seats.

As the 1972 season ended, Williams resigned as the Rangers manager. He had had enough. "Managing is essentially a loser's job," he later wrote, "and managers are about the most expendable pieces of furniture on earth." For the control freak, overseeing twenty-five men, whom he could not even pick, as opposed to confronting a single dumb pitcher in the batter's box, left too much to chance.

Under his cushy contract with Short, Williams could keep collecting his checks for another year while remaining a team consultant devoid of any responsibilities.

He turned his attention back to being Ted Williams, a demanding full-time job in its own right. Everyone from Hollywood A-listers to politicos of all stripes was eager to rub shoulders with him, but he came out of his cocoon only occasionally. While he relished the social clout that his hitting had wrought, he exercised his newfound freedom to the fullest extent possible. Like Holden Caulfield, the adolescent anti-hero created by the late J. D. Salinger, the perpetual "Kid" had no interest in sucking up to anyone he considered a phony. "Ted don't do mucha anything he don't want to," said his longtime Florida neighbor and fishing guide, Jimmy Albright. For this man of modest means and simple tastes, life would once again revolve around the pursuit of the Big Three. At home in the Florida Keys, he would go after tarpon and bonefish; and every summer, he would retreat to his cabin on the Miramichi River in New Brunswick to fish for Atlantic salmon. "I am as nuts about it [salmon fishing] in a cold, pouring rain as I am in bright sunshine," he later wrote. "I love it that much."

But not long after calling it quits with both the Texas Rangers and his third wife, Williams stumbled upon something unexpected: love. It came in the form of Louise Kaufman, a white-haired woman six years his senior, whom he invited to move into his home in Islamorada, Florida, in the mid-1970s. Nearly two decades earlier, as her own first marriage was crumbling, Louise first became entranced by Williams, and she was devastated when he kept passing her up for his assorted lot of short-term lovers and part-time spouses. Though Louise was no looker—Williams's Red Sox teammate Johnny Pesky nicknamed her "Grandma"—her résumé was ideally suited for the nearly impossible position of being Ted Williams's live-in girlfriend. A card-carrying member of the International Women's Gamefishing Association, she once caught a 152-pound fish (and she weighed only about 120). An avid nonfiction reader who liked to collect facts, she, too, could hurl F-bombs. But most important, Louise knew how to stand up to the rageaholic without losing control herself. For the first time, Williams would manage to organize his existence through a bond with another human being rather than with an implement. The anti–May Williams, Louise would keep his houses spick-and-span; she not only cleaned his clothes, but she even ironed his underpants. While order was still his summum bonum, he was now accompanied on his quixotic quest by a flesh-and-blood companion with whom he shared both his wounds and his aspirations. As he neared his sixties, Ted Williams was finally starting to understand what human connection was all about.

In 1978, Williams also reconnected with baseball when he was hired by the Red Sox to come to Winter Haven every spring to work with young hitters. For a new generation of Red Sox minor leaguers, "the Corpulent Clouter," as a *Globe* columnist dubbed the 260-pound retiree, was not a Greek hero, or even a Greek god, but God Himself. One awestruck teenager was future Hall of Famer Wade Boggs, who first met Williams when they both happened to be standing in line for a movie. Within seconds, as Boggs recalled in a recent phone interview, Williams emitted his standard salutation, and Boggs, who had pored over *The Science of Hitting* in high school, was suddenly shaking with excitement. As the other patrons started filing into the theater, the pair kept demonstrating batting stances and discussing hip action. "Ted was bigger than life," stated the former third baseman with the .328 lifetime average. For Boggs, who also "never could get enough hitting practice," Williams's monomania would serve as inspiration.

The former catcher Rich Gedman, who also played with Boggs both in the minors and on the 1986 Sox team that lost a classic World Series to the New York Mets, recalled the hush that shrouded the field at the team's minor-league complex whenever Williams started issuing his profanity-laced running commentary from behind the batting cage. "It was like the old E. F. Hutton commercial," Gedman told me. "We sensed that we were in the presence of greatness, and we listened intently to every word." Besides hitting coach, Williams also served as cleanliness consultant. Soon after his return to the Sox, according to Leigh Montville, then a *Globe* reporter, Williams asked the club's equipment guy: "What detergent do you use to clean these uniforms?" When he heard Tide, his inquisitive mind was far from satisfied: "Now why do you use Tide? Is it better than all the other detergents? Is it cheaper? Is there some secret ingredient? Why do you use Tide?"

After Louise Kaufman died unexpectedly in August 1993 during the couple's annual sojourn in New Brunswick, Williams's health quickly deteriorated. As with Estée Lauder after the loss of her husband, he was devastated; he immediately shut down emotionally. Six months later, he suffered a major stroke, which robbed him of 75 percent of his vision. The seventy-five-year-old would now require round-the-clock nursing care. At the end of 1994, his youngest child, John Henry, then twenty-six, moved into his Florida home and promptly took control. "The Kid's Kid," as he was called in the Boston papers, had the same volatile temperament. "Dealing with John Henry is like sitting on a powder keg," an auctioneer once told the *New York Times*. But the six-foot-five JFK Jr. look-alike had little talent or ingenuity to go with the touch of madness. He could not even hit minor-league pitching and never made it anywhere near the bigs in several cracks at a baseball career. And just about every one of his many business ventures, which he kept concocting in the attempt to cash in on his father's fame, flopped miserably. As Williams careened from one health crisis to another, all that the self-absorbed and combative John Henry seemed to care about, according to a slew of observers, was whether his autograph machine could still function. In the fall of 2001, as an exceedingly frail Williams recovered from major heart surgery, his former cook, Jacques Prudhomme, noticed that he was doing special exercises to strengthen his right wrist. "Just for the autographs," Prudhomme told Leigh Montville. "I went into my car and cried....I would never come back to...[his home] again."

As soon as Williams died on July 5, 2002, John Henry had the body flown to Alcor, a cryonics firm in Arizona, which promptly put him in a freezer. The reason? Unlike Lindbergh, Williams himself rarely, if ever, expressed an interest in immortality; however, John Henry, who held power of attorney, insisted otherwise. He also produced an oil-stained scrap of paper containing his father's signature to back up his claim that his father wanted to be frozen until medical science could figure out how to bring bodies back to life. His older sister, Bobby-Jo, was shocked and horrified. In an interview with a Boston TV station, she stated that John Henry had told her: "We can sell Dad's DNA and people will buy it because they'd love to have little Ted Williamses." Supported by a host of family friends, Bobby-Jo sought legal action to stop her brother. Six months later, lacking sufficient financial resources, she reached an out-of-court settlement; in exchange for a couple of hundred grand, Bobby-Jo gave up her attempt to have her father cremated, in accordance with the request that he had made in his will. Today "a splintered Splendid Splinter" is still frozen. But as an ex-Alcor employee, Larry Johnson, claimed in a controversial *Sports Illustrated* feature story and subsequent book, *Frozen: My Journey into the World of Cryonics, Deception, and Death* (2009), the job may have been botched. According to Johnson, the firm ended up severing Williams's head from his body and storing each part separately; moreover, during the surgery, his head was accidentally cracked in nine places. (Alcor ended up suing Johnson for defamation, and in early 2012 the two sides reached an out-of-court settlement. Avoiding a protracted legal battle, Johnson issued a public statement, which included the following carefully worded retraction: "My account of the Ted Williams cryopreservation, which was not based upon my first-hand observation as noted in my book, is contradicted by information furnished by Alcor.") In a rare interview with ABC News in 2012, Claudia Williams defended her brother, whose body was also shipped to Arizona after his death from leukemia in 2004. By way of explanation, she alluded to her father's lifelong obsession with science—a word that, as she noted, made it into the title of his treatise on hitting. She added: "We [the family] did this together because it made us feel like it had something of hope. That's all. A hope." But as a good obsessive, Williams was much more about complete control than idle hope. And especially in something as monumental as possible resurrection, it is likely that this god would have done everything in his power to ensure at least a reasonable chance of success—say, .400.

Future Obsessives

The movers and shakers have always been obsessive nuts. Name any mover or shaker you like—I don't care if it's Attila the Hun or Jesus of Nazareth or Karl Marx or F.D.R. or Winston Churchill. They were all obsessive nuts. They were not even-minded people who saw both sides of the question. Far from it.
  —Theodore Sturgeon, late American science fiction author
  and screenwriter

Particularly in these tense economic times, America could certainly benefit from a new generation of obsessive innovators. What baseball general manager wouldn't want to sign the next Ted Williams, even if he too displayed screwball antics on the diamond? (A few might even be willing to acquire some DNA of the last one, no matter how slim the odds are that cryonics will turn out to be anything but a bust.) What venture capitalist wouldn't be eager to support a new business led by the next Henry Heinz or Estée Lauder?

It's hard not to fantasize about a little army of obsessives suddenly coming along and single-handedly jump-starting the entire economy. Heck, you might even be tempted to rush out and become one yourself. Soon after publishing his book *The Hypomanic Edge*, Johns Hopkins psychologist John D. Gartner received many calls from people asking, "How can I get hypomania?"

Unfortunately, or fortunately—depending on your angle—one can't suddenly come down with a deeply entrenched form of mental illness such as OCPD or hypomania. By the time you reach adulthood, either you've got it or you don't. America will just have to settle for those obsessives who happen to come down the pike. "There is no formula for making them," psychiatrist Kerry Sulkowicz, head of the Boswell Group consulting firm, told me. "If there were, it would be some form of child abuse. And we wouldn't want to try that kind of social engineering. We would probably get it wrong, and the kids would end up in a mental institution."

However, as successful as some obsessive innovators have been, should we even look up to them? After all, they also come weighed down with the kind of self-absorption that can humiliate underlings, wreck marriages, and traumatize children. Do they all belong in the Hall of Shame rather than the Hall of Fame? As this book demonstrates, upon close examination, some of those very same super-achievers who have long defined the American character—such as Jefferson, Lindbergh, and Ted Williams in particular—were themselves defined by major character flaws. If truth be told, these were not the kind of men whom any of us would want our daughters to marry. But though we may not approve of how these obsessive innovators lived their lives, we can unequivocally admire both how they solved particular problems and the attributes that they brought to their respective crafts—the thoroughness, the dedication, and the passion.

Can obsessives perhaps maintain their drive and focus while shedding the emotional volatility that also has the potential to destroy their own careers? That is the bailiwick of business consultants and therapists to whom they are sometimes forced to turn after a major meltdown or business failure. (Both the depressed twenty-eight-year-old Melvil Dui and the burned-out sixty-year-old Alfred Kinsey could well have used such a professional tune-up.) While medications, most clinicians agree, have little effect, other treatments can sometimes steer them back toward productivity. In his work with executives with personality disorders, Michael Maccoby, head of the Washington, D.C.–based consultancy the Maccoby Group, teaches what he calls "strategic intelligence." "They often pick the wrong people to work with, such as those who flatter them. They can benefit by learning how to partner with and motivate others," stated Maccoby.

Psychologist Stephen C. Josephson, an OCPD expert who teaches at the medical schools of both Cornell and Columbia University, relies on cognitive-behavioral psychotherapy. "Homework assignments can be useful," he noted. "To help obsessives become less rigid, I sometimes start by asking them to try eating different foods or even walking home a different way. The ultimate goal is to get them to learn how to tolerate the anxiety associated with imperfection both in themselves and others."

How about a cure? For obsessives, full-scale transformations are possible, but rare. The emotional pain is just too deep. John Oldham, an international authority on personality disorders who runs the Menninger Clinic in Houston, cites his thrice-weekly psychoanalytic treatment of a patient with OCPD, whom he calls "Dr. B.," as one of the highlights of his forty-five-year career as a psychiatrist. Oldham, who recently stepped down as president of the American Psychiatric Association, mentioned the case in his presidential address at the annual APA convention in 2012. A high-powered young academic, Dr. B. sought therapy after he failed to get tenure and his wife left him. "After some time in treatment," Oldham complained to his fellow shrinks, "I thought I understood how his wife must have felt." The problem? Dr. B. was disconnected from his feelings, and in the clinical setting he was so emotionally controlled that the sessions were "amazingly sanitized, colorless, and cerebral." However, after a few years, the patient started to open up about his early history. "His father was distant and detached," Oldham explained to me in a recent phone interview. "And his mother died when he was four. He was raised by a highly critical stepmother who was a mess." Dr. B. also confided in Oldham that he would spend hours fingering memorabilia of his dead mother to soothe himself. Eventually, he was able to mourn her loss and begin anew. Dr. B. got remarried and ended treatment by giving Oldham a bear hug. He later sent Oldham photos of his kids. It's unclear, however, whether Dr. B.'s newfound happiness reduced his potential for staggering success.

While one wouldn't wish the distress of the young Dr. B. on anyone, those types of childhood wounds can have an upside; they are the stuff out of which America has long been—and will likely continue to be—built.

Sources

My project was inspired in part by Lytton Strachey's 1918 book, *Eminent Victorians*—the authoritative new edition released by Oxford University Press (New York, 2003) was edited by John Sutherland. This landmark work, which forever changed how we view the Victorian Era, contains profiles of Cardinal Manning, Thomas Arnold, Florence Nightingale, and General Gordon. Bothered by the hagiographic tone that pervaded nearly all biographies back then, this founding member of the Bloomsbury Group described his approach as follows: "To preserve...a becoming brevity...that, surely, is the first duty of the biographer. The second, no less surely, is to maintain his own freedom of spirit. It is not his business to be complimentary; it is his business to lay bare the facts of the case, as he understands them."

While I drew on the major biographies of each of my subjects, I also sought to break new ground by digging into various archives and conducting numerous interviews. For each chapter, I retrace the steps that I took in my research, list key sources, and provide suggestions for further reading.

Prologue

Michael Maccoby, "Narcissistic Leaders: The Incredible Pros, the Inevitable Cons," *Harvard Business Review* (January–February 2000), pp. 69–75. Michael Maccoby, *Narcissistic Leaders: Who Succeeds and Who Fails* (Boston, 2007). Jim Collins, *Good to Great: Why Some Companies Make the Leap...and Others Don't* (New York, 2001).

John D. Gartner, *The Hypomanic Edge: The Link Between (a Little) Craziness and (a Lot of) Success in America* (New York, 2005). Nassir Ghaemi, *A First-Rate Madness: Uncovering the Links between Leadership and Mental Illness* (New York, 2011). Though Gartner and Ghaemi both view mental illness from a biological rather than a psychological framework, their work linking madness and great-

ness actually has much in common with that of the psychoanalytically oriented
Maccoby. For another recent take on the advantages of a major mental disorder,
see Kevin Dutton, *The Wisdom of Psychopaths: What Saints, Spies, and Serial
Killers Can Teach Us About Success* (New York, 2012).

The late British psychiatrist Anthony Storr provides a concise analysis of the obsessive
character in his classic work, *The Dynamics of Creation* (New York, 1972). While
obsessive über-achievers abound, to date, biographers have rarely paid attention to
this character type, except for a few literary critics who have analyzed the lives of
canonical authors and their fictional characters. See, for example, Andrew Brink,
Obsession and Culture: A Study of Sexual Obsession in Modern Fiction (Cran-
bury, NJ, 1996), which features chapters on five twentieth-century writers, including Vladimir Nabokov and John Updike, and Marina van Zuylen, *Monomania:
The Flight from Everyday Life in Literature and Art* (Ithaca, NY, 2005), which discusses, among others, the novelists Gustave Flaubert and Thomas Mann.

Jack Welch and John A. Byrne, *Jack: Straight from the Gut* (New York, 2001).

Amy Chua, *Battle Hymn of the Tiger Mother* (New York, 2011).

Walter Isaacson, *Steve Jobs* (New York, 2011).

Karen Southwick, *Everyone Else Must Fail: The Unvarnished Truth About Oracle
and Larry Ellison* (New York, 2003).

Jon E. Grant, Marc E. Mooney, and Matt G. Kushner, "Prevalence, Correlates, and
Comorbidity of DSM-IV Obsessive-Compulsive Personality Disorder: Results
from the National Epidemiologic Survey on Alcohol and Related Conditions,"
Journal of Psychiatry Research (2012), pp. 469–475.

While research suggests that OCPD is largely environmental in origin, this finding
does not rule out the possibility of a biological component to this personality disorder. As a wealth of studies now show, adverse early experiences such
as neglect can permanently alter brain chemistry. For a jargon-free overview
of the scholarly research linking childhood trauma to impaired brain development, see the pamphlet written by public health researchers Jennifer S.
Middlebrooks and Natalie C. Audage, for the Centers for Disease Control and
Prevention, *The Effects of Childhood Stress on Health across the Lifespan* (Atlanta, 2008).

For more on the difference between OCPD and OCD, see my article, "Field Guide
to the Obsessive-Compulsive," *Psychology Today* (March–April 2008), pp. 43–44.

At the time of writing, the American Psychiatric Association is still debating the final
format of the fifth edition of its *Diagnostic and Statistical Manual*, which is due
out in May 2013. While OCPD is to remain a personality disorder, the diagnostic criteria are likely to undergo some changes. The criteria that I list come from
the edition known as the *DSM IV-TR* (Washington, DC, 2000).

Author interviews: Debi Coleman, Dr. John D. Gartner, Dr. Nassir Ghaemi, Nancy
Wheeler Jenkins, Dr. Stephen Josephson, Dr. Lorrin Koran, Kate Mitchell, Dr.
Michael Maccoby, Dr. John Oldham, Dr. Dan Stein, and Dr. Kerry Sulkowicz.

1. Politics: Thomas Jefferson

The weather diary entries for 1776 are reprinted in Thomas Jefferson's *Memorandum
Books: Accounts, with Legal Records and Miscellany (1767–1826)* (Princeton,
1997), edited by James A. Bear and Lucia C. Stanton. I also had the privilege of
examining Jefferson's personal copy of the 1776 almanac at the Massachusetts
Historical Society, the nation's largest repository of Jefferson manuscripts. For
more on Jefferson and the weather, see Alexander McAdie, "A Colonial Weather
Service," *Popular Science* (1894), pp. 331–337; and "America's First Great
Global Warming Debate," my article for Smithsonian.com, the online edition
of the *Smithsonian* magazine (July 15, 2011).

Princeton University Press will eventually publish all of the nineteen thousand letters
that Jefferson wrote and the twenty-five thousand that he received in a projected
sixty-volume set, *The Papers of Thomas Jefferson*. The first editor was Princeton
history professor Julian P. Boyd, and the first volume appeared in 1950. As of this
writing, thirty-six volumes in the main series, covering 1760 to 1801, and seven
volumes in the retirement series, covering 1809 to 1814, have appeared.

The two most comprehensive biographies are the three-volume *The Life of Thomas
Jefferson* (New York, 1858) by Henry S. Randall and the six-volume *Jefferson and
His Time* (Boston, 1981) by Dumas Malone. Of the numerous one-volume bi-
ographies, the most authoritative is *Thomas Jefferson and the New Nation* (New
York, 1970) by Merrill Peterson, the scholar who also edited the Library of Amer-
ica's *Jefferson's Writings* (New York, 1984), which features all the major works
such as the *Autobiography* and *Notes on the State of Virginia* as well as key
letters. I also consulted numerous other biographies, including Fawn Brodie,
Thomas Jefferson: An Intimate History (New York, 1974); Andrew Burstein, *The
Inner Jefferson* (Charlottesville, VA, 1995); Joseph J. Ellis, *American Sphinx:
The Character of Thomas Jefferson* (New York, 1996); Kevin J. Hayes, *The Road
to Monticello* (New York, 2008); Jon Kukla, *Mr. Jefferson's Women* (New York,
2007); and Willard Sterne Randall, *Thomas Jefferson: A Life* (New York, 1993).
Jon Meacham's biography, *Thomas Jefferson: The Art of Power* (New York, 2012),
was not available at the time of writing.

On Jefferson's relationship with Sally Hemings, the recent volume edited by Robert
Turner, *The Jefferson-Hemings Controversy: Report of the Scholars Commission*

(Durham, NC, 2011), challenges the position of Annette Gordon-Reed, as articulated in her two books, *Thomas Jefferson and Sally Hemings: An American Controversy* (Charlottesville, VA, 1998) and *The Hemingses of Monticello: An American Family* (New York, 2008).

In *Burr* (New York, 1973), novelist Gore Vidal paints Jefferson as a pedantic obsessive. While this portrait is solidly researched, it seems unduly harsh, as Vidal downplays Jefferson's considerable brilliance.

Jonathan R. T. Davidson, Kathryn M. Connor, and Marvin Swartz, "Mental Illness in U.S. Presidents between 1776 and 1974: A Review of Biographical Sources," *Journal of Nervous and Mental Disease* (January 2006), pp. 47–51.

Douglas Wilson has edited *Jefferson's Literary Commonplace Book* (Princeton, 1989). For a lively analysis of this work, see Kenneth A. Lockridge, *On the Sources of Patriarchal Rage: The Commonplace Books of William Byrd and Thomas Jefferson and the Gendering of Power in the Eighteenth Century* (New York, 1994).

For more on Jefferson's two terms in the White House, see the first four volumes of Henry Adams's nine-volume masterpiece, *History of the United States of America 1801–1817* (New York, 1962).

Robert C. Baron has edited *The Garden and Farm Books of Thomas Jefferson* (Golden, CO, 1987). For a good secondary source on Jefferson as a builder, see *Thomas Jefferson as an Architect and a Designer of Landscapes* (Boston, 1913) by William Alexander Lambeth and Warren H. Manning.

For more on the birth of the University of Virginia, see John S. Patton, *Jefferson, Cabell and the University of Virginia* (New York, 1906). On Jefferson's books, the Library of Congress has issued *Thomas Jefferson's Library: A Catalog with the Entries in His Own Order* (Washington, DC, 1989), edited by James Gilreath and Douglas Wilson.

The original manuscript of *The Jefferson Bible: The Life and Morals of Jesus of Nazareth Extracted Textually from the Gospels in Greek, Latin, French and English*, bound in a red leather book, now resides in the Smithsonian Institution's National Museum of American History. The Smithsonian has recently published a beautiful facsimile edition (Washington, DC, 2011), which includes scholarly essays on both its history and conservation.

2. Marketing: Henry Heinz

E. D. McCafferty, Heinz's private secretary, published the first book about the founder, *Henry J. Heinz: A Biography* (Pittsburgh, 1923). Businessman and attorney Steve Lentz has republished this privately printed work as *It Was Never About the Ketchup! The Life and Leadership Secrets of H. J. Heinz* (Garden City, NY, 2007). Another early impressionistic work is Stephen Potter's *The Magic Number 57: The Story of '57'* (London, 1959), which, while focusing on the emergence of the H. J. Heinz Company in Britain, contains interesting tidbits about the founder. Likewise, both Eleanor Foa Dienstag's corporate history *In Good Company: 125 Years at the Heinz Table (1869–1994)* (New York, 1994) and Nancy Koehn's chapter on Heinz's career in *Brand New: How Entrepreneurs Earned Consumers' Trust from Wedgwood to Dell* (Boston, 2001) also contain valuable biographical information.

H. J. Heinz has also been the subject of two scholarly biographies. Using previously unexamined diaries and manuscripts supplied by the family, Robert C. Alberts wrote *The Good Provider: H. J. Heinz and His 57 Varieties* (Boston, 1973). While the originals of these Heinz manuscripts are kept by the Heinz Family Foundation in Pittsburgh and are not available to the public, Alberts deposited copies (and/or transcripts) of some manuscripts in Pittsburgh's Heinz History Center. I examined these materials, as did Quentin R. Skrabec Jr., author of *H. J. Heinz: A Biography* (Jefferson, NC, 2009). The biography started by John F. Cowan was never completed. However, Cowan did write a manuscript about the family, "Diary of My Life at Greenlawn, Pittsburgh"; though it was never published, a typescript is available at the Heinz History Center.

Simone Wendel, the director of the forthcoming German documentary *Kings of Kallstadt*, which traces the roots of the Heinz and Trump families, supplied me with information about the ancestors of both Henry Heinz and Donald Trump.

Elizabeth Beardsley Butler's reporting on the Heinz Company is featured in *Women and the Trades: Pittsburgh, 1907–1908* (New York, 1909), the first of the six-volume set *The Pittsburgh Survey*, issued by the Russell Sage Foundation under the editorship of Paul Underwood Kellogg.

Howard Heinz's remarks about his father's legacy are taken from his 1927 address before the Pittsburgh Chamber of Commerce, "Pittsburgh and the Food-Preserving Industry," published in *Pittsburgh and the Pittsburgh Spirit* (Pittsburgh, 1928).

Ralph Vartabedian's front-page story in the *Los Angeles Times* on Heinz's eccentric heirs, "Family Has Seen Share of Turmoil: Along with Power and Wealth, the Clan Teresa Heinz Kerry First Married into Has Lived through Tragedy and Estrangement," appeared on October 27, 2004. This item was then considered particularly newsworthy because the presidential election involving Mrs. Heinz Kerry's husband, Democratic senator John Kerry, was held a week later.

To write about Heinz, one must also devour the literature on the condiment for which he has become a synonym. The king of ketchupologists is Andrew Smith, author of *The Tomato in America* (Columbia, SC, 1994) and *Pure Ketchup* (Columbia, SC, 1996). Malcolm Gladwell's classic *New Yorker* article "The Ketchup Conundrum," has been reprinted in his collection, *What the Dog Saw and Other Adventures* (New York, 2009). For more on the early history of ketchup, see Bee Wilson, *Swindled: The Dark History of Food Fraud, from Poisoned Candy to Counterfeit Coffee* (Princeton, NJ, 2008) and Clayton Anderson Coppin and Jack C. High, *The Politics of Purity: Harvey Washington Wiley and the Origins of Federal Food Policy* (Ann Arbor, MI, 1999).

For information on Heinz's activities at various World's Fairs, I looked at the respective catalogs — e.g., *International Exposition, 1876: Official Catalogue* (Philadelphia, 1876) — and such secondary works as Robert W. Rydell, *All the World's a Fair: Visions of Empire at American International Expositions* (Chicago, 1984).

Author interviews: Clayton Coppin and Jack High.

3. Information Technology: Melvil Dewey

Wayne Wiegand, an emeritus professor of library and information studies at Florida State University, has published the authoritative biography, *Irrepressible Reformer* (Chicago, 1996), which includes a frank discussion of Dewey's racism and sexism. This preeminent Dewey scholar has also written the informative article "The 'Amherst Method': The Origins of the Dewey Decimal Classification Scheme," *Libraries and Culture* (Spring 1998), pp. 175–194. In contrast to Wiegand, early biographers ignored his dark side. The first life, *Melvil Dewey: Seer: Inspirer: Doer 1851–1931* (Lake Placid, NY, 1932), was compiled by Grosvenor Dawe, a former student of Dewey's at the New York State Library School, under the close supervision of Dewey's second wife, Emily Dewey. Though an idealized portrait, it is a valuable resource that contains numerous letters and diary entries. It also features a full list of Dewey's scholarly publications. The short biography *Melvil Dewey* (Chicago, 1944) written by Fremont Rider, the husband of Dewey's niece, and a librarian at Wesleyan University, also presented Dewey as a hero.

Over the course of several chapters on Dewey in her lively book *Apostles of Culture: The Public Librarian and American Society, 1876–1920* (New York, 1979), the late historian Dee Garrison was the first to allude to his obsessive-compulsive tendencies.

To learn more about the birth of the first Columbia Library School under Dewey, see the volume assembled by the School of Library Service (as the second incarnation was called), *The School of Library Economy of Columbia College, 1887–1889; Documents for a History* (New York, 1937), which includes a copy of the famous application in which he asked for photos so that he could exclude "pumpkins." Cecil R. Roseberry's *A History of the New York State Library* (Albany, NY, 1970) gives a useful overview of Dewey's tenure as the head of that library.

As Wiegand notes in his appendix, Dewey manuscripts are now scattered in dozens of libraries across the country. I examined archival material at Columbia University's Rare Book and Manuscript Library—the largest repository of Deweyiana, it houses his diaries, his memoir, "3/4 of a Century," as well as hundreds of letters, including that startlingly frank 1927 note to Anne Colony—the New York Public Library, Harvard's Houghton Library, and the Amherst College Library. I also obtained by mail various Dewey manuscripts held at the American Library Association Archives at the University of Illinois in Urbana. At Harvard's Widener Library, I read the first edition of his classification system, *A Classification and Subject Index for Cataloguing and Arranging the Books and Pamphlets of a Library* (Amherst, MA, 1876), which was personally signed by Dewey, even though his name does not appear as the author in the book.

At the Boston Athenaeum, I was delighted to find several books on the Lake Placid Club, including the *Handbook* (Morningside, NY, 1901), Reginald Townsend's *A University Club in the Wilderness* (Essex County, NY, 1923), and T. Morris Longstreth's *Lake Placid and an Experiment in Intelligence* (New York, 1923).

Dewey's pedantic and unintentionally amusing treatise, "Office Efficiency," appeared in the three-volume collection *The Business of Insurance: A Text Book and Reference Work Covering All Lines of Insurance, Written by Eighty Eminent Experts* (New York, 1912), edited by Howard Potter Dunham.

The volume edited by Sarah Vann, *Melvil Dewey: His Enduring Place in Librarianship* (Littleton, CO, 1978), features numerous professional and personal writings such as his ten-page eightieth birthday letter.

Regarding Dewey's "shady reputation with women colleagues," see Claire Beck, "A Private Grievance against Dewey," *American Libraries* (January 1996), pp. 62–64.

4. Sexuality: Alfred Kinsey

To write about Kinsey's college career and his graduation speech, I drew upon information contained in various issues of his college newspaper, the *Bowdoin*

Orient—the text was printed on June 22, 1916—which I downloaded from the website of the Bowdoin College Library.

Both Cornelia V. Christenson, author of *Kinsey: A Biography* (Bloomington, IN, 1971), and Wardell B. Pomeroy, author of *Dr. Kinsey and the Institute for Sex Research* (New York, 1972), were former staff members of the Kinsey Institute and reveal little about the man. In contrast, *Alfred C. Kinsey: A Life* (New York, 2004) by James H. Jones and *Sex the Measure of All Things: A Life of Alfred C. Kinsey* (Bloomington, IN, 2000) by Jonathan Gathorne-Hardy both address his personal life, including his sex life. T. C. Boyle's novel *The Inner Circle* (New York, 2004), which is essentially the fifth Kinsey biography, draws extensively from these two books. Bill Condon, director of the 2004 biopic *Kinsey*, has published the script to his movie, based on the Gathorne-Hardy biography, in *Kinsey: Public and Private* (New York, 2004), a volume that also includes a couple of interesting essays on Kinsey's life by other contributors.

While Jones and Gathorne-Hardy, authors of the two major biographies, are largely in agreement about the main facts of Kinsey's life, their interpretations differ. Jones argues that Kinsey was scarred by childhood traumas and that his personality and bizarre sexual behavior "bear the unmistakable stamp of compulsion." In contrast, Gathorne-Hardy sees in Kinsey a free spirit who simply knew what he wanted sexually and went for it. "By the time he got going," the British author told the *New York Times* in 2004, "he was more unrepressed than practically anyone." The best living authority on Kinsey, Gebhard has praised both books but has called Jones's massive tome, which took twenty-five years to complete, "definitive."

While Werner Muensterberger's *Collecting: An Unruly Passion: Psychological Perspectives* (New York, 1994) relies heavily on Freudian jargon, the basic insights seem well-grounded.

Theodoor Hendrik van de Velde (trans. Stella Browne), *Ideal Marriage: Its Physiology and Technique* (New York, 1930).

In his book, *The Kinsey Data: Marginal Tabulations of the 1938–1963 Interviews Conducted by the Institute for Sex Research* (Philadelphia, 1979), Kinsey's colleague Paul H. Gebhard, who was assisted by Alan B. Johnson, provides useful insights into Kinsey's method of interviewing.

The Kinsey Institute, located on the campus of Indiana University, holds tens of thousands of letters and documents that cover every aspect of Kinsey's long scientific career. After the death of his wife, his personal papers were divided equally among his three children, Joan, Anne, and Bruce, and they remain in the hands of the family. I examined original Kinsey manuscripts at both the

Kinsey Institute and at Harvard University's Pusey Library, where I read his application to graduate school and his correspondence with his advisor, William Morton Wheeler.

For information on Kinsey's academic career, I consulted Thomas D. Clark's *Indiana University: Midwestern Pioneer, Volume III: Years of Fulfillment* (Bloomington, IN, 1977). And to learn more about his friends, associates, and enemies, I looked at Samuel Steward's *Chapters from an Autobiography* (San Francisco, 1981); *Secret Historian: The Life and Times of Samuel Steward, Professor, Tattoo Artist, and Sexual Renegade* (New York, 2010) by Justin Spring; *Continual Lessons: The Journals of Glenway Wescott, 1937–1955* (New York, 1990), edited by Robert Phelps and Jerry Rosco; as well as Warren Weaver's memoir, *Scene of Change: A Lifetime in American Science* (New York, 1970).

Author interviews: T. C. Boyle, Paul Gebhard, James H. Jones, Consuelo Lopez-Morillas, Reed Martin, and Judith Riesman.

5. Aviation: Charles Lindbergh

I derive my account of Lindbergh's childhood visit to the White House from a letter written that night (February 21, 1916), by his mother, Evangeline Land Lindbergh, to his grandmother, Evangeline Lodge Land, which is held at Yale's Sterling Library. Yale holds the vast majority of Lindbergh's papers—its Lindbergh Archive includes hundreds of boxes of materials—and I focused on manuscripts related to his first few decades. However, I also examined several other slices, such as his detailed notes on the work of early biographers contained in a box called "Biographical Treatment of Himself." According to Yale's archivists, A. Scott Berg spent years at the library, going through every box, in order to complete his biography, *Lindbergh* (New York, 1998), which was authorized by Anne Lindbergh. The other major repository is the Lindbergh Collection at the Minnesota Historical Society, which I did not visit. I did, however, find a handful of letters at Harvard's Houghton Library—of particular interest was the correspondence between Lindbergh and the late Boston writer J. P. Marquand—which A. Scott Berg did not track down. Reeve Lindbergh, Lindbergh's literary executor, kindly gave me permission to quote from these unpublished documents.

Other biographies include *The Hero: Charles A. Lindbergh and the American Dream* (New York, 1959) by Kenneth S. Davis, *Lindbergh: A Biography* (New York, 1976) by Leonard Mosely, and *Lindbergh Alone* (New York, 1977) by Brendan Gill. For more on the trip to Paris, see *The Flight of the Century:*

Charles Lindbergh and the Rise of American Aviation (New York, 2010) by Thomas Kessner.

Lindbergh's three children with Brigitte Hesshaimer—Dyrk Hesshaimer, Astrid Bouteil, and David Hesshaimer—are listed as coauthors of the biography written by Rudolf Schroeck, *Das Doppelleben des Charles A. Lindbergh* (Munich, 2005). Dyrk Hesshaimer's fifteen-minute interview with Swiss talk-show host Kurt Aeschbacher aired on September 9, 2005, and can be downloaded from the Swiss TV website's SF Videoportal page (www.videoportal.sf.tv/?WT .zugang=front_sfe).

A careful writer, Lindbergh wrote eloquently about both his flight and various chapters of his life in *We* (New York, 1927), *The Spirit of St. Louis* (New York, 1953), and *The Autobiography of Values* (New York, 1978). Other less well-known autobiographical writings are *The Boyhood Diary of Charles Lindbergh, 1913–1916: Early Adventure of the Famous Aviator* (North Mankato, MN, 2000), edited by Megan O'Hara; and *Lindbergh Looks Back: A Boyhood Reminiscence* (St. Paul, MN, 2002), which features a foreword by Reeve Lindbergh and an introduction by Brian Horrigan, a curator of the Minnesota Historical Society. Lindbergh himself also wrote the foreword to the major biography of his father, Bruce Larson's *Lindbergh of Minnesota: A Political Biography* (New York, 1973).

For details on the scandal involving psychiatrist John N. Rosen in the 1980s, see Edward Dolnick, *Madness on the Couch: Blaming the Victim in the Heyday of Psychoanalysis* (New York, 1998) and Jeffrey Masson, *Against Therapy: Emotional Tyranny and the Myth of Psychological Healing* (New York, 1988).

Anne Morrow Lindbergh, *Gift from the Sea* (New York, 1955).

On Lindbergh's scientific research with Carrel, see David M. Friedman, *The Immortalists: Charles Lindbergh, Dr. Alexis Carrel, and the Quest to Live Forever* (New York, 2007).

My account of the first dates of Charles and Anne Lindbergh comes from *Bring Me a Unicorn: Diaries and Letters of Anne Morrow Lindbergh, 1922–1928* (New York, 1972). In the last of the six volumes of personal writings, *Against the Wind: Letters and Journals, 1947–1986* (New York, 2012), edited by Reeve Lindbergh (who also wrote a thoughtful introduction), Anne alludes to her affairs with Dana Atchley and Alan Valentine. For more on Lindbergh's wife, see Susan Hertog's *Anne Morrow Lindbergh: Her Life* (New York, 1999) and Joyce Milton's *Loss of Eden: A Biography of Charles and Anne Morrow Lindbergh* (New York, 1993).

Reeve Lindbergh has written eloquently about her childhood in *Under a Wing* (New York, 1998). In a subsequent memoir, *Forward from Here: Leaving Middle*

Age and Other Unexpected Adventures (New York, 2008), she discusses with wit and sensitivity her reaction to learning that her father also had three German families.

Author interviews: Brian Horrigan, Tom Flanagan, Dyrk Hesshaimer, Judith Schiff, Kristina Lindbergh, and Reeve Lindbergh.

6. Beauty: Estée Lauder

Marylin Bender wrote the first short biography of Lauder, which was based on her 1973 *New York Times* story "Estée Lauder: A Family Affair," which she included as a chapter in her collection, *At the Top* (New York, 1975). As noted, the only full-scale biographies are Lee Israel, *Estee Lauder: Beyond the Magic* (New York, 1985), and Lauder's own *Estée: A Success Story* (New York, 1985). Most other accounts of Lauder's life rely heavily on these two sources, such as the chapters in Gene N. Landrum's *Profiles of Female Genius: Thirteen Creative Women Who Changed the World* (Amherst, NY, 1994) and Doris Burchard's *Der Kampf um die Schoenheit: Helena Rubinstein, Elizabeth Arden, Estée Lauder* (Hamburg, 1999). The one notable exception is Nancy Koehn's thoroughly researched chapter in *Brand New* (cited under chapter 2), which also draws on her own interview with Leonard Lauder. The brilliant *New Yorker* profile "As Good As It Gets" (September 15, 1986), by the fashion writer Kennedy Fraser, provides an excellent snapshot of the nearly eighty-year-old entrepreneur. Lindy Woodhead's *War Paint: Madame Helena Rubinstein and Miss Elizabeth Arden: Their Lives, Their Times, Their Rivalry* (New York, 2004) also contains some useful tidbits about Lauder.

To learn more about Lauder's early years in Queens, I downloaded the relevant census records that are available on the website Ancestry.com. For more on the 1916 public health crisis that affected her family, see the monograph compiled by the New York City Department of Health, *The Epidemic of Poliomyelitis (Infantile Paralysis)*, (New York, 1917).

Rebecca Mead's telling profile of Ronald Lauder, "An Acquiring Eye," appeared in the *New Yorker* (January 15, 2007). Kai Falkenberg discusses the seven-year affair between William Lauder and Taylor Stein in "The Secret Tale of William Lauder," *Forbes* (March 10, 2010). For a recent profile of Jane Lauder, see Jenny B. Fine, "Jane Lauder: The Natural," *Beauty Inc* (August 10, 2012). For more on William, Jane, and Aerin Lauder, see Daniel Roth, "The Sweet Smell of Succession," *Fortune* (September 19, 2005).

Cathie Black, *Basic Black: The Essential Guide to Getting Ahead at Work (and in*

Life) (New York, 2007). Andrew P. Tobias, *Fire and Ice: The Story of Charles Revson—the Man Who Built the Revlon Empire* (New York, 1976).

While Estée Lauder didn't leave much of a paper trail, the Arthur and Elizabeth Schlesinger Library on the History of Women in America at Harvard University's Radcliffe Institute for Advanced Study contains a few original Lauder manuscripts. One interesting item is a brief undated letter from 1983, enclosing some samples, which Lauder sent to Julia Child after reading in the *Los Angeles Times* that the cooking guru used her perfume Aliage. Child did not respond. This library also houses Hazel Bishop's notes on a brief talk Lauder gave to her class at the Fashion Institute of Technology in the mid-1980s, to which I refer in the chapter. Leonard Lauder describes his love of collecting in his preface to *The Postcard Age: Selections from the Leonard A. Lauder Collection*, coauthored by Lynda Klich and Benjamin Weiss (Boston, 2012).

In her controversial memoir, *Can You Ever Forgive Me? Memoirs of a Literary Forger* (New York, 2008), Lee Israel talks briefly about her own disappointment with her Lauder biography.

Mark Tungate, *Branded Beauty: How Marketing Changed the Way We Look* (Philadelphia, 2011).

Author interviews: Agnes Ash, Marylin Bender, Mary Randolph Carter, Ann Friedman, Michael Gibbons, Fayette Hickox, Lee Israel, Aerin Lauder, Jane Lauder, Leonard Lauder, Ronald Lauder, William Lauder, Vincent Tomeo, and two sources—a family member and a former coworker—who did not wish to be identified.

7. Sports: Ted Williams

Ted Williams's complex personality has inspired some of America's best sportswriting. Two shining examples are John Updike's 1960 *New Yorker* article, since rereleased as a book, *Hub Fans Bid Kid Adieu: John Updike on Ted Williams* (New York, 2010), and Richard Ben Cramer's 1986 *Esquire* article, rereleased as a short biography, *What Do You Think of Ted Williams Now? A Remembrance* (New York, 2002). The collection *Ted Williams: Reflections on a Splendid Life* (Boston, 2003), edited by Lawrence Baldassaro, contains numerous lively pieces published between 1940 and 2002.

At present, Leigh Montville's *Ted Williams: The Biography of an American Hero* (New York, 2004) remains definitive. Benjamin Bradlee Jr., a former editor at the *Boston Globe* who, unlike Montville, has the full cooperation of the Williams family—namely, his daughter Claudia—has been working on a biography for more than a decade, but it's still unclear when this book will be published. Earlier biographies include Ed Linn's *Hitter: The Life and Turmoils of Ted Williams* (Orlando, FL, 1993) and Michael Seidel's *Ted Williams: A Baseball Life* (Lincoln, NE, 1991). The baseball aficionado Bill Nowlin has written two comprehensive books on particular segments of Williams's life, *The Kid: Ted Williams in San Diego* (Cambridge, MA, 2005) and *Ted Williams at War* (Cambridge, MA, 2007). For information on Williams's early years in San Diego, I also consulted Bill Swank, *Echoes from Lane Field: A History of the San Diego Padres* (Paducah, KY, 1999).

John Underwood has coauthored three books with Williams: *My Turn at Bat: The Story of My Life* (New York, 1969), *The Science of Hitting* (New York, 1971), and *Fishing "the Big Three": Tarpon, Bonefish, and Atlantic Salmon* (New York, 1982). After the slugger's death, Underwood also wrote a moving book of reflections, which comes with a CD containing interviews with Williams, *It's Only Me: The Ted Williams We Hardly Knew* (Chicago, 2005).

David Cataneo, *I Remember Ted Williams: Anecdotes and Memories of Baseball's Splendid Splinter by the Players and People Who Knew Him* (Nashville, TN, 2002).

The ex-Alcor employee Larry Johnson was assisted by Scott Baldyga in the writing of the controversial book about Williams's remains, *Frozen: My Journey into the World of Cryonics, Deception, and Death* (New York, 2009). For more on his career as a manager, see Ted Leavengood, *Ted Williams and the 1969 Washington Senators: The Last Winning Season* (Jefferson, NC, 2009).

In April 2012, I examined many of Williams's household items at Fenway Park where they were being auctioned. The beautifully illustrated catalog, *The Ted Williams Collection at Public Auction* (Exton, PA, 2012) prepared by Hunt Auctions, shows what he kept in his Florida home—his memorabilia, his hunting gear, and his books. Among the volumes in his personal library was a copy of Charles Lindbergh's *We*, which he apparently obtained as a young boy.

Williams's nephew, also named Ted Williams, shared with me some letters that Williams had written in the late 1950s, including the one that I cite that concerns the health of his elderly mother.

Author interviews: Steve August, Yogi Berra, Wade Boggs, Dick Bresiani, Bobby Doerr, Mike Epstein, Dave Ferriss, Suzanne Fountain, Rich Gedman, Richard Johnson, Frank Malzone, Leigh Montville, Bill Nowlin, Jim Prime, Dan Shaughnessy, Nathan Stalvey, Bill Swank, John Underwood, Russ White, Dick Williams, Sam Williams (nephew), and Ted Williams (nephew).

Epilogue

The epigraph from Theodore Sturgeon, né Edward Hamilton Waldo (1918–1985), comes from an interview with David D. Duncan published in *Phoenix*, the University of Tennessee literary magazine, in its fall 1979 issue.

John D. Oldham, "Presidential Address: Integrated Care," delivered at the 165th Annual Convention of the American Psychiatric Association, Philadelphia, PA, in May 2012.

Author interviews: See under Prologue.

Acknowledgments

I would like to thank my agent, Suzanne Gluck of William Morris Endeavor, for suggesting that I turn my obsession with the obsessed into a book. Every time I found myself amused by the discovery of yet another obsessive quirk in one of my subjects—which was often—I couldn't believe that I had a day job that I loved so much. Eric Lupfer, her colleague at William Morris Endeavor, also offered invaluable assistance on the proposal. At Grand Central, I am deeply indebted to the tireless efforts of my editor, John Brodie; in the hurly-burly world that is twenty-first-century publishing, it's a distinct pleasure to work with someone so deeply committed to bringing out the best in his writers. His assistant, Meredith Haggerty, has also been helpful at each stage of the process. I also thank Rachel Youdelman for reading a draft of the manuscript and for her expert photo research.

While numerous archivists from across the country responded to my queries, several deserve special mention. Judith Schiff, chief research archivist of the Yale University Library, helped me find what I was looking for in the vast collection of Lindbergh manuscripts located at Yale's Sterling Library in New Haven. Likewise, Thomas G. Lannon, assistant curator of Manuscripts and Archives at the New York Public Library; Peter Nelson, assistant archivist at the Amherst College Library; Kajsa Anderson, archives graduate assistant at the University of Illinois at Urbana; and Tara C. Reid, reference services supervisor at Columbia University's Rare Book and Manuscript Library, were all instrumental in helping me track down various Melvil Dewey manuscripts. At the Kinsey Institute, Shawn Wilson, library public services manager, made sure that I made the most of my trip to Bloomington. And Art Louderback, the chief librarian at the Heinz History Center, was a big help during my visit to Pittsburgh.

I am grateful to everyone who agreed to be interviewed (and their names are all listed in the notes section). I also owe a particular debt to those individuals who helped me contact difficult-to-reach family members and associates of my subjects. Tony Schwenk set up my interview with Dyrk Hesshaimer in Munich. Samantha Goldsmith, Enid Kemmer, and Bari Seiden of Estée Lauder Global Communications arranged for my visit to the company's Fifth Avenue offices and for my interviews with Leonard Lauder, Ronald Lauder, William Lauder, Jane Lauder, and Aerin Lauder. And Bill Nowlin helped me locate Ted Williams's nephews, Ted Williams and Sam Williams, whom I interviewed by phone. And thanks to Steve Alexander for setting up my phone interview with Hall of Famer Wade Boggs.

And I am grateful to Carrie and Thomas Kupka, the current residents of the fifth-floor apartment at 44 Agnesstrasse in Munich, where Lindbergh first met Brigitte and Marietta Hesshaimer, for inviting me to visit their home.

A fellowship from the Virginia Center for the Creative Arts funded a three-week residency in December 2010.

Finally, I want to acknowledge the friendship of the late Andrew Brink, a former professor of English at McMaster University and a prolific literary scholar, to whom this book is dedicated. I first met Andrew in 1995 at an academic conference. In the early 2000s, as I was starting out as a biographer, he took the time to read whatever I sent him and provide insightful feedback. And his thoughtful work has helped me find my own niche. As he noted in the first line of his 1996 book, *Obsession and Culture*, "Obsession is a term in broad popular use whose value in studying culture has been underestimated."

Photo Credits

p. 12: "A philosopher, a patriote and a friend. Dessiné par son ami Tadée Kociuszko et gravé par Michal Sokolnicki." Ca. 1800–1816. Library of Congress Prints and Photographs Division [LC-USZC4-7084].

p. 48: Henry Heinz on a horse. Ca. 1907. H. J. Heinz Company. Reprinted by permission of the Library and Archives Division, Sen. John Heinz History Center.

p. 84: Attendees, including Melvil Dewey (front center, holding hat), American Library Association Twenty-First Annual Conference, Atlanta, Georgia, May 8–13, 1899. Photographed by Moore and Stephenson, Atlanta. Gift of Mrs. William C. Lane, Cambridge, to Harvard College Library, 1931. Portrait Collection, Fine Arts Library, Harvard University.

p. 118: Alfred Kinsey with Clyde Martin, Paul Gebhard, and Wardell Pomeroy. Ca. 1953. Photographed by William Dallenback. Reprinted by permission of the Kinsey Institute for Research in Sex, Gender and Reproduction.

p. 154: Charles and Anne Lindbergh in flight gear, 1930. Lindbergh Picture Collection, 1860–1980. Photographed by R.W.G.H., St. Louis. Manuscripts and Archives, Yale University Library [MS 0325B].

p. 196: Estée Lauder putting makeup on a woman's face, 1966. Bill Sauro/*World Journal Tribune*/Library of Congress Prints and Photographs Division [LC-USZ62-109674].

p. 230: Ted Williams kissing bat. From the *Daily Boston Globe*, September 29, 1941.

Index

Page numbers in *italic* type indicate illustrations.